Afterlife Conversations
with
Hemingway

Books by Frank DeMarco

Fiction

Babe in the Woods
Messenger: A Sequel to Lost Horizon

Non-Fiction

The Cosmic Internet: Explanations from the Other Side
The Sphere and the Hologram: Explanations from the Other Side
Chasing Smallwood: Talking with the Other Side
Muddy Tracks: Exploring an Unsuspected Reality

Afterlife Conversations *with* Hemingway

A Dialogue on His Life, His Work, and the Myth

Frank DeMarco

Author of *The Cosmic Internet*

RAINBOW RIDGE
BOOKS

Cover art © 2012 by Patty Ray Avalon
Cover design by Patty Ray Avalon

Published by:
Rainbow Ridge Books, LLC
140 Rainbow Ridge Road
Faber, Virginia 22938
434-361-1723

If you are unable to order this book from your local
bookseller, you may order directly from the distributor.

Square One Publishers, Inc.
115 Herricks Road
Garden City Park, NY 11040
Phone: (516) 535-2010
Fax: (516) 535-2014
Toll-free: 877-900-BOOK

Visit the author at:
www.facebook.com/frank.demarco.10

Library of Congress Cataloging-in-Publication Data applied for.

ISBN 978-1-937907-06-8

10 9 8 7 6 5 4 3 2 1

Printed in Canada on acid-free recycled paper

Dedication

For my brother Paul,
who first called my attention to what I was doing,
and said it was wonderful.

Contents

Introduction
This Business of Afterlife Communication

"What a book would be the real story of Hemingway, not those he writes but the confessions of the real Ernest Hemingway. It would be for another audience than the audience Hemingway has now but it would be very wonderful."
—Gertrude Stein, *The Autobiography of Alice B. Toklas*

What if Papa Hemingway could speak from beyond the grave? What would he say about his life and work?

And what if a skilled and wise psychological practitioner like Carl Jung could join with Hemingway in speaking from beyond the grave? What if he were to say that Hemingway is a good model of the Complete Man, developed physically and intellectually, exhibiting highly developed intuitive and sensory functioning? And what if their considered judgment was that Hemingway's life had meaning beyond what had been seen to date? What if they felt it worthwhile to make the effort to communicate with us, to try to correct certain harmful aspects of The Hemingway Myth? What if they thought that correcting that myth was important, not to Hemingway but to those of us living now and in the future?

That's pretty much what this book is about. This interaction with Hemingway is neither biography nor autobiography. It is more a series of conversations, hitting certain highlights; Hemingway as I experienced him.

≈2≈

I communicate well with disembodied others, working from a mildly altered state very little different from my ordinary consciousness. How I learned to do this, I told in my first non-fiction book, *Muddy Tracks: Discovering an Unsuspected Reality*. What I've done with it so far, I have told in three other books. I don't intend to recap even the highlights of my story here, as anyone interested can consult my other books, or my blog, "I of My Own Knowledge ..." (www.hologrambooks.com).

For most of my life, what I knew about Ernest Hemingway was primarily his posthumously published novel, Islands in the Stream, a moving portrait of a man's love for his children and his desolation when they were taken from him. I felt emotionally very close to the man who had written that book. One day it occurred to me that just as I had learned to talk to others who were no longer in the body, so I could talk to him. Immediately it was as if a two-dimensional field had become three dimensional, or a black-and-white photo acquired color.

This book is about Hemingway, and Hemingway's place in our time, and Hemingway as a model for what humans may become, which gives that life importance for us all, even those who think they know who Hemingway was.

His interests were so wide ranging! His life touched so many extremes! He was a writer of genius, a renowned and skillful hunter and fisherman, a charismatic personality who became a celebrity. He had friends in every social stratum, from his poor neighbors in Cuba to the rich on three continents. He was praised and damned, admired, and contemned. His stories and books made him rich, but were frequently entirely misunderstood, as was he. No adequate picture of 20th-century literature can ignore his considerable legacy. But what that legacy is, history hasn't quite decided. He didn't run with packs, but the pack came to run after him, which sometimes has left him at the mercy of those who claimed to be upholding his legacy.

I had thought of calling this *Hemingway: A Man Alone*, quoting Harry Morgan in *To Have and Have Not*, who famously decides, at the end, that a man alone doesn't have a chance. And I thought of calling it *A Hemingway Nobody Knows*, to emphasize the difference between the man and the myth. But neither title quite caught the gist of the story and the reason behind the story. *Afterlife Conversations with Hemingway* better captures it, I think. We're out to correct the record, Hemingway and Jung and I—two giants from beyond the grave and their still-embodied editorial assistant.

Or, to quote Papa [Tuesday, July 20, 2010]:

> *Remember, in all this we are proceeding along more than one track. There is the correction of The Hemingway Myth for the sake of providing a model of completeness that the world misunderstood—not for the sake of doing me justice, although there is that, so much as for the sake of providing the model. The model is needed! And to correct the myth, it is necessary to understand; therefore it can't be a whitewash job, and it can't be superficial. But it isn't a matter of research for new facts; mostly it is a matter of interpreting what is known. That's one strand.*
>
> *A second is to provide a model of possibilities, showing how communication proceeds and showing what can be done, and how easily. This could be a great encouragement to people. And just as correcting the myth can't be a whitewash if it is to do any good, so explaining the process can't overlook the difficulties and pitfalls, which involves your giving the process a certain amount of thought so as to be useful.*
>
> *Then, most important of the three but depending on the other two, this will provide people with a new model of the physical/non-physical interaction, hence the true function of 3-D existence, and by implication we will show that the non-physical exists—that is, that the afterlife is not only not a fantasy but is a necessary part of life, without which life wouldn't have meaning or make any sense. And it will do so in a way that shows that religious belief was tapping into the same reality.*

Of course I am aware of the danger of leading myself and others astray. All along, others have asked me, and I have asked myself, how much of what I think is happening can be proved. The answer has to be, none of it. In matters of contact with non-physical intelligences, all we can really know for sure is that the material does or does not resonate. That, we can *know*. Anything beyond that is a matter of belief, only. I am left with Jesus' test, "by their fruits you will know them." So far the fruits of each day's task are enthusiasm, and joy, and new insight. But as to proof? You're going to have to use your discernment, and see what resonates.

〜3〜

How is the interaction possible? Here's how I think of it.

Any minds that ever existed *within* time-space continue to exist *outside* of it, as alive as we are. Since our own minds extend into the non-physical world, we can connect to these non-physical minds, often when we aren't even aware of doing so. We seem to be in continuous connections with those who are on our particular wavelength. This is what some people call guidance. Yet there will be a core group of contacts that connects to what is most deeply you.

I call my core group "the guys upstairs" (TGU), and neither they nor I see any advantage in my putting them on a pedestal. We have the same kind of easy, joking relationship that I have with many of my embodied friends. I would suggest that you think of your own guys upstairs as friends who drop in or out of conversations depending on whether they have anything to add. We don't necessarily know at any given time who is participating, because different individuals fade in or out depending what's going on. Different particular interests elicit different minds, just as in ordinary life. From time to time our TGU may include relatives, friends, "past lives"—and perhaps famous people with whom we have certain resonance, or with whom we share a certain task.

A very important thing to keep in mind: When we are in connection with other minds, they know what we know. Thus, Hemingway knows about *Star Trek*. That is, he knows what I know about *Star Trek*. When he connects with others, he knows what they know. Minds on the other side are no longer bound to one time and space as we seem to be. (I say "seem to be" because in fact our minds are as non-physical, hence as unbounded, as theirs. But we are tethered to a body that repeatedly brings us back to a focus in one space, one time.)

So who are we interacting with? It isn't always possible to know, and it isn't always necessary to know. A message has to stand on its own, to resonate or not, rather than lean on someone's presumed authority. Sometimes I recognize the presence of Carl Jung or Ernest Hemingway or another specific individual, but I try to remain aware that what I think I know may or may not be true. I proceed on that understanding, and so should you.

≈4≈

The conversations with Hemingway and others that make up this book occurred between the years 2006 and 2011, inclusive—with most of it coming in the last seven months of 2010. Mostly it came in sessions of about an hour to an hour and a half. I would sit down with my journal and sometimes pose a question, sometimes merely indicate my availability, and would write what welled up, and would respond to that, much like a normal conversation with someone in the body.

The material did not come in the same order that Hemingway's life was lived, nor for quite a while did I realize that a book was intended. Our conversations skipped around, sometimes examining this aspect of his life, sometimes that aspect, sometimes in one session connecting bits of his life that were widely separated in years. I tried three different ways of arranging the material. For a while I thought it should be divided into three themes: his life, his work, and the myth. Then I thought to arrange it chronologically as much as possible, to follow the life as he had lived it. Then I thought to arrange it according to a different chronology, presenting it in the order it had been given to me.

Each way had its disadvantages, mostly because the conversations skipped around so much even during the same session. To arrange it by themes sometimes meant that to put a session where it logically belonged, I would have to leave another part of the same session where it did *not* belong, or would have to break the session into two or more parts, with some loss of clarity. To arrange it by the chronology of Hemingway's life resulted in conspicuous gaps and unevenness—for, after all, this is neither a biography nor an autobiography—and did not assist in placing many large sections that could have gone in any of several places, or (because they were too conceptually abstract) in none at all. So finally, with reservations, I decided to present the material in the order it had come to me—that is, chronologically according to the date of the session. This prevented the kind of confusion that arises when things are presented out of order.

More importantly, though, it gave a better sense of how the relationship gradually developed, for *the process itself* is at the heart of this book. This series of conversations provides one example of how to learn to communicate with the other side. That's one reason why I have left in some of the perplexities, hesitations, obstacles, and fears that I had to work through. (I did silently edit both my entries and those of others to enhance clarity. As the guys upstairs told me long ago, the aim is not to produce words to be treated as scripture, but to provide increased understanding of whatever we happen to be talking about.)

You will notice that I have made no attempt to dramatize either the information or the process of obtaining it. I don't know of any single factor that has tended to discredit the whole business of such communication than this over-dramatization that so often happens. I'm with Jack Webb (*Dragnet*'s Sergeant Friday): "Just the facts, ma'am." The facts are dramatic enough; they don't need enhancement. It would be like making a big drama over somebody talking on the telephone.

One more thing. The Hemingway I connected to is not the entire person, any more than anyone is the entire person to anyone, ever. We relate to each other according to who we each are. Some traits and interests are shared, some are not. There never has been and never will be a relationship without mystery. How could there be? Thus the Hemingway I met was not the hunter and fisherman—the outdoorsman in general— nor the *bon vivant* or the cut-throat competitor. Those are not the traits I possess. It isn't that these traits do not have their legitimate place in his life; it is merely that they were not part of the common language we spoke in the way that literature and writing and art and other things were. So, even if you accept this book at face value as a genuine communication from Hemingway, you must not expect it to be the final word. Any new combination of traits that contacted him would encounter a somewhat different person. And this is as it should be.

I no longer get up before dawn, eager to have a talk with Papa Hemingway, as I did for so many happy, fulfilling months. I miss that, but life goes on. The very process of putting together the book imposed some distance, but in any case our shared task was accomplished, as best we could accomplish it, and so he and I have moved on to other things. But what a gift, my God! To spend so much time talking to Hemingway, and Jung, and even Abraham Lincoln, and to do so not as acolyte but as co-worker—what a wonderful experience!

This won't be the book that Gertrude Stein wished she could read, but you'll get at least a little of that here, Hemingway's commentary on Hemingway (and other things), from the life we come to by way of the grave.

Hemingway's Timeline

The following timeline will help orient those less familiar with the flow of Hemingway's life, but if you want to read Hemingway's life told as a story (which, after all, is the nature of biography or autobiography), you'll find plenty of sources available, a few of them listed at the back.

(1899-1918)

Born July 21, 1899 (second child and first son) to gifted parents. Grew up in an exclusive suburb of Chicago. Graduated from high school in 1917, just after the United States entered World War I. Ineligible to join the army because of defective eyesight, he spent several months as a reporter for the *Kansas City Star*; then was accepted as an ambulance driver for the Red Cross.

(1918)

Shipped to the Italian front, he was voluntarily in the front lines distributing chocolates and cigarettes to Italian troops when, on the night of July 8, 1918, an Austrian mortar shell made him the first American to be wounded in Italy. [One had been killed, but Hemingway was the first to be wounded and survive.] Months of recuperation among veterans followed, as did the experience of falling in love and being jilted.

(1919-1921)

He spent a year at home recuperating; found a job in Chicago, talked his way into a job with the Toronto *Star*, and married Hadley Richardson.

They moved to Paris, armed with introductions from Sherwood Anderson to very important literary figures.

(1922-1923)

While filing feature stories for the Toronto paper, he worked hard at learning to write fiction. He and Hadley moved back to Canada in the latter half of 1923 so that their first child could be born there, where they thought the medical care would be better. But within months after the birth of son John they were back in Paris, this time living entirely on Hadley's inheritance, Hemingway having given up his job with the *Star*.

(1924-1929)

Within these few years, Hemingway went from first publication to acknowledged master. Among the works published were *In Our Time (1925)*, *The Sun Also Rises (1926)* and *A Farewell to Arms* (1929). But this period also saw the marriage break up, as Pauline Pfeiffer went from being Hadley's and Hemingway's friend to being his lover and then his second wife.

(1929-1939)

Hemingway lived ten years in Key West, arguably the most consistently creative decade of his life. While there (besides fathering second and third sons Patrick and Gregory) Hemingway authored *Death in the Afternoon* (1932), a book of short stories, *Winner Take Nothing* (1933), *Green Hills of Africa* (1935), *To Have and Have Not* (1937), *The Fifth Column and the First Forty-Nine Stories* (1938) and did the initial part of *For Whom the Bell Tolls* (1940). During this period, the Hemingway Myth—the hunter, the deep-sea fisherman, the all-around tough guy— became firmly established in the public mind.

(1936-1939)

His Key West years were punctuated and ultimately ended by the coming of the Spanish Civil War and by Martha Gellhorn. He loved Spain, hated fascism, and went three times to Spain to report on the war. During that time he carried on a long affair with Gellhorn. That war ended in the defeat of the Spanish Republicans in March, 1939.

(1940-41)

Hemingway wrote *For Whom the Bell Tolls,* his novel of the Spanish Civil War, which became a huge best-seller. By this time he had moved to Cuba with Gellhorn, who then cajoled him into accompanying her on a long trip to see the war in China in early 1941.

(1942-1943)

After Pearl Harbor, he edited a massive anthology of war stories, *Men at War*, became involved in counter-espionage work ("the crook factory") [a surreptitious informal spy network Hemingway set up and ran for a few months in 1942, with the approval of the American ambassador and the disapproval of FBI Director J. Edgar Hoover], and employed his fishing boat, Pilar, as one of a vast net of Q-boats, searching for clandestine U-boat refueling dumps and U-boat sightings.

(1944-1945)

Again repeatedly prodded by Gellhorn, Hemingway signed on as a correspondent for *Collier's* magazine and in May flew to London in time for the D-Day invasion. He soldiered along with the infantry until early 1945, his marriage breaking up meanwhile.

(1946-1960)

After the war, now married to Mary Welsh, Hemingway worked for years on what he called his "land, sea, and air book," never completed. In 1950 he published *Across the River and Into the Trees,* and in 1952, *The Old Man and the Sea,* for which he won the Nobel Prize for Literature. But a second safari in Africa in 1954 ended in two plane crashes in two days, inflicting injuries from which he never fully recovered. His last years were marked by physical and mental illness. After the Castro revolution of 1959, living in Cuba became increasingly difficult, and in 1960 he left his beloved Finca Vigia for the final time.

(1961)

Following two hospitalizations in which shock treatments successfully destroyed his ability to work but did no good that anyone had noticed, on July 2, 1961, Hemingway took "the family exit" as he had long foreseen he would, shooting himself to death as his father had in December, 1928.

(1961-)

In the years since Hemingway's suicide, interest in his life and work has grown continually, resulting in biographies, critical studies, blogs, articles and books examining specific aspects of his life. Hemingway works posthumously published includes *The Snows of Kilimanjaro and Other Stories* (1961); *A Moveable Feast* (1964); *The Fifth Column and Four Stories of the Spanish Civil War* (1969); *Islands in the Stream* (1970); *The Nick Adams Stories* (1972); *The Dangerous Summer* (1985); *The Garden of Eden* (1986); *The Complete Short Stories of Ernest Hemingway* (1987), and two alternate editings of his African journal of 1954, *True at First Light* (1999) and *Under Kilimanjaro* (2005). Nor, of course, is this likely to be the end of the torrent.

Typographical Conventions

I use a few conventions to make the dialogues clear.
Normally, in dialogue:

- *my words are in italic, like this.*

- material from the other side is in normal Garamond, like this.

- words added to their statements are in square brackets [like this].

However, when I am speaking directly to the reader at some length,
I omit the brackets for the sake of easier reading.

I

May 2006 - July 2009

Gone Fishing • The Sun Also Rises • For Whom the Bell Tolls • Spain and the Modern World • The Old Man and the Sea • Beisbol and Santiago • Harry Morgan and Paul Potts • Pretending and Lying • Plotting • Novels and Self-revelation • Reputation • Unfinished Business • Opening Pathways • Fame and Relationship • Life Always Slipping By • The Edge • The Hemingway Patrols

[The beginnings of anything are often more strange and wonderful than they at first appear. Many impulses that we think are ours later turn out to have someone else's fingerprints on them. One Saturday morning it occurred to me that I could communicate as easily with Hemingway as with anyone else, and I thought to introduce him to my father.]

Gone Fishing

Saturday May 13, 2006

Mr. Hemingway, meet my father. I always thought you two would have liked each other.

You are right. One thing I couldn't stand is phonies, and another is pretentious phonies, and a third is pretentious phony fools—and your father is none of the three.

The fact that the two of you looked somewhat alike—does that show any inner likeness? I mean, can that be generalized?

Neither your father nor I were very interested in that kind of generalization. What good does it do?

Now that you have been introduced via me—if in fact you didn't know each other previously—will that cause some kind of change on your side?

You forget, your dad read my books. That's a direct connection.

[In my experience, contacting people simultaneously thereby puts them into contact with each other, regardless when they lived. However, the fact that Dad had been a Hemingway fan means that there was already a connection. Those unnamed discarnate personalities that I call The Guys Upstairs have said that anyone who reads a book is connected not only to the author but to everyone else who reads the book!]

(2:05 p.m.) All right. Mr. Hemingway—you presumably know my situation. Can you help me? [This referred to writing a novel I was planning.] And if so, would you? And if so, is there something I can do for you?

Something you can do for me? You mean something like a retrieval, I suppose. [That is, help in realizing that he was no longer alive on earth, as is sometimes needed.] No, I'm not in need of that kind of assistance— although now that you mention it, I can see that perhaps even this part of me ought to be moving on to other things.

I don't understand.

The spirit is always fine, you know that. The soul can get stuck by not being aware that it is not in the Earth any more, or it can go to do other things or it can bask in its surroundings, so to speak. I have been on vacation a good while now. Maybe it is time to move on.

I still don't quite get it, though I get the sense you are going to fill me in a little.

When I left the body—when I blew myself out of that situation—I knew what I was doing, and why. I wasn't emotionally distraught, I wasn't out of my mind, and I wasn't even depressed—once I'd figured out how to get out. So when I got over to this side—as you always put it—I knew where and who I was and how I'd gotten here. I was fine, despite what you've heard about suicides. The bad effects of suicide have a lot more to do with attitudes than with a given act.

I went back to being in my mid-thirties. I was happy then. I'd taken my lumps and I'd already left Hadley, which was a stupid thing to do but there you are, and I was in the prime of life. I was healthy, able, clear-sighted, and I could do about anything I ever had a reasonable chance to do. I could shoot, I could fish, I could ride, I could write. I saw beauty everywhere and I *loved* being alive! It was people and their actions and emotions that were hard, and here that isn't a problem.

As you are beginning to discover, loneliness is not a factor here, either. We're all connected. So you're as alone as you wish and as con-nected as you wish. It's perfect! If you want to go fishing, it's as real as going fishing on earth—especially to the degree that you release control.

I think I know what you mean, but—
Not much fun fishing if every time you throw the line you know you are going to catch a fish, and even less fun if you know that every one is going to be prize category. So—release control and it's just like earth. You are deliberately renouncing your ability to create what you want, you see, or maybe I should say you are creating a range of results and renouncing timing and control over which one manifests and where and when and how often. Maybe there'll be days you don't catch anything. You might think that would spoil it, but it doesn't—it enhances it when you do catch something. Just like in your dimensions.

Well, just as you do that with fishing, you do it with relationships. What's the point in having a perfect romance, day after day, with a pre-dictably adorable other person who adores you too? You'd get sugar dia-betes of the emotions! So you relinquish control and you let people come to you sometimes—as you did. As Hadley does. As my children still do.

You were reading *Islands in the Stream* last night and thought how the impact is different when you don't think of death as The End.

And you just happened to be in my mind this morning, suggesting that we talk?

It was only a suggestion. You might have said no, or not noticed.

What is my attraction, to you? That I read your books? That I too am trying to write?

That you read my books makes it more possible because for one thing it puts me in your mind—I mean that you are thinking about me. That you want to write a novel puts us into a different relation when you read my book; it's like talking shop. But the important thing—the reason you have been contacted by so many people, whether on your initiative or theirs—is because you are the model for a new way for people to relate to the past. It is alive to you as it is to few—now you are seeing how much *more* alive it is and can be.

It is an amazing blossoming out of richness.

Available to all, and it will be much more so as others realize it by reading about it and trying for themselves.

[Following this exchange, I began buying and reading everything he had written. But more than a year went by before these conversations really began.]

≈ 2 ≈

The Sun Also Rises

Sunday, June 10, 2007

Dear Ernest—

Yes?

I envy your life. Yet at the end your life was insupportable.

Well you know when you have had a lot and much of it was very fine and you know that there is nothing ahead of you as satisfying—that you will never again be clean and whole and young—why not step through the doorway?

The family exit. [Which is how Hemingway referred to suicide.]

I didn't talk too much about my out-of-body experience. [In World War I, on the Italian front.] I died before Bob Monroe's experiences even began—the ones he remembered—and certainly long before anybody was talking about them. But why should I fear death after that? And why should I fear *life*? [However, as became plain over many sessions, he did fear death, and some aspects of life. In these conversations, as in anyone's, it is important not to take any one statement as set in stone.] Your life is your undiscovered country. No one else will ever live it, and it wouldn't be good for anybody if they did—but it was good that *you* did.

People imitated yours.

They imitated what they thought they could see—and not even all they could have seen, let alone what they did not see and were not smart enough or thoughtful enough to see. They saw sea-fishing and bullfight-studying, and physical enjoyments, but did they think about the reading and thinking and the passions and what was behind the passions? I became a Catholic. Did they think that was a sentimental gesture to Spain? Yet I was not a comfortable Catholic—can an American become a comfortable Catholic, I wonder? Did they think about that? No, imitation may be flattery, but it is more like counterfeiting. Who wants flattery from someone who would flatter?

Do you regret anything in your life?

Of course, but what good does it do except to shine light on who you are and where you are doing the regretting?

None. Well, maybe it helps steer your course.

Don't believe it. Good resolutions—how many good resolutions do you suppose have ever been carried through in this world? On either side of this world, come to that. You don't do what you resolve to do, you do what you mean to do, what you have to do, because you are whatever you are. If you're doing it, you see, you don't need to make resolutions. If you aren't, you aren't going to keep them anyway.

Have you been used to create others in this past 45-plus years? [I meant, had his energy on the other side been used as a template for others coming in to this life, a process often misunderstood as reincarnation.]

That's a long subject involving people catching contagion from my writing, and others from my publicity, and others from the qualities they infer. The short answer is yes; the longer answer is no. One Ernest Hemingway was enough and cannot be reproduced. But many of my qualities and characteristics are common enough, and here and there some people combine various threads and produce something more like me.

[I quoted some dialogue from *The Sun Also Rises*, where Brett says it makes her feel good that she decided not to be a bitch: "It's sort of what we have instead of God," and, after Jake says that quite a lot of people have God, she says, "He never worked out very well with me."]

The dialogue I quoted—

Yes. That is more the gist of the book in a way than the lines everyone always quotes. But [most people] wouldn't quote those lines because they don't like the message. The people who understand them and approve of them mostly don't read it. Or if they do they don't notice because it's plain as day to them, as it was to you.

The rottenness of society was plain enough in the book, by contrast to the simplicity and cleanness of the same people in simpler surroundings. But the underlying cause of the rottenness wasn't. It seemed like some vague result of the war.

Different people read different things into it. The war exploded an awful lot of hollow containers, platitudes, and conceited complacent self-assurance. Naturally it affected most those with the shallowest roots—and of course Spain hadn't been involved in the war, and Spain was Catholic in the way that France was rationalism, or was money. France was modern and it drew all the rottenness of people with too

much money and not enough work to do—and France had also lost the
war and didn't acknowledge it, although they knew it well enough—so
money and pleasure were hollow but were more important as something
to sell than they had been as something to live. Again, we are talking
about the cities, and about the upper classes. The poor and the peasants
always bear the burden and always will, but their very helplessness keeps
them closer to what is real. It stops them from racketing along and going
off the rails. Of course it just as often sinks them into the mud beyond
hope of ever seeing the stars.

Plus, perhaps, the peasants in France are still Catholic?

A Catholic Frenchman is Catholic and French in the way that you
were Catholic and American. You can look at one side or the other and
lose sight of the opposite pole.

*Still they were Catholic and that surely differentiated them from the
urban rich.*

Distinctions look clearer with distance in time or space, and more so
with distance in both. But broadly, yes.

*In a way it is as if your book, and Fitzgerald's and others, gave people
an excuse to give up.*

That isn't what you intended to say at first, but in any case our books
succeeded because our editors correctly sensed that we were saying something that many others would have said if they could have, and therefore
that we would succeed because we were speaking for our generation, who
would support those who gave it a voice. Remember, in years we were still
very young. We were forced, like hothouse flowers.

Forced by your war experiences?

More like your generation was forced by the 60s, except that we
were *doing* things rather than spending years in college *reading about*
things. When an old phase of civilization is abruptly replaced—when
it ends with a bang instead of imperceptibly, little by little—it is a shock
that brings some people to consciousness. Others, it may knock out, or

anyway stun. But some are carried outside of the common dream and see as from outside looking in. You yourself are in that situation because of the life you lead and have led, that you are tempted to complain of or repent. It is being outside the dream that produces a full consciousness that forces you.

Yes. Thank you, I will pass this on.

Do you think you're not living? Do you think your life is dull?

I get the point. I know this is a gift to me and from me.

Good. Don't forget it.

⁓3⁓

For Whom the Bell Tolls

Wednesday, June 13, 2007

Oh, Papa, your For Whom the Bell Tolls! Does it not tell the truth! Such a relief from political lying, even by those on our side—so to speak. [Even] Upton Sinclair [for instance] did not tell the truth as you did.

Upton Sinclair told the truth as Claude Bowers told it—as a form of weapon, as a club to beat the fascists and reactionaries with. But I was trying to do a deeper thing than that.

I know—and yours surely had a wider appeal.
You think wider because you think that fewer people would discount it as merely the result of propaganda, or a political agenda. But that isn't as true as saying that it offended everyone because it attacked their stereo-types, but [on the other hand] it got by them because it also seemed to attack their enemies. What was not so easily seen for some reason was that it was a portrait of the idealistic American who genuinely knew and loved Spain. He was in a place that didn't even see him as an American, in a way: They called him ingles even after he corrected them, even though he spoke their language to them, and could think inside their heads. He was very much a product of America, an America they could never be brought to understand.

He was forced to use the terms of the left—which quickly hardened into Stalinist cant—but he knew that he wasn't really one of them. He just knew that he hated injustice and that while the Russians might not be trusted to hate injustice, at least they pretended to be, and said they were, and they were providing real material assistance to those who were, fighting the fascists—and about the fascists there could be no mistake.

So Roberto Jordan was in no man's land, and by 1937 he was used to it, and saw no way forward but to continue with the only allies he had, or rather to subordinate himself to the only armed organized force that opposed all he opposed.

I liked that you showed what the peasants did in 1936, the complications of their reactions. [In other words, that he had showed the bad as well as the good.]

A story about their war was no place for whitewashing or for the creation of two-dimensional pictures that time would reveal as false. I tried to write it as true as I knew it, because it was already clear that this was going to be an elegy.

I liked that you suffused it with the total foreshadowing of defeat.

It is a very Spanish sentiment. The people know defeat, and they know how to endure. But don't forget, nobody who read the book in 1940 could be ignorant that the Republic had been doomed, no matter what they felt about it. No, nor in 1941 or 1942 or for a long time afterward, until other events buried the cause with its partisans.

Do you think—from your vantage point now—that the endurance of the Spanish did help defeat the Nazis?

Spain was to be taken in a coup in the month of July, and [Jose] Calvo Sotelo was to have been the new *çaudillo*. Unlike Franco he understood politics and would have been with Muso and Hitler in a way that might have been very damaging among the Spanish American republics. But more, it would have disheartened the French left—which was a major goal of the enterprise, from the German viewpoint. If the *frente popular* could be defeated so quickly, how much faith could the workers have in the *frente popular* of France? [I don't know the French words and had hoped that Hemingway could put them in. Basically he said, don't worry about it.]

Much more to the point, the Spanish resistance put the fascist intervention on the world's front pages—and kept it there. It was supposed to happen in the dark, you see. It was to be a three days' wonder, not even a nine days' wonder, and then be done but for the killing. But when the workers took over cities, and the Air Force didn't come over, and the Navy, suddenly the coup was in trouble. A coup that doesn't succeed in a few days is doomed, because it means that it has shot its bolt, no surprise remains, and it has not met response. So it could not be presented as the will of the people, even by the boldest lying, which of course was immediately employed.

So then if Muso wouldn't provide troops and equipment—equipment particularly—the fascists were going to lose.

They couldn't afford to lose, and Mussolini thought anyway he was going to get another cheap victory. It was the next step up from Ethiopia, you see. First the niggers of Africa—that is how he would see it—then the played-out Spanish, with their reds like the ones he had put down at home, and then who knows? Spain had a big empire and who knows? Also, it would show the frightening upstart to his north that Italy too could play at empire building.

So when the Republic didn't fall to a coup, it provided an opportunity for Muso to show what his troops could do (which, too bad for him, it did) and for Hitler to give his Air Force practice in actual war conditions, which the British and French later paid for, as did the Poles and Russians who had nothing to do with letting him in there.

All this helped wake up the West, because you have to understand the situation in 1936. Liberals were split between their anti-fascism and their pacifism. This rendered them totally ineffective against Hitler the master politician, who used that masterfully. Conservatives in England and France were not happy to see Germany growing so strong so quickly but they were more afraid of Russia which might be geographically more remote but was actively meddling in politics everywhere and seemed to have, in the poor, a vast fifth column in every country.

If Spain had not resisted—if Spain had not shown that the Republic had not fallen from lack of support but was being murdered—all the clarifying of position that took place between July of 1936 and March of 1939 would not have taken place in the same way. Hitler would have been enabled to do much more perhaps, and have gotten even further entrenched, before the West awoke.

This is a complicated subject because what also happened is that the world saw Russia come to the aid of the Spanish Republic with arms and equipment and experienced officers—but it also saw it bring commissars and purges and little Stalins, and so there was concrete evidence too that Spain might become a Soviet republic at the gates of the Mediterranean. It wasn't a chimera. So that hardened the domestic lines as well, and confused the situation.

Still—the war started, and continued. The Western governments refused to sell arms to the Republic, and the peoples of the West gradually learned outrage. The British left in particular learned that their government was their enemy—and they did not forget it in 1945 when they got the chance to overthrow the government and the social system. The Labour government of 1945 and its various socialist reforms is one direct result of the Spanish resistance in 1936, and should be seen as such but generally isn't.

Politically, too, the war discredited a lot of anti-Communist slogans that otherwise might have gotten quite a bit more use. After three years of lies about Spain resulted in a fascist victory at the time that Czechoslovakia had been swallowed up, people weren't as willing to hear all the same fairy tales yet again. Truth can get tiresome, but it prevails, though it takes forever. Lies though have a definite half-life and after a while people see through them.

See it this way. Suppose Spain had been lost in July 1936. No Soviet intervention. No German Air Force training grounds. No Italian Army fiasco. No Neutrality Act debate in the United States. No clarity to the British opposition [about] the Spanish or the French weakness in the face of threats. Continued pacifism in France without correction by facts. Continued pacifism, in fact, all through the West on the left—leaving a clear field for the fascists.

With Spain absorbed into their coalition, Hitler and Muso had France surrounded by hostile neighbors as in 1870, and a little before it actually occurred. Hitler's moves against Czechoslovakia and Poland would have proceeded against a far more tranquil background.

No, don't ever doubt it. Spain bought time. Time for liberals to decide between anti-fascist and anti-militarism; time for Western statesmen particularly in England to reveal themselves as hopelessly unable to combine with workers against fascists; time for the world's populations to have their attention fixed on the snake-like advance of fascism. That time was bought with Spanish blood. They didn't die for that purpose, but that was the result. Also—but it didn't do as much good—the Civil War showed clearly what Stalinism was, if any in the West on the left were willing to see and didn't already know. And so it helped to prepare for the impact of *Darkness at Noon* that, as you know, saved France from going communist after the war.

Thank you. That was quite an interesting discussion. It isn't where I had thought we would go. I thought it was just one question. But that will have to do for now.

≈4≈

Spain and the Modern World

[I entered what I had gotten into the computer, and prepared it as a post for my blog. But I worried about "hearing" some things wrong. A couple of days before, I had hesitated, trying to feel if Hemingway had been "raised a Catholic" or "converted to become a Catholic," not then knowing which it was. Similarly, on this day when I wrote that the Navy had stayed loyal to the Spanish Republic, I then thought, maybe not. I finally decided to go with what I was given, because if I were to insist on 100 percent verification I would cut off access, whereas if I were to take what came as it came, at least I would create a track record that I could judge after the fact. Giving myself permission to get some of it wrong without assuming that the whole process is invalid was a liberating step, one that would be necessary for nearly anyone trying to do this work, I think.]

(12:40 p.m.) So, Papa—and this is because I feel so much closer to you as I read your work and I have now read so much in so short a time, that "Mr. Hemingway" no longer seems appropriate—about For Whom the Bell Tolls.

Well, the title gives away the message, of course. The West looked on and thought it didn't concern them, and then over months that became years they learned that it did, very closely. And in a larger sense, Robert Jordan had learned, and was living, the same lesson. He joined because he loved Spain. He stayed because it wasn't just about Spain and Spaniards.

I liked, too, that you had him at one point violently enraged with them as a people, such that as you said "if she had spoken at that moment he would have struck her," or words to that effect.

Anyone could tell you, they are an exasperating people—and that same anyone, if he or she has truly lived among them—would immediately begin to list exceptional individuals, and then countervailing virtues, and reasons to make allowance.

So what was it about them? You said they hadn't been touched by the Reformation—but neither had Russia, or that end of the Mediterranean world.

Spain did not receive nor even have to overthrow and defeat the [Protestant] Reformation in its home territories, only in [its possessions in] the low countries and east, where it wasn't particularly successful. At home, church and state remained fused by emotion and identification no less than by mutual self-interest. "His Catholic Majesty" was a great boast, and a reassurance that the faith in Spain was purer, better reverenced and in all ways better—as anything Spanish was bound to be, if one discounted non-medieval, non-aristocratic pursuits as technology, finance and anything the British (particularly) were good at. [Recording this, I felt a gentle irony, which I hope comes through.]

It was because Spain was in no way modern that it was so deeply appealing, so deeply human. It had escaped our modern drawbacks and the dwarfing by technological forces and "modern ideas" that killed Europe. But it is also the fact that Spain was not modern that made it so infuriating, so alien, so incomprehensible unless you learned to understand with your heart. Now, you understand, "modern" in this case doesn't mean up to date technologically or scientifically, certainly not militarily. I mean a way of looking out at the world.

You distinguished Spain and France very economically and clearly in The Sun Also Rises, I thought.

You had eyes to see. But I did not try to say *why* they were different, only one instance of *how*.

The modern world when it finally came to Spain was very cruel to it—as cruel as *la leyenda negra* could ask. ["La leyenda negra"—the black legend—is what Spanish people called their reputation for cruelty that foreigners ascribe to them.] It was the communists and the anarchists, the POUM [Trotskyists] and the anti-clericals, the people who would have collaborated with Napoleon to "modernize" Spain, who were responsible for some of the hatred that lead to implacable warfare instead of even a vestige of compromise. It was the fascists and Falangists and monarchists—the Carlists and the Alfonso-ists (so to speak) and every brand of reactionary who resisted that force; they were the rest of the hatred.

In Spain there was no reconciling force. The middle class, that in our country gave stability even at the price of great inertia, did not exist as a *modern* middle class. It existed as a sort of middle class in a feudal society, which is why so few of the middle class ever served the Republic. It wasn't just fear of the peasants and workers. The workers and peasants represented, to them, 1789, and they were sure would be the end. The miniature jacqueries of 1936 seemed to them to prove them right.

So then what of the modern world is poison that they were still exempt from?

They were not economic digits, nor grains of sand in the universe, nor accidents of creation. They were still creatures of God, with dignity and individuality and their own importance regardless how hard their lives or how unjust or incompetent their economic or technical or social arrangements. They were ignorant of trends but immersed in deeper currents, scarcely consciously. You might compare them to yourself, living without television in a hypnotized land. Of course this is only partly true. The modern world was coming in, a bit at a time. But it came not in an overwhelming tidal wave as in France in 1789, nor in a steadily rising tide as in, say, England, nor even in a patchwork as in geographic Italy in the 1800s, or German states. It came only by exception. The Civil War brought the modern age though it didn't mean to. So many Italian soldiers, so many German influences, so many foreign novelties on both sides—not gadgets but viewpoints—could have no other effect. War always modernizes while it destroys. It almost doesn't matter who wins, in that respect.

So the Spain of today would be fundamentally different from that of 80 years ago—fundamentally, beneath changes in technology and economics?

Think of the changes in the American national character in that time and ask again. Some of those changes would have seemed very unlikely, if not impossible. War may be the health of the state; it isn't the health of the country.

Thank you for all of us. Is there a message you'd like to give us? Beyond what you have already?

Read "El Viejo y el Mar" [*The Old Man and the Sea*] or in English if need be.

That's on my list. Haven't read it in a long time.

≈5≈

The Old Man and the Sea

(10:30 p.m.) Mr. Hemingway—Mr. phenomenal writer Hemingway—talk to me about The Old Man and the Sea.

It is a love story, of course. The old man loved the world, and his life, and everything in his life, and he particularly loved the boy who loved him. He loved the fish he caught, and God who had put him there, and even certain things about the sharks.

He was a tough old man of great unconscious pride and no arrogance.

Yes, that is right. He would have seemed arrogant in his strength in his middle years but he had learned humility, and not by being beaten down or humiliated by anyone or by anything or circumstances, but just in the way a man at night in the ocean would see his size and the size of all around him and know that he is not nothing, but he is not the be-all and end-all either. Only those who get close enough to the source of living get to understand that, though perhaps some people are born knowing.

Somehow "he was dreaming of lions" makes it clear that he was not defeated in what he was, but just in one thing that he had tried to do.

It is a matter of perspective, merely. He had had a full life and it had come down to a few symbols that came to him when he dreamed. He didn't know what caused them to come and not other things, he just knew that in a way this is what he had left. He didn't dream of his wife, or of women he had known, or the Negro he had beaten at arm wrestling. He did not dream of triumphs or defeats, but of lions as he had seen them and heard them on a far-off shore long before when he was a boy, and when he was a young man.

The symbols—the lions—didn't go away or change to something else just because he had triumphed and then been defeated.

No. They were beyond being taken away by anything that could happen to him. He could break the connection by being unworthy, but no external event could break the connection.

What else about el viejo or the boy or anything?

If you could have found it in Spanish or if you find it now and spend the time with it, you will see things you cannot see so easily in English. It is short enough that with the dictionary you can make your way through it without great trouble, and with pleasure, and you may absorb it through the skin.

≈6≈

Beisbol and Santiago

Thursday, June 14, 2007

Papa, the talk of beisbol and Joe DiMaggio was to show us that Santiago was not a philosopher but a simple man?

It was to show that he was not an educated man. It also showed a valid aspect of their lives, tied in second hand to Yanqui baseball teams that practiced in Cuba. What can be older than being a fisherman? Yet he followed the box scores and sometimes wished for a radio so that he could hear the games. He had heard of DiMaggio having a bone spur and knew that it was painful but didn't quite know what it was. He used that to give himself courage against pain, not knowing how the one shaped up compared to the other.

You used it, too, to link them closer to the American reader?

It gives a common reference point, and that it means something different to the old man reminds the reader that it is a different society. That the boy and others share the obsession and the way of seeing it reminds the reader that it is not the old man's peculiarity.

[Later]

So. A sus ordenes.

You wonder, will you see Spain?

I wonder, more, why am I being drawn there again when there is so little chance I can see it. Even if I go I cannot see.

You might say some more about your feelings about travel, and learn something thereby.

All right. When I travel alone, or with another stranger, I feel like I am looking through a plate glass window. I can't get to the lives of the people, I can only look on.

And this is different from the rest of your life—how?

No, you are absolutely correct. In that too it is the same.

And so?

And so I look at what was, and what can be understood by means of books or movies.

Or psychic experience, or interpersonal relations.

Yes.

So you are never immersed?

No, it seems not. It isn't much of a life.

No? What would you do?

Well that's a point. I don't know.

There is nothing to be done but to play whatever cards one holds. If you are an intuitive you cannot expect to live a sensory life. If you are a mystic you cannot expect to be immersed in the everyday life. No one is everything because in duality to be everything would be to be nothing, or to be the opposite of some other part of a larger something.

I must write.

Sure. Not for publication so much as for company.

Yes, I can see that. I can write and thus talk to myself, nothing more.

Nothing more, nothing less. Cervantes talked to himself, and so do all storytellers. Emerson and Thoreau are bad influences for you in one sense: their world was very much more grounded in experience than yours. Emerson's more than Thoreau's, but both. It is in the internal experience that you connect with them—but you are going where they never did, and you should recognize that with joy. Write your novel as [in the way that] you hear these conversations and you will be at home.

This is what you did too, then.

Of course. It is what storytellers do: they create their re-creation. They live in another world in this world. They make manifest what was only a glimmering. Santiago lives, now, and the boy, and they will live a long time. Are they less real than I was? No, a better way to put it is, are they less real than I am now?

The way you put it, it is like borrowing from the other [non-physical] side to bring into this side so it can be put into form on the other side.

That's *exactly* what it is—and your gift for putting that into words is what you were shaped for. You are no more and no less real than Santiago or me. It is only while we are passing through the physical side that there appears to be a difference.

The guys would say, I think, only while that wave of the present is passing over us.

You see? You can grasp it, you can translate it, you can convey it. You are fishing in deep waters and you can describe the process as carefully as I could describe fishing in the Gulf Stream and *we are describing the same process.*

≈7≈

Harry Morgan and Paul Potts

Wednesday, June 20, 2007

[A video from a television show called "Britain's Got Talent" showed an unassuming man named Paul Potts suddenly revealing an amazing voice as he sang opera. He went on to win, and Hemingway, being in touch with my mind, knew what I knew.]

Papa, what do you think of Paul Potts and my reading of his life?

You wouldn't think to connect him with Harry Morgan, but think of what I was showing in *To Have and Have Not*: Everything had gotten so big, interconnections were so far beyond the individual, that it was hard for the individual to go his own way as he always had. That is what broke Harry Morgan: he had to get into things involving too many unreliable or hostile people, and it got beyond his ability to control the situation.

Paul Potts was bullied and he found refuge in his talent. He pushed on and found himself on the brink of ruin. Only by staying true to his gift, which means true to himself, did he save himself by entering the competition that put him into another world that until then he could not enter. Will he be able to stay true to himself? If he stays true to the gift and not the trappings, he can do it. Otherwise I'd say his chances aren't much better than Harry Morgan's: he will get into deep waters, into a situation he can't control or direct or even understand, and it will kill him.

We will hope for the best, and trust that he was fashioned to provide a model for people needing hope.

The question is simple but as always it is the crucial question: can he stay true to himself, true to his gift? But there wouldn't be much point in fashioning an experiment that couldn't fail. Even Jesus could have failed. Think how tedious it would be, if we could not!

≈ 8 ≈

Pretending and Lying

[When I travel, I read, and one day in a bookshop in Chester, England, I bought *The Young Hemingway*, by Michael Reynolds. That purchase turned out to have big consequences! What I read troubled me, and two days later, in a hotel in Manchester, I set down my thoughts.]

Tuesday, July 31, 2007

Mr. Hemingway, you said you couldn't stand phonies, and clearly you couldn't. How do you reconcile this with so much pretending and rearranging and lying and misremembering and leading people on?

That is quite an indictment, but I have to concede it. In my defense I could say this. It is one thing to pretend until you can achieve—fake it until you make it, as your business partner says—and another very different thing to pretend that you are what you are not. It is true, there isn't much difference in a boy.

I am sorry, I can't see much difference in a grown man protecting a territory of lies however young he was when he created them.

Perhaps you can see it this way. Lies, stories, imaginings, have consequences. Some are internal, the stories you tell yourself in order to bring a better you into existence. Others are external, and you have to live with them. If you tell someone you are 22, and you are barely 20, at some point you may have to overcome the consequences of even so small a thing. The internal consequences may be small or nonexistent—you were, after all, merely wishing yourself a little farther along the path. But the external consequences may be larger, or even maybe important, depending on what that lie or exaggeration does to the person you told it to. Will she then know to distrust your facts? Will she distrust *you*? But there isn't any going back once you've made the wrong step.

Why isn't there?

If I said I was in the Italian army when the truth is that I *wanted to be* with the Italian army, and *wanted to be* a soldier among the soldiers, to correct this story would be merely to adjust it to the externals rather than the internals. Why do you think I was in harm's way in the first place? I wanted to be a soldier among soldiers, a man among men. There was no reason for a Red Cross man to be at a forward post except wanting to be among the men at the lines, and do what I could even if it was only bringing them little comforts. To correct my story would have been to dishonor that aspiration, as I saw it then.

You were improving on the truth.

I was reporting what I was experiencing on the inside.

And wearing the uniform and the cape afterwards?

You should understand clinging to what had been.

And I understand your needing to remind yourself that you were not merely what you appeared; were not fated (doomed) to return to your hometown and revert to being seen as what you didn't want to be.

I had an eye that would have kept me out of it entirely, so life found a different path for me to get the taste I needed, then pay prolonged consequences.

≈9≈

Plotting

[Nearly four months had gone by. Then I thought to ask Hemingway if he could help me to plot my prospective novel, which I ultimately called *Babe in the Woods*.]

Of course. It isn't difficult if approached from a certain angle.

You somewhat misconstrue me in thinking that I merely set characters into a situation and see what they would do. That was Thomas Hudson's advice to Roger, not my advice to the reader. Thomas Hudson gave him that advice because Roger had been misusing his talents and had lost his ability to formulate anything that wouldn't sell to Hollywood. Also, remember, Thomas Hudson was a painter, not a writer, but the caveat on the advice is the same. You are not in danger of perverting your story for the sake of selling. Your danger is self-induced paralysis.

Consider what you know. You know the setting, the characters and the central issue you wish to illustrate. You know the various side-trails you would like to shed light on. What you lack is a logical progression of incidents of dramatic power that will embody and illustrate the issues. So the easy fix is to list the issues and the characters and fix them in relation to Angelo [the main character]. You could easily do this with cards that you can physically arrange and rearrange as desired.

Could you do this for me? With me?

Or in fact help you eliminate the process? No, not to any good effect. What would that do but reinforce your fears that you can't do this? I have given you what you need. Do the arranging and re-arranging and then come back and we can talk some more, whenever you require. For this way you will see the logic and structural stability of it better than if it were handed to you. It will be yours, arising from your own experiences and beliefs. If you get stuck devising events or relating things one to the other in some form that gives dramatic power, we can talk.

[The novel got written, and of course I experienced it as myself doing the work. The final result did not resemble a Hemingway story, and the process did not include a sense of Hemingway's day-by-day presence. The only sign that something unusual had happened is that it came easily and quickly, and was done more skillfully than I had been able to do previously. Having produced a first draft, I returned for advice.]

≈ 10 ≈
Novels and Self-revelation

Wednesday, April 2, 2008

Papa Hemingway, I have been reviewing Babe in the Woods. Is the story too slight? And if so why and how can it be fixed? I already instantly hear some of your response but for clarity let's set it out in order.

You might say I've been waiting for you to ask. It's as if I were leaving the manuscript uncompleted and I always hated to do that if I got that close to the end.

You *know* what is missing—the elements of self-revelation that cut closest to the bone. Nothing on sex, nothing on family, nothing on boredom and spiritual stagnation, nothing on metaphysical despair or wild unreasoning hope. All of that is out of the picture. Now it would be one thing to deliberately mute and even suppress them to keep Angelo in character, but that isn't what you are doing. You are suppressing them lest they say too much about you. But in that case you should choose another profession. Novel writing is strip-teasing if it is anything. You can't pretend and be a successful prophet—and what else do you want to be but a prophet? If your stories don't move *you*, how should they move anyone else? To the degree that you have been honest—about healing, even a bit about asthma—people have been taken by it. Spiritual seeking, too, or anyway psychic exploration. But if it is still slight, it is because in too many areas you have not dared to take the lid off and see what would emerge. [Etc.]

Can I thank you enough?

The work is fun, and is thanks enough.

≈11≈

Reputation

[Revision completed, I self-published the novel and went on to other things. More than seven months went by.]

Wednesday, Nov. 26, 2008

In re-reading The Sun Also Rises, I realized for the first time that Hemingway did not admire or entirely approve of his narrator. At least, that was my conclusion. Papa? That right?

Is your narrator [in Babe in the Woods] you, however many of your traits you may have given him? Yes, I didn't approve of his pimping his love to Romero. It amounted to betraying himself and his aficion. "It was not pleasant," I said, meaning not that he was misunderstood but that he was reaping where he had sowed. A man may share one of our passions as he may share our politics or our taste in art, and yet have no fundamental connection to us.

Of course. Thank you. Is there anything that we who have profited from your life and words can do for you?

Our reputations don't mean anything to us now in terms of ego or career building—but they do matter in that they can make it easier or harder for someone who needs us to find us. So merely spreading the word about *how you see us* helps us.

≈12≈

Unfinished Business

Tuesday, January 27, 2009

[My reaction to a novel about Hemingway's overlooked World War II Q-boat operation made me wonder if I were being prompted to obtain access to whatever reports he must have filed with the Navy, to get that period of his life onto the record.]

All right, Papa. I have been fighting this for a variety of reasons, not least of which is fear of self-deception. But I guess I'm out of excuses. The thought occurred to me a minute ago that perhaps this is the beginning of another book like Chasing Smallwood. Papa, is that it?

If you will consult some of the things you have read—The Secret Vaults of Time and its story about Glastonbury Cathedral, for instance—you will realize that unfinished business [among those who have left this life] is not perhaps as rare as you might think. You could look at it as us having unfinished business, or you could look at it as the unfinished business in us being activated by someone's intent who is still alive. There are other ways to look at it as well, but those two should be enough to help you to realize that what is going on is not automatically something to be dismissed. Maybe it will turn into nothing, maybe not, but in any case you can't dismiss it out of hand as a possibility.

You may remember that in our first exchange you asked me about the stories that I had fabricated about my early life, and I told you then that it was a way of imaginatively re-creating life as it ought to have been. But in a way you could say that people have been imaginatively re-creating my life for me, after the fact, because serious portions of it have been suppressed for reasons good or bad. So, if somebody writes about Hemingway during World War II, they are inclined to say, "Oh, he was only a drunkard, or a partygoer anyway, romanticizing his involvement in the war and unintentionally demonstrating that he didn't really care about it." You have seen critical reports dismissing my work in France as playacting, with me in the center of the play. It was only later, with Carlos Baker's book, that the truth of what I had done began to emerge.

It was a solid achievement. It saved American lives. It cost me not only a certain theoretical danger of prosecution for acting outside the Geneva Convention, but it cost me the additional bitterness of being dismissed as a playboy and having to lie about something I was deeply proud of. Had we been able to tell the truth, people might have understood better why I retained the respect of people like Buck Lanham. Instead, they assume that I somehow blinded them with my reputation, as though a good soldier in wartime is going to have his judgment warped by factors like reputation, literary or otherwise.

If people had seen what I really did, it would have showed them some things. First, that I was practical. I really knew how to get results. Second, that I was intensely patriotic, although you would think that would have been obvious even to that stupid son of a bitch J. Edgar Hoover. Third—and this is what they would have found hard to forgive—that I was thoroughly without illusions about that war or any war. No, I wasn't a soldier in World War I. But I was the first American to be wounded, and I spent months in the hospital surrounded by veterans who were happy to talk veteran to veteran, and like Jack London in Alaska, I learned more from talking and listening than perhaps I would have by several months' experiences even in the Army. I knew war and I knew that sometimes there is no alternative but that even when there is no alternative war is not a good thing for anybody. There is a rottenness to it. Brave things are done with it. Splendid examples of manhood and you almost might call it godhood are produced out of the hell that it is. But the brave things in the splendid examples are not justifications for the hell. It's just that if you get into a fight you have to win it, no matter who got you there or for what reasons and no matter how clearly you can see through the bullshit that is spun around it.

But you see, if people took into account the fact that I had spent months among the wounded in World War I and that I had spent months first as an unofficial sub-hunter and coordinator of The Crook Factory and then, after Hoover shut that down, as informal leader of the temporary band of partisans who found which ways were clearest and cheapest for our army to get to Paris, they would have to reevaluate their opinion of me. But *because* I was not a phony, I couldn't explain why I was not a phony. So, they took me as a poseur.

It hurt. Of course it hurt. If I had been a private figure, probably the respect of the people whom I respected would have been enough. But I was a public figure and had been for years, and so I never had the luxury of the anonymity that would have left public opinion indifferent to me. I'm not complaining, I'm just saying that I as a public figure was liable to misinterpretation. Liable to libel. It was the very kinds of people who theoretically opposed war and in practice did nothing to get the war finished who were delighted to be able to attack me as inauthentic, as playing at war, as self glorifying and lying.

A lot of time has gone by, where time goes by [in 3-D]. I don't want you to get the idea that time passes in the same way over here and we spend it drinking and reminiscing and reading old press clippings and brooding over bad reviews. But, as I say, active interest from a living person sort of activates any given unfinished business. So, you get incensed at Marty's [second wife Martha Gellhorn's] treatment of me as portrayed, or at Marty as an individual whose traits annoy you, when you aren't even thinking of her particularly at all. Your interest is focused on me. Yet she hears your opinion, and therefore that portion of her life is somewhat activated. It is a price of fame that has been very little understood in the days since we left off praying to saints and cursing demons.

You think I have an agenda for you. That isn't exactly wrong, but it isn't like anybody can make you do anything either. You will find that it is easier to perceive on this side than to act and easier to contact those in the body than to come up with a clear contact and develop clear communication. Go get something to eat and read some more if you want, and we can always continue when and if you want to.

All right, Papa. I know there's some link between us. You know I'll do what I can, if I can persuade myself that I can do it and that there's something to do.

[This was a big leap for me. It's one thing to have these conversations in private; another to put it out in the open for people to criticize and perhaps discredit.]

≈ 13 ≈

Opening Pathways

Wednesday, January 28, 2009

All right, Papa. I have never faced stronger resistances than I am now. I have a feeling this is the deepest water I've ever swum in—or rather hesitated to swim in.

Well, I understand the point. That's just part of the price of doing something new. It isn't that much different from starting a new project, a book, a painting. But you can't create anything new without facing it, so in the end that's the choice you have to make one way or the other.

You are wondering what the agenda is. You're right that it is not strictly about my wartime service from Cuba. It's true, it would be nice to have that story told sympathetically and accurately, but that doesn't mean you're the person to do it and that doesn't mean that it would be the best use of your time and energy. Your function could be as simple as being the finger pointing to the moon. If someone could just get it across, the deceptive blank spot in the Hemingway biography, someone else with nothing better to do and with the requisite skills could come in and do a better job than you could. This would have the advantage of freeing you from a task you don't particularly feel qualified to do and at the same time having that task performed by a professional, which means it would find easier acceptance not only among academics but among the general public. Those are two good reasons to have a professional historian do the research and writing.

But if it isn't about your finding my records—the reports to the ambassador, the reports to the Navy, which, you are correct, still exist—then what is it about?

The task involves you more than it does me. It's more about opening up pathways within your mind than it is with uncovering information about my life. As you see with this prospective task, anything that could be falsified still fills you with apprehension, almost paralyzes you. This is the next hurdle for you to get over. And who better to help you through this bottleneck then I? Like your friend David [Poynter, a Welsh journalist of the 19th and 20th centuries, a "past life" of mine, if the story I was given is right], I am a writer, but unlike him I am a writer whose work can be found, whose life is somewhat known. You may not know the connection between yourself and me, but it's clear enough that it exists, surely. Nor need it be a tie between a part of you and a part of me that is Hemingway in particular. But that's neither here nor there, since the Hemingway persona is what offers you the tools required.

≈14≈

Fame and Relationship

[My friend and former business partner Bob Friedman was following these conversations with interest. Having met Mariel Hemingway, he wondered if her grandfather had a message for her.]

Thursday, June 25, 2009

Papa, I know that Bob would love to have a message from you to your granddaughter. So would I if you wanted to send it, but on the other hand— well, you know.

I do, and I recognize the crosscurrents within you. Tell Bob, I know of his [Ph.D.] dissertation on men and war because you know of it because you know him and *he* knows it. If you had read it, it would have been a shorter circuit, but everything connects sooner or later. Just because you're interested, I'll say a little about the process as we experience it.

I'm famous and I die and on your side people keep reading me and keep writing about me. It all sorts out automatically in degrees of closeness. My family talking about me is one thing, my friends, another; acquaintances, another level further away, people reading me in school, say, another. It isn't organized in any way; I'm trying to show you that there are different degrees of closeness, just like in your own lives. The world has billions of people—that doesn't mean you're equally affected by all of them, and how could you be? There's close and there's far and there's might-as-well-not-even-exist. There are degrees of relationship in everything. Some things are closer than others, it's that simple. It's true of spatial relationships and it's true of people. You have your family, your lovers, your close friends, your acquaintances, etc., as I said. The nearer ones have more effect on you than the farther ones do.

But it sorts out another way, too. There are those who are closer or farther from you temperamentally. My mother and I weren't at all close intellectually, or even emotionally except in opposition. Her reaction to the story-telling part of me isn't nearly as close to me as [F. Scott] Fitzgerald's, say, or even Morley's [Morley Callaghan]. They came closer to my writing *center*, you might say. And I don't mean to pick them out, particularly. They're just examples. Max Perkins certainly understood me better than Fitzgerald, for instance. But see, there is an example for you. Scott Fitzgerald was close to my emotional life *and* my writing life *and* my—what do you want to call it? My *emotional everyday* life. So that's three categories.

Oh hell, this is getting too theoretical. The simplest thing is to say that those who know you best may know you in different ways. They may be related to you, they may spend a lot of time with you, they may have shared common tasks, or maybe they just *know* you because you're the same thing somehow. Hotchner and me, for instance. So what I wanted to tell you is that over here, somebody who has been famous has left lots of cords hanging down that people can yank. But not everybody's yank is of equal strength, and not every yank goes past a certain threshold. So mostly we aren't particularly aware of it.

Some things get our attention. Hotchner spending enough time to write a book about us couldn't help but get my attention even if I hadn't known him. But him being a pal *and* reading my stuff *and* writing about me, of course he's going to be front and center. Mary writing about me (good or bad) or Marty or anyone I lived with—of course I am going to be there. But somebody reading my stuff and not even particularly understanding it or being moved by it—how can that get through to me, and why should it? What would it add for me or for them?

Besides, it matters if people think you're dead or if you're alive to them. Bob [Friedman] thought I was dead [when he wrote his dissertation], and so he wrote about what he could conclude I thought and felt by what I had written. That didn't touch me. But if he had had deep feelings about me and had written from them—I am not saying he should have, I'm explaining differences—if he had written from deep feelings about me, I'd have heard. If he'd written from deep instinctive sympathy with me, I'd have heard. Writing more or less as an exercise, however sincere and interested he may have been, I didn't. But now, you see, there is another hook. It is as if I met him through you and now I pick up his dissertation with the interest you acquire when you know the author. You see?

I do, I think. You're saying that we can make the acquaintance of "the dead" through our own sympathetic response to them, and they will respond and perhaps be changed.

That's it exactly, and isn't that what you've been doing since December 2005?

I'll have to tell Bob. If he can believe it, he can open a whole new world— Edgar Cayce, or anybody else who ever meant anything to him.

Yes—and this is the point of the book you're working on now [*The Sphere and the Hologram*], isn't it? You don't talk to people just for what you can learn, and not for what you can get out of them, but for companionship.

Thank you, Papa. That's the point. I'll bear it in mind.

≈15≈
Life Always Slipping By

Thursday, July 2, 2009

[It was now nearly two years since I picked up Reynolds' *The Young Hemingway* in England. The 2nd of July is, of course, the anniversary of Hemingway's suicide.]

I hope you are happy, Papa. You are, of course, much in my mind today.

Thank you. Understanding is always appreciated; it is like a cat must feel when somebody is stroking him. And you have a saying, don't you, about getting "strokes" when people complement each other? I believe you do understand why I had no good choices left, so you understand what my suicide did and didn't mean to me. But more, you *somewhat* understand and must put more effort and thought to it if you are going to *really* understand, that I like other people was a different person at different times of my life. You could say, different every single day, and with the perception of that difference comes a sort of background desperation sometimes, a sense that it's slipping away, that it could never be held in the first place. That background realization was always there, and it ought to tell you something.

I am sort of distracted at the moment, don't know why. Fragments of a movie seen again last night (Dead Again).

Coincidence?

Until I wrote down the title, the connection hadn't occurred to me. Okay—since you can probably see it more clearly than I can—what does it suggest?

I can't necessarily be responsible for your associations! But think of your father to understand me better.

Yes, I get that. Different life circumstances, but a similar wish to enjoy the day rather than living in past or future.

When you realize that your life is *always* slipping out from under your feet, as a boy you look forward to when you will be a *man* and can participate fully in life. It doesn't occur to you that life will still be slipping away behind you. As a grown man you feel the slippage but you're thinking of where you're going, what you hope is coming to you. And at some point you see that the best actual action is behind you and the best you can hope for is whatever wisdom you've accumulated, plus the use of skill you've acquired, plus you can still enjoy lots of things. But if you don't have any sense that there's more coming *after life*, the pointlessness overwhelms you, plus there's no use just sitting around waiting for death if you don't want to and aren't afraid to die. That monk John Tettemer you read about—he was old enough to be my father, and he died a good while before I did.

In 1949. [Tettemer was author of the very interesting book, I Was A Monk.]

Yes. He knew the value of the fact that the present moment doesn't exist, or is *all* that exists, however you want to look at it. He set his eyes on eternity because he could see that this life in a body is just a fast ride there.

So—your life is just an expression of carpe diem?

My life is an expression of living life to the fullest as best I could, physically and mentally. And emotionally. If I could have had a more satisfying framework for the spiritual longing that was at the core of me, I might have been happier, but maybe I couldn't have done that. You yourself have seen how hard it is to live when you don't believe in the *reality* of things.

Yes. So few things are worth much effort, unless I can persuade myself to throw myself into them, and that doesn't last.

"And that doesn't last" could sum up everybody's life, could it not?

Thank you, Papa. Your life certainly was a success in that you gave so much to the rest of us.

It's funny, isn't it? You work so hard to succeed and at the end of it, the only thing that matters is your effect on others. Not true, exactly, but in a way close enough.

≈16≈
The Edge

Friday, July 10, 2009

[My friend Hank Wesselman sent me an email in response to one of these dialogues, saying that he had been put off by Hemingway's obsession with boxing "and the fact that he proclaimed that he would rather beat someone up than read a good book." He suggested I bring it up.]

Papa, you will have read Hank Wesselman's somewhat pugnacious question to you. At first I wasn't going to ask it, but then I thought, if it was a sincere question it deserves to be asked, and deserves an answer.

All right. And this answer may illustrate for you one of the problems always attendant on this kind of work. Who are you talking to? In this case I mean, what age Hemingway? The answer you'd get from a 20-year-old isn't what you'd get ten years later, or thirty, or after-the-fact entirely.

Yes, I do see that. We're not the same person from year to year.

The whole point of living is *not* to be the same, year by year, but to change—hopefully for the better, hopefully learning something, but anyway changing with inner and outer experiences. Of course, you gain and you lose as you go along. You outgrow some things and develop new problems, maybe.

Now, one part of this question is easily dealt with. I *didn't* prefer beating somebody up to reading a good book. Just count the number of people I beat up, and the number of books I read! And, more to the point, I never said that. I may have said something like it; I may have said I love boxing even better than reading a good book, but that was in a moment of exuberance. Would you want anything you ever said—in whatever passing mood—to be taken to be your philosophical stance?

But if the problem is that I loved boxing, well, there's no defense possible, and none needed. Tastes differ. If he doesn't like boxing any more than you do, fine. But just because you don't like it doesn't mean there's anything wrong with it. I liked my life to have an *edge* on it, and boxing is a very good edge, pretty harmless except if there's an accident somehow, and great fun. You tend to think of it as beating people up, but that's because you're not considering that *you're* as likely to get beat up, unless you're the kind of guy who only fights patsies. There's nothing wrong with getting and giving a bloody nose, or bruises, or cuts, or anything, as long as you're taking the same risk and it's a fair fight.

It's like bullfighting. The *torero* isn't exactly taking advantage of the bull! If the man had armor plating, or a safe platform, or he went out there with a rifle, it would be one thing. But he goes out there with his skill and his courage and his sword and cape, and he is not as likely to die as the bull is, but it happens; and he's plenty likely to get wounded. In fact, it's damn near certain that he will be, sooner or later—and the trick then is to go back into the ring *the next time*, when his body knows full well what could happen. And that's the edge, you see. That's feeling the life within him. That's *living* right in that moment. And that's why some people get addicted to the edge.

Well, you can't fight bulls every day, and you can't do it in Paris in the 20s or Key West in the 30s. You can't risk your life in a war, or on safari, more than a few times at most in a lifetime. And who would want to? That's the edge of the edge. But boxing, it's good exercise, it's a fair fight, it's not likely to really hurt anybody, not on a friendly-match basis. You'll notice from Morley Callaghan's book, he continually gave me bruises and cut my mouth, and I didn't hold it against him—why should I?— and I kept coming back for more

Betting more money than you can afford to lose, too—that can give you the edge. If you lose, you aren't going to be killed or wounded, though you might not eat so well for a while, but while they are running you are *right there*. And then it becomes less about whatever you're betting on, and more about the bet itself. *Winning*, or the chance of winning, especially at long odds, and the chance of losing—the good chance of losing—gives you the edge. That's why betting can become an addiction, and the more a person has, the more he has to bet, so he's putting down insane amounts on something that can't be calculated—because it takes that much to give him the *edge*.

So, that's me and boxing. And me and hunting and gambling too, for that matter, as a sort of bonus. What people don't get about me for some reason—and I can't figure out why—is that I wanted *first-hand* experience of life. I didn't just read about it, I wanted to live it. *I enjoyed living in a body.* But if I [hadn't needed] to write it, to re-create it, you never would have known I existed. There are plenty of people like me only they don't write. Gregorio Fuentes, for example. All the men I hung around with who knew how to *do* things and enjoy them and do them perfectly. You just don't hear of them unless they happen to be inside your world.

≈17≈

The Hemingway Patrols

Monday, September 7, 2009, Labor Day

[Browsing in a bookstore, I found The Hemingway Patrols, by Terry Mort, and I thought, hmm.] Papa, when you were talking to me about your wartime service, it seems to me you should have known that Terry Mort was researching The Hemingway Patrols. When that thought occurred to me, then I thought I heard that you knew but I didn't, and therefore it affected the transmission. True? And in any case please comment on the questions you know I have in mind. Let's start with the question—did you know?

Like most questions asked from your side to this one, it sounds more clear-cut than it is. Your guys ["the guys upstairs"] always say "yes, but no," and that's what I'm going to do too. It's a question of focus, from either end. In other words, the more you on your side *intend* to contact us, the easier to get our attention (in a manner of speaking). The more we on our side *intend* to get your attention, the better chance we have. Common sense, after all. But there are all sorts of intending, and all sorts of hearing. For instance, if you, yourself, were to try to write a book about me, it would be a different process, with different levels of available intuition, because you'd expect to be able to contact me or at least hear from me. I'm not "dead" to you. But someone who researches my life, no matter how much he may like me or my work, is going to have a different experience if he thinks I'm dead.

Some people are stronger flashlights than others. Your intensity of purpose affects how strongly we feel your presence. I know that doesn't sound very likely to you, but think of it this way. It's the difference between someone thinking of a song in his mind, or humming it, or singing it full-throat. And distance factors in, because not everybody is at the same level of resonance. Some are connected in many ways, others only peripherally or—so to speak—accidentally, meaning tangentially because of some other interest.

And, not everybody persists in a given line of preoccupation. Not everybody thinks of the same person year after year, as you do of so *many* people—the Kennedy brothers, Churchill, Lindbergh, Thoreau, Lincoln—you know. They become themes, well-worn grooves. It is natural that with time your connection becomes deeper, more natural. Think how ours has developed—speaking only of present-life connections— since your father-in-law gave you *Islands in the Stream* in 1970!

And since I began re-reading parts of it every so often, being deeply moved. So, to go on. You were aware of Terry Mort's research?

How could I not be? He and I connect on a different wavelength than you and I do, of course. Though he is also a writer, he is much more a sportsman, and understands that sort of thing intuitively. Similarly, war and soldiering.

Not so much into talking to dead people, though, eh?

Well—not deliberately and in public!

So when I was talking to you and you were saying you wanted your war-time service revealed—when I was considering the research etc. that would have had to be done—couldn't you have said, it's being done?

In the first place, it *isn't* and *wasn't* being done. This is one small piece, more or less disregarding the Crook Factory except as background to the patrols, and, of course, not extending to France at all. By the way, notice how he got my attitude to the war exactly right, though he didn't factor in my disgust with the French and British governments. He saw that it was going from being a participant on my own to being a spectator within the big machine. Who else has ever seen that?

In the second place, the writing of the blog entry [about maybe researching Hemingway's Gulf Stream war experience] was itself worth something. It made people think who maybe never did. Now, I know that to you it looks like dropping a pebble into a stream, and it disappears, but what you can't ever see while you're functioning within time is the eventual impact of things. If Henry Thoreau getting thrown into jail for one night helped liberate India from the English, how can you tell what affects what, unless you're on this side where a given moment of time ("the present") doesn't have the same exaggerated importance?

In the third place, though in a way it ought to be "in the first place" for you—you are very stubborn and very little inclined to hear things that don't make sense to your present moment. So, if you have an assumption—and assumptions are pretty much always unconscious at base—it is hard to move you. You're easy enough to convince if you can be led to consider something, but leading you there can be a trick! So—you assumed that because nobody was doing all of it, nobody was doing *any* of it.

But do you see evidence that he examined the reports I filed? Weren't you disappointed not to have lengthy excerpts from the log, and the FBI reports, and the reports to the Navy via the ambassador? What Terry Mort did very well was to put it into focus within my life and within the war effort. That has now been done, and will have its effect. But the job isn't finished. So, there you are. I didn't mislead you, you didn't, quite, mislead yourself, and the work you did do, even though only a couple of blog entries, will have its effect. Now, meet Terry Mort, if only electronically, and see what happens.

He'll assume I'm a nut.

If not for his own inner counselors, he might. But—

Interesting. Well, we'll see.

[However, I was unable to find a way to contact him. And more than half a year went by, during which I presume (but can't remember) that among other things I was still re-reading Hemingway (for I am a great re-reader) and reading *about* Hemingway. And then the curtain rose on the next act. As usual, I had no clue what was coming.]

II

April and May 2010

[I didn't suspect it, but this entry began a series that would go on nearly every day, week after week, for months.]

The Central Experience

Thursday, April 29, 2010

I find myself recurrently thinking about—brooding on—Hemingway's emotional life. I feel that I understand him as perhaps his biographers do not, quite. What you think, Papa?

Yes, you do. Not because you have any particular insight into [the facts of] my life—many of them see the externals much more clearly—but because you know more, consciously, about the fluctuations of moods and almost possessions that we are. You could write that.

Maybe. I don't have any kind of handle on form. Oh—as I did with Joseph? [I.e. Joseph Smallwood, a "past life" I described in Chasing Smallwood.]

The bar isn't higher, just different. Joseph might not exist. I might be demonstrably different from what you get. But it is the same thing either way.

So, Papa—what would you like to say about your life and/or reading and/or experiences.

I came out of the hospital in Italy as Jack London came out of the bars in the Klondike, with no first-hand experience, but a wealth of secondhand experience. After all, I had never fired a rifle at an opponent, and hadn't even had the preliminary fear of going into combat. The shell that injured me was a bolt out of the blue to a boy who assumed his own invulnerability. So, what I *knew* was pain and suffering and irrational fear. Everything else was second-hand; the life in the lines, the comradeship of arms, the mixtures of fears and courage that filled people at different times, the nature of the Italians.

I was on slightly more first-hand ground with the love affair, except I glamorized it, adding an older man's perspective on a very young man's experience. I killed Agnes as I had had to kill my love for her when she rejected me—but the emotions and experiences Frederick Henry had were those I learned much later in life than 18. So to that extent there is a fairytale element in the love story.

All right, I romanced, telling my story to the press and to my fellows at home. I told it as I dreamed it, rather than as it was. You could look at it as novelizing without the writing of it. But the things that I pretended had happened to me, I *knew*, even though secondhand.

I do see that. And of course you and I discussed this somewhat three years ago when I read The Young Hemingway while in England.

Well, this is the foundation for understanding my later life, you see. Not Paris, not my upbringing, not the things that happened in Spain and all. Being wounded without warning, being the first of the Americans in the hospital, listening for many months to the real veterans, being able to pretend I was a veteran too, and sort of feeling that because of my wounds, I *was*. And then knowing that I had a whole extra life to lead, for I could have been killed, even *was* killed, but came back—. This was the central experience of my life, and it came before I was 20.

≈2≈

Home from the War

Friday, April 30, 2010

All right, Papa, you came home from the war and what happened externally is on record. What happened on the inside, and how conscious were you all that at the time? And—if you don't want to talk about this but about something else instead, we can do that.

Getting off the gangplank in New York worked well. A nice piece of theater, but it was sort of necessary, too. I didn't want to be crowded in any sense of the word. Not physically, not in terms of attention. But I was 19—I didn't realize that what I was doing was going to have consequences that couldn't be blotted out later when they would be embarrassing. Besides, maybe I didn't care that much. It was important that I not go back to be that school kid. And the war was over; no more chances for glory, and what I had was going to have to do. So if I glamorized things, and made myself out to be more than I had done—notice that, to *be* more than I had *done*—it seemed worthwhile, necessary.

I hadn't been in the Army—but I would have been, if they'd taken me. I *was* wounded, legitimately, and for being where I hadn't needed to be. Shouldn't I use those wounds, since I'd gotten them?

People write that yours were wounded heroes, and they psychologize you extensively, as you know.

Yes, but they don't see things whole. A lot of them never *wanted* to see me whole, because they weren't seeing *me* at all. They took me to be a cardboard recruiting poster for things they hated, like war, and the military, or hunting and fishing. Boxing. Anything too physical for them. So—if they're using you as a punching bag, you can't expect that they're going to play fair. Understanding me is the last thing they wanted—they wanted to destroy me.

I can see that among some of the critics in your day. But others really did try to understand, I think.

The point is, what I stood for, what I loved to do, wasn't popular; wasn't in style.

≈ 3 ≈

Q-boat

Saturday, May 1, 2010

[Speaking about the decade of the forties] Ten years out of your life, eh, Papa?

Fucking right. Ten years out of my *writing* life, which is my closest, most precious, part. Everything else in my life was sort of relaxing from it, or holding it away.

And from 1940 to 1950 you weren't able to publish anything but Men at War.

Bearing in mind that writing is one thing and publishing is another. But the real chunk out of my writing life was between the rest period after Bell and the time after the war was over when I could start working again.

But so much was changed, lost. That is what Islands was about: irretrievable loss and what you had to do to deal with it in a manly way, instead of falling into self-pity or despair. A man had to know how to use his despair to build something.

Assuming you could retain faith in the value of building something.

Exactly. Or—if you couldn't—you had to proceed anyway. What else was there to do? Having fun isn't fun if you don't offset it with some meaningful work.

The Q-boat work was meaningful.

Yes it was, but it wasn't *my* work, particularly. I mean, it was work that I was fitted to do, and it was necessary work, but it wasn't writing. Accumulating raw materials, maybe.

And the work in France?

Well, more than anything, that was the cause of bitterness. I did a good job and couldn't talk about it. The Army knew I did a good job, and had to pretend I didn't, had to pretend it didn't know, had to pretend to investigate, even. And the end result was that I couldn't even use it in my writings.

What did you think of your war reporting?

It didn't have much permanent value, and I acquired the knowledge it gave me at too high a price. I didn't realize it at the time, but that concussion in London was too high a price even all by itself.

I found your "First Poem to Mary" very revealing. Maybe more revealing than anything else you put into poetry.

You—knowing me and knowing my life—could read *into* that poem and *see* things.

Yes—like you expected to die in that boat, and so did those around you—or was that just romancing?

You go attack a submarine in a 38-foot boat and tell me if you expect to survive. But the war gods smiled on us, and we couldn't catch the son of a bitch, so we lived.

Pardon a naïve question. If you expected to die if you engaged the sub—why engage it? I mean, what good would it do anybody for you to be killed without doing it any harm?

You couldn't know that. We had our plans and we had been out there hoping for just a chance. So here was the chance. What should we have done? Play possum? Run? What would that say about us and our way we had been thinking of ourselves? Would you want to live with that memory for the rest of your life? And—maybe it would've worked! Probably if it did work, it would be the only time in the war it would. *That* would be something to remember.

And something to show [third wife] Martha?

I was already past worrying about impressing Marty. She had her mind made up that I didn't care about the important things and was just fishing and boozing out there. If we'd come in with a sub, or had a confirmed kill, signed off by CINCLANT, she'd have just said, "The sub must have interrupted the fishing." She wasn't going to give me the time of day, as you put it. She'd washed her hands of me, even if she didn't quite know it. And I was about finished with her, too, and I was a lot closer to knowing it than she was.

Was Wolfie [Hemingway's friend and shipmate Winston Guest] a British agent? I presume you know, now.

He was who he was, and that background assured his loyalty. America and England thought of themselves as having common interests in those days. There wasn't the strain in him that such a straddle would cause today.

So—yes?

Yes, but not formally. He was willing to keep his friends informed. He wasn't spying on me, if that's what you mean (and it is, a bit). He was a good man and a valued friend.

Your portrait of Henry [modeled on Guest] certainly is unclouded, if a little vague.

There were some things I didn't think I should say. And anyway, fiction isn't history.

Who is the original of Willie?

Nobody in the singular. I patched together some GIs from France and used a liberal imagination and put in a couple of Marines from the Pacific.

Peters?

His *function* was Don Saxon, but he was invented otherwise.

≈ 4 ≈

Hemingway and Perkins

Sunday, May 2, 2010

Papa, I know you liked Max Perkins, and I know that you nonetheless struggled with him. Tell us about your relationship.

The thing about Max was that he listened. He knew what worked and didn't work. Didn't always know how to fix a problem, but he could hear, loud and clear, that the problem was there. That's the only thing he *could* hear loud and clear! [This refers to Perkins' increasing deafness.] And of course, the fact that he could hear the manuscript meant that he could hear the author (as author). I mean, simply, that he knew when to pay attention to somebody because he had something. When Perkins believed in you, he believed in you. Max knew writing, so he knew what a writer could or couldn't do—subject to revision if you showed him different. The fact that he had perfect pitch for writing meant that he couldn't be fooled by externals, not about writing. Somebody might fool him about what they weren't going to do anymore, or how they were going to work harder, all that—but nobody ever fooled him about was this or that passage right or not.

You know what it is worth, to have someone knowledgeable believing you. There's nothing like it. And to have that person be in a position to advance your career—to plan it with you—was invaluable. But of course, he worked for Scribners. That meant he had divided loyalties always, that he had to try to keep going in the same direction. But if the author's needs and the company's needs diverged, who was he going to stay with? I always knew that, and it gave an edge to our business relationship sometimes.

Let me try to express it again. Max's professional life was to ride two horses at a time—one foot on the company's horse, one on whichever author he was handling at the moment. Most of the time, he made it work, because most of the authors knew they needed Scribners on their side, and Scribners knew they couldn't go around alienating their stable. So mostly the horses ran in the same direction, and he could ride with one foot on each. His personality helped him do it, because he did care about his authors. They were, many of them, his friends. And we all knew it, even [Thomas] Wolfe. But it's always a hazardous thing to mix business with friendship, and that's what we had to do, by the nature of things. So when I invited him to come fishing or hunting with me, we both knew there were two things going—friendship, yes, but also a maneuvering for future advantage, a binding by affection. You should know!

I can't imagine what my life would have been if not for Max being my editor. When I was in my early twenties, he believed in me. I know that the story is that Scott Fitzgerald puffed me to him and he bought my novel sight unseen, but that leaves out two things. First, he was binding Fitzgerald to him by a courtesy, a sort of taking him seriously as a talent scout, and second, he had seen enough of my journalism—don't think he hadn't—to hear something, and take a chance. That's what makes great intuitive editors and publishers.

But to have the editor at Scribners believe in me, and take a chance on me, and then understand what I was doing, and struggle for me and with me to get as much of what I was trying to do into print as was possible in the laws and habits and climate of the day was remarkable! Especially since he himself was so refined, repressed, un-profane, however you want to put it, but didn't let that interfere with his hearing what I was doing. If he and I hadn't had to argue money; if he hadn't been riding both horses; if we could have concentrated only on the actual writing and nothing more—but then, maybe we couldn't have accomplished so much.

Papa, will you introduce me to Maxwell Perkins? That's the way for him and me to meet, I think.

You and Max are already well acquainted. Why do you suppose [author] Sydney Omarr suggested [in a book I edited] that you might be the reincarnation of Max? It wasn't entirely flattery—Omarr intuited a connection through traits.

Well, Mr. Perkins—if you're here, welcome, and thank you for the work you did so well. I know only a bit of it—Hemingway mostly and a bit of Fitzgerald—but your reputation is formidable. Would you like to talk about your relationship with Hemingway?

[MP] Not "Papa," you'll notice. That would have made my job impossible. In fact, if I hadn't been so much older, so as to make straight competition impossible, it would have been impossible anyway. He was Ernest to me, and he never tried to be anything different.

I get the impression that you never cared about being an "alpha male" and all that.

[MP] No more than you, and for the same reasons. Competition for its own sake isn't nearly as interesting as competition for quality—and is boring, in fact. It's like trying to be the most popular in high school, in your day.

What do you think of Papa's description of your horse-riding career?

[MP] Accurate. It was in the nature of the job. For me to give up acting as Scribners' representative would have reduced me to a copy editor, and wouldn't have done him—or any of my authors—any good, because they would still have had to deal with some representative of Scribners, and he couldn't have known, as well as I did, the value of their work.

Were you a stockholder in Scribners?

[MP] I was. I had a small piece, as an executive bonus. Now—look that up and check! But—good that you could ask a factual question at the risk of not getting the right answer.

Well, I figured you weren't just a salaried employee, but I've never seen any sign that you were a stockholder.

[MP] I was in the inner circle who decided the course of Scribners' future, remember!

[Later that next day, I was relieved to read, in A. Scott Berg's Max Perkins, that Perkins was receiving liberal amounts of private stock. However, I had read the book before, years ago, and may have subconsciously remembered it.]

Papa?

Max and I did our dance for 20 years and more—and then he goes and dies of pneumonia on me! It was a blow.

[MP] I was worn out, and we all have to go sometime. And how much longer did you last, year for year?

Oh, I know. But it was a terrible thing. And then Charlie Scribner five years later. It left me isolated.

[MP] You did brighten my life, Ernest, you know that, even more than you did for others. Your life was a vicarious life lived for us, letting in a huge draft of fresh air. We liked to think of somebody actually living that way.

I just wish you had had more fun

[MP] No need to think that. Think of your always reading. Suppose somebody had looked at you and said "Poor Hemingway, he spends so much time looking at books or magazines or newspapers, and doesn't do anything!" They'd miss your real life.

Well, I know. But fishing was good for you, and getting out among men having fun.

[MP] I'd never deny it. It was a window into another world. But you know that my inner world was plenty bright. That's one reason I went deaf—to cut down on distractions. It had its inconvenient points, though.

Your sense of humor is one thing that never translates, Max. People don't remember.

[MP] I was surrounded by too many colorful characters. I looked like the wallpaper. But I had my fun, as you know.

You had a great satiric eye.

This has been fun, but I think I've done what I can do for now. Thank you both.

≈5≈
Hemingway and Scribners

Monday, May 3, 2010

Well, Papa, I don't want to veer off to Max Perkins. You and I are perhaps in the middle of something but I don't know that it centers on your relationships with others, even important others. I must say, reading of Perkins' life, I sympathize so actively with him, because I spent nearly 20 years in increasingly the same position, though in a vastly smaller field. Always connecting, always encouraging—it becomes a strain.

Dealing with people like me, you mean.

Relationships bring demands, if only of time and attention. You can only slice the pie so many ways.

Anybody could see that Max was slicing himself too thin, but there wasn't anything to do about it. If I stayed out of his way, that didn't mean everybody else would. So why should his time and energy be taken up with chicken shit?

I got the feeling—in fact I know it—that you were among the very least demanding in terms of his having to work over your manuscripts. But he paid in other ways.

He *paid his way* in other ways. I wasn't begging; I was playing my trade and making them a lot of money. Look, I know I look unreasonable in those angry letters. Nobody is at their best when they're worried, and sick, and they suspect they are on their own with no one looking out for their interests. But I had valid concerns. Max was a great guy and a great editor. He was supportive in so many ways. Nobody denies it, how could you? It was clear. But he was a businessman, and like I said, he was riding two horses. Sometimes he would press me to do things that were in Scribner's interest, sure, but not necessarily in mine. And if I didn't stand up for myself, who would?

Do you think you should have had an agent?

Then I would have had one more guy to watch. I don't know. I read—through you—the analysis that said that I lost more than I gained by not having an agent do my negotiating for me. Maybe so. But if I had had an agent, maybe he'd have gotten between me and Max, you know? Maybe he'd have always been looking to maximize his commissions even if the deal might not work out for me in the longer run. The thing is, if I had had one person I could trust to look out just for me, through thick and thin, I could have relaxed. But that's just theory. Who's going to find that? Even Max had divided loyalties, and he was a prince. Why do you think an agent would have been any better?

You were often generous with the company, and they with you.

It was a great relationship. Great to have *one* publisher. But it did have its disadvantages.

Yes. You felt taken for granted.

This time as you're reading Berg's book I am reading it with you, in a way. So I see Scribner's side of it both in the text and in your own experiences. But that doesn't change how I felt then—and it doesn't mean I was necessarily wrong.

No, not at all. I guess my concern here is centered on your emotional life as I intuit it, inside your behavior.

Yeah, I hear you psychoanalyzing me as you go along. If I couldn't see you from the inside, I'd resent it.

You'd misunderstand it.

That's the point of all this, isn't it? What I misunderstood, what people misunderstood about me.

Well, it's a defense of you, in a way. A defense against your own actions.

An interesting approach, and at least one that nobody else could take except in the same way.

≈6≈

The 20th Century and God

Tuesday, May 4, 2010

The 20th century could be called The War About God, and that would be as close a clue to it as any. Started re-reading For Whom the Bell Tolls last night. What an achievement. Papa, what do you know of the war against God? You certainly left enough clues scattered about in your writings.

It was there to be seen, if you had eyes. But it was harder to see it impartially in those days.

You, though, did. Or seemed to.

I was caught between the lines, as usual. Take Spain, since that's what you're reading about at the moment. The Republic was tied in with freedom from the church, because the church sided with the aristocrats from which its own top ranks came. In the minds of the people, somewhat confused with so many things, not only the Church had to go, but God and Mary and the saints, because their only allies, the Soviets, were militantly certain—or pretended to be—that all such things were superstitions of the past. These peasants wanted to be "modern" just like writers in New York, and they did the same thing—they jumped on the bandwagon, and for the same reason, because they didn't want to have to stand alone. The peasants had the Soviets, and they had the Western liberals, and in both cases atheism, open or politely disguised, was taken for granted as the only belief possible for free men of goodwill.

And it was a lot deeper than that, as you showed by reflection—ricochet, really—in The Sun Also Rises and in True at First Light.

You caught that easily enough when Brett said not being a bitch was her substitute for God, but said it in a way that showed that she took it for granted that the idea of God was obsolete, suitable only to simple or ignorant people, and Jake quietly made it clear that he didn't agree. He didn't really have a connection but he *wanted* it; he "wished he was a better Catholic."

And yes, the meditation about whether we had souls, that you picked out of *True at First Light*, I agree that it showed confusion. But the point is, it *showed* confusion. It wasn't just *my* confusion; it was common.

Somebody noticed that you were most at home, or felt most deeply about, Catholic countries: Italy, France, Spain, Cuba. How much did that even occur to you?

Not at all. And there *was* the US, you know. Not a Catholic country, and so close in my heart that I could scarcely bear to live there sometimes.

You mustn't make the same mistake as Spanish peasants! It wasn't really about being Catholic; it was about a civilization having a different center of gravity. Now, these are sort of abstract thoughts, and I always distrusted great abstractions, but I *felt* that difference first in Spain when I went there in the 1920s, even more than in France. The French knew how to live, and we refugees from America could appreciate the contrast from our more driven society. (But of course in the absence of that driving, we were left on our own, and either drove ourselves, and did very good working, regardless how well the work turned out, or did nothing, and fooled ourselves that we *were going to* work, soon.)

But the French were if anything even less connected to the other side—as you put it—then the Americans or English. I'm talking about the Frenchmen we would see in Paris, you understand, not the peasants a hundred miles away. The French society, the self-important thinkers, the international set (to the extent that a Frenchman ever *is* international) had the same view of religion and the things of the spirit that the smart set anywhere did. It was superstition, charming or irritating or dangerous by turns, but superstition. There was no life in it, for them.

These are vast abstractions, as I've said. In my writing I would put it into tiny glimpses or thoughts—like Jake's being relieved to deal with French mercenary service that reduced everything to a cash basis, without Spain's individuality that always was there regardless.

Now, you might think this doesn't have much to do with your War About God idea, but it does. I am showing you France as I saw it: mercenary, self regarding, incurably small-minded in its daily ways, yet a breath of fresh air to Americans and English chiefly by its contrast to our own homeland's relative philistine nature.

But Spain! Spain was far older than France, and it wasn't tamed or mechanized as France was (and as England and the US were). In Spain, you could go into a *culture*, a way of being, so much older than Europe, so much purer. It's the difference between a bullfight and a long-distance bicycle race. That's why I put in the bit about the bicycle racers, for those who could catch it. Not that there was anything wrong with them as individuals or even as a product of their civilization, but Jake didn't have any interest in them. Their life and cynical work ("the money could always be arranged") were European, as Spain was not.

Now—to keep coming back to it—Spain didn't have the war about God as part of its official culture. Nobody had ever worshiped the Goddess of Reason there! And they aren't likely to! At least, I hope not. It was only the cut-off intellectuals who tried to follow the intellectual life of Europe against their own contrary life who do that.

Let me go at it a different way. When Napoleon made the mistake of taking on Spain, there was a definite pro-French, pro-"modern" group who aided and abetted him. This was an earlier Spanish Civil War. That group and its descendents considered themselves more cultured, more civilized, more modern, more European, than their government or countrymen. They rejected the Church not as the peasants did, as rapacious landlords and officious busybodies and as irresponsible legislators (for the bishops and all did appear in all these roles to the people, day by day throughout life) but as *theoretically* obsolete, as *abstractly* wrong, as *philosophically* superstitious and backwards.

These *franceses* were Spain's fifth column working for Napoleon. When they lost, by 1814, naturally reaction came with a vengeance—and nobody embodies vengeance like the Spaniards!

Still, there was always the liberal underground. In Spain it was always an anti-Catholic underground, for always the Church's hand was against it. Even Leo XIII's encyclical on social justice didn't make any difference to the Spanish church. It *thought* it was part of the universal church, but it was Spanish first, last, and always.

So when they declared the Republic in 1931 the people who did it were motivated by a couple of ideas: They wanted to make Spain "modern"—which meant following the rest of Europe—in technology, in ideas, a government, in social justice. They failed at all of these, of course, because those things can be held up by a government but they can't be advanced by anything but the people's own energies—and where is the government that is going to liberate the people's energies? It would have to curtail itself, and governments *never* do that. No new government—not even a revolutionary new government—can change things overnight, even if it has the will. The only thing it can do is oppose change or welcome and channel it.

Until the generals rose against the Republic in July 1936, the government was about as ineffectual as usual. But the rebellion burst the bounds. People took things into their own hands—on both sides—and so the middle ground was destroyed. Everything went to extremes, as it always does when the bars are down. And then when the Western countries wouldn't let the government buy arms or planes or *anything* it needed to protect itself, then in came Stalin's boys, and before very long they were in charge, or as much "in charge" as anyone ever is in Spain.

And then God had to go out the window. It became that you were for the Republic or for the Church, and then for the Republic or for those who believed in God. And of course that was a weakness because not only did it make the Republic seem wicked, with its Soviet allies, and its official anti-Catholicism, and then its war on God—but the feelings of two thousand years of ancestors couldn't be uprooted in a few years of indoctrination. That's what I was showing when the boy started by quoting La Passionaria but ended by reciting the little his terror left him of the Hail Mary.

And there you were between the lines.

As usual. I hated fascism, but that didn't mean I couldn't see communism clearly enough. It's just that Spain didn't have anything else; not a friend in the world except Mexico and the International Brigades, which were also mostly communists except the Americans.

You've been going great, but I'm feeling a little worn out. More another time, I hope. Who ever said you weren't capable of abstract thought, Papa?

Critics. Professors and what you in your day would call wannabes. They didn't understand my methods, they didn't approve of my subject matter, and they were threatened by my life. And all that was enough [ammunition], even without any ammunition I gave them by things I did or said or was supposed to have done or said.

Okay. More later.

∼7∼

Spain and Modernization

(11 a.m.) So, Papa, more about Spain?

There is always more about Spain. I just wish you could see it for yourself—and I wish you could see it in the 1920s, as I saw it.

Nobody brought it closer than you did.

And I can be there now, if you help focus me, or someone else directs my attention there. But the whole tragedy was lying there waiting. They'd missed [World War I], so they had to have one of their own, or continue dozing in the sun, and that wasn't possible.

Not sure I understand that.

All the world was knocking down the doors. The telegraph, the radio, the airplane, the automobile, banking, foreign ideas, everything. Even tourism had its effect. You can't keep a country like a hothouse, isolated at its own temperature. And the more disruptive the elements, the more the forces of reaction fought against change—even, or especially, when they themselves were introducing the things like radio or cars that were changing everything.

You've got to go back at least to The Generation of '98, the shell-shocked witnesses to the end of Spain's leftover dreams of empire in the summer of the Spanish-American War. Suddenly Cuba, Puerto Rico, the Philippines were all gone. There was no remaining excuse for not realizing that it wasn't the 16th century any more. So—la generacion de noventa y ocho thought they'd better reform things. But as usual, it amounted to trying to change without changing. How do you modernize one compartment? How do you put new wine into old wineskins? The result was something that nobody liked—not the peasants, not the landlords, not the workers, not the factory owners, not the church or the Army or the bureaucracy or the intelligentsia. What you had was something that no longer had any unity, any structural integrity. Instead, you had a bunch of pieces moving in different directions at different speeds.

Everybody could see that what existed couldn't last. But nobody could see what should, or even could replace it. Nobody could see how to get from here to there, either—even when they had an idea of what "there" should look like. So what happened is what always happens when people are confused and without any agreed vision. The loudmouths and the know-it-alls and the impractical visionaries all took center stage and started to fight one another. It was like Yeats' poem. ["The Second Coming"] Politics is depressingly stupid and dishonest at best—and by "dishonest" I don't mean just crooked financially, I mean intellectually dishonest, and full of lies. But when the crooked non-fanatics are displaced by crooked fanatics, watch out. How many times did we see it?

So when [Jose] Calvo Sotelo [the political leader of the Falange party] got killed, it didn't cause the army revolt, it just disorganized it a little, because he was supposed to head up the government they were going to form. Probably if he hadn't gotten killed, the army wouldn't have been left as the only power broker, and Mussolini and Hitler might not have been needed, and Stalin might not have had an opening, and instead of a civil war there might have been a coup and a few thousand shootings and that would have been the end of it for the moment. And if it had happened that way, would the West have woken up to Hitler in time, the way it did watching Spain bleed for three years? No telling, of course. It didn't happen that way. Foreign ideas destroyed it, just as they had in the time of the Napoleonic wars. All those outside forces rushed into a vacuum chamber.

And afterwards?

Well, Spain in the late 1950s wasn't exactly a fascist country. It was very authoritarian, sure, and Franco was careful to keep the lid on, even if he had to play the Americans carefully—sub bases in return for non-interference. And I see that the liberalization finally did take place in the 1970s. So maybe all the war did was delay things a couple of generations—but actually I think (beyond what it did in disrupting the fascist dictators' plans) it mostly held Spain firmly to its past, even while the forces of the outside world went on burrowing into the fabric, changing this and that until the essence changed. It would be interesting to be in some small Spanish town and see if much has changed. Between television—and now the Internet—and cheap travel and decent wages, and opportunities to work overseas and send home money (and new ways of thinking, eventually), much must be very different. But I'd still bet on the old Spain being right there under the surface.

≈8≈

Harry Morgan, Values, and Rules

Wednesday, May 5, 2010

I wake up, Papa, thinking about you and the Communists (having still been reading For Whom the Bell Tolls, of course). Is that what you want us to talk about next? If not, where would you like to go?

Do you really want an abstract disquisition about politics and government?

More, I'd like something on you and government.

You know my views. Government is a form of necessary protection racket. They have the ability to make you pay, and make you do things, and they use it as much as they dare. You have to have it, I'm not saying you don't, because if you don't have one protection racket, you're going to have another one—but you don't have to like it, and you certainly don't have to see it as anything but what is. I mean, you don't have to put a lot of hopes on it.

How are you going to win World War II, say, without a government? And *not* having a government won't make you any safer—won't keep you out of war. Just the opposite. You're in the position of one man alone—with a family or others he needs to protect—surrounded by gangs. You can't count on it, you can't trust it, but you *have to have it* there.

That's what Harry Morgan learned, part of it.

People don't get what I was getting at with Harry—not that I did as good a job on it as I should have done, but I got distracted. The point about Harry isn't that I was trying to jump on the "social relevance" bandwagon and become a New Dealer—or, even less, a revolutionary! The point was, Harry found that things were closing in. At one time he could function alone, in a sort of tribal way, just him and his family and community. They didn't get anything special *from* the government and they didn't owe anything special *to* the government, and they sure as hell didn't confuse themselves by thinking the government was anything but an impersonal machine trying to milk them (and everybody else) of anything it could get. They lived their lives without paying much attention to the law one way or another. If some law made smuggling rum financially attractive, they noted the fact and did it if they could and didn't consider themselves as bad men or as lawbreakers except in a technical sense. They didn't figure that a thing was right or wrong according to how it was or wasn't legal. They tried to do what they considered to be right, and fit it in as safely and profitably as they could, depending on conditions.

So, for instance, Harry kills one man in Cuba so he doesn't have to kill the whole illegal cargo of men, and he figures to kill Eddy even though he likes him, just for his own safety, and he is just as glad when it proves to be unnecessary. He did what *he* thought was right and necessary, you see. He didn't take the law into consideration except as one risk among many.

You'll notice that Max Perkins liked Harry Morgan "even though he was a bad man—almost *because* he was a bad man." I doubt that Max ever thought it through, but [Perkins liked Morgan] because Harry *wasn't* a bad man, he was a good, responsible, reliable, well-intentioned competent man; it's just that the times had made his virtues look like vices. If Harry had been a cowboy in the old West, nobody would have thought him a bad man in any respect, and he wouldn't have been. He would have been a self-sufficient man raising his family, providing for them, reliable to anything his community legitimately asked of him. And there wouldn't have been government enough to molest him. Not like the 30s—let alone your times!

Harry had his rough side, sure. He was hard as a board and blunt as the side of a hammerhead. But that doesn't have anything to do with right and wrong, or good and bad. That's just the temperament he was born with. Fishermen in the Gulf couldn't be soft, and Harry didn't have any mannerisms to soften what he was, clean through.

Part nature myth! That's how much people understood about what I was doing. Sitting there in New York or in some college town, they thought Harry Morgan was an impossible romantic abstraction. I knew a *dozen* of him. More.

So—to get back to the point I started—government is a necessary protection racket, and the closer the world gets tied together by technology, the more necessary and the more intrusive government gets. It doesn't have anything to do with intentions, and not much to do with ideology. It's a matter of technical necessity, you might call it. If you have sailing ships, they go where they want and they can take their chances. But if you have coal-fired ships, now they have to have coaling stations. And if you go to motor ships, now they have to have access to refueling docks. You see? More complex things require a more complex network of support. And then when radio comes, you can do more to help, so you set up stations to help seamen know where they are by triangulating, and to let them have somebody to broadcast to if they are in trouble. But if you have radio, you have to have some sort of *regulation of* radio, or it becomes chaotic.

And so one thing keeps leading to another, and regulation keeps getting piled onto regulation, and it's always in response to somebody seeing a new need, whether the need is real or not. The thing that is moving it is technical elaboration—or what people call progress. Well, progress always leads *toward* something, but it also leads *away* from something, at the same time, and what it's leading away from had its value; maybe more than what you're moving toward. No matter what, you can count on the fact that to some people, what you're calling progress is progress in the wrong direction. By the way, this is why so many people in your time see conspiracy everywhere. They can *feel* that current, always pushing toward one goal of more complexity, more regulation, more regimentation.

They think it's *designed*, when it is really gravity, with some people taking advantage of the downhill slope for purposes of their own.

Do you think we are pretty much doomed to a more complex life, then?

Didn't Joseph [*Smallwood*] tell you your life seemed like living inside a machine, to him? And it gets more so every day, you can't help it. If the stream is carrying you in a certain direction, you can fight it, but that's still the direction you're going every minute that you *don't* fight it. At some point you realize, this is the trip I've signed up for. I can fight it, I can make it compromise with me, I can compensate for it, I can live around it, but that's the current. How many times did I have my characters say, in effect, what you draw is what you get? That's how it is and that's always how it is. How you play the cards is up to you, but the cards get dealt by somebody else.

So what do we do, to play our cards as well as we can?

Well, that's the point, you see. You have to have a solid place to plant your feet, and to me, that place is in the values you choose for yourself, and then try to live up to. If you don't choose your own values, you live by somebody else's. Now, maybe they fit you well enough and maybe they don't, but you're fitting yourself into somebody else's shoes. And even there, you're going to have to live up to those values or not.

Now you might say, the only values you can live by are the ones you already have, but let's look at that. Yes, your traits are those you are born with. But you have enough choice that you can turn around, after all. If you're naturally timid you can choose to be bold. If you're naturally inhibited, you can become extroverted. If you're naturally irresponsible you can train yourself to do your duty. So it isn't like it's fated, entirely. What is fated is what you start with, what you are most comfortable being or remaining. But you can make yourself into something else (if that possibility of choosing is in you).

When you choose a set of values, or when you take seriously whatever set of values you are born with, or pick up unconsciously from others, you confine yourself—or you accept confinement, let's say—to the rules that follow from those values. If you value honesty, then whatever honesty means to you, you have to do, or know that you are breaking your own rules, going against your own values. Well, who doesn't? But it doesn't come free, that's the point. To have a firm place to stand is the thing. It lets you *stand* instead of drift. It lets you hit back.

Harry Morgan had a place to stand. Now maybe you look at that and you say, he wasn't broad enough, or wise enough, or flexible enough or even smart enough—and that all misses the point. He was somebody in particular. He was a man planted on the earth. It didn't have a thing to do with him being a tough guy, though he was tough, or with being a cruel hard man, though he could be that, or with being any given characteristic. The point was, he was a definite person, and so he was not just drifting with the tide. Sometimes governments realize that they need guys like him—when they have wars to fight, say, or natural disasters to deal with—but often enough they've driven them away, or sent them underground, or turned them into the enemy, and when they need help they've got jellyfish. Too bad.

And so?

And so you are in your own peculiar fix, in your times, just as we always are. That *fix* wasn't an accident and it wasn't a plot and it isn't even, exactly, what you could rightly call a predicament. It's a fix in the sense of a mariner getting a fix on his position. It's where you are. Live it.

Wonderful thoughts, Papa. The more I study you, the more amazed I get at how little even the scholars understand you.

That's because you're seeing me from the inside more than from the outside. Don't forget that. Anybody looks different from his own view of himself.

Well, you look pretty good to me. Thanks.

≈9≈

World War II in Europe

Friday, May 7, 2010

[VE Day] All right, let's talk about the war—or, actually after the war. You flew home (I think) from Europe, and stopped in at New York and went

right on down to Cuba. What was on your mind, and what were you plan-
ning, and what was your emotional state?

That's a good enough starting point.

I left Europe older than I had gotten to it, and I wasn't in all that
great shape when I got there. Certainly not emotionally, as you noticed
in the poem to Mary. A year at sea—even if Marty thought it was just
drinking beer and fishing and playing—was serious business, and it took
its toll as a year of warfare does anywhere. Most people in a war aren't in
the front lines, you know, so they aren't in daily terror of their lives—but
it wears them down nonetheless. The mere physical hardships that come
with it are hard enough. And the strain of uncertainty. And the strain of
responsibility. And the worry—stashed in the back of your mind, but it's
there—that you'll never get back to your real work.

On the other side of the ledger, the time at sea had been a chance to
see some real, worthwhile *action*. I don't mean combat, though we easily
might have had that if we had stumbled onto a refueling station, but—
action. Movement. Something external with consequences, not just editing an anthology of war stories. On the boat, I'd been in command, and
we had a small picked crew, and we knew what we were doing. In Europe
it was going to be different and I knew it. A war correspondent's job is
not as serious as the commander of a Q-boat, however small the boat and
however widely distributed the byline.

And there was the concussion. You picked up (it's funny how few
do) that being in the air took away the headache for the time I stayed
in the air. Something about air pressure at sea level, I suppose. But continual pain that can't be endured and can't be evaded wears you down. It's
almost worse to be able to get away from it for a couple of hours when
you are in the air, knowing that it's waiting for you on the ground.

Yes, I can hear you think I should have stayed in the hospital and let
it heal—but there was no time! Were they going to call off the invasion
until I felt better? Besides, that isn't how I handled weakness or injury
or pain. Germs and colds and all were something different. With them,
I went to bed. That was more serious, because I didn't know how else to
handle them. But you'll notice I didn't put myself to bed in France in the
Fall! It would have been silly, when we were any of us liable to be killed at
any odd time for any or no particular reason.

≈10≈

A Shipboard Romance

I was finished with Marty, yes. You can see clearly enough that I wasn't considering her at all, by the time I went to Europe. We had crossed the line, and it was just a matter of legal formality. I was in a continual slow burn about her. You know the feeling. It was impossible to remember how we'd felt—and how we'd been—in Spain. It was a passing emotion, or put it this way, she and I were in the same place and the same time for a while, emotionally, and we sort of forgot that fundamentally we were on different courses. I'm not going to come up with some complicated military metaphor about it, but you get the idea.

[Second wife] Pauline's political ideas weren't very developed, and they were always bounded by her Catholicism and her wealth, with the insularity those things bring, particularly in combination. In comes Marty, making her way with ambition and journalism, passionately interested in politics against the fascists and for the people, and the contrast made it look like she and I belonged together. Plus, she was younger and admired my work, which made her and me think she admired *me*. And then in Spain we shared danger and work and fun and bed and friends and, again, it looked like we belonged together. In a way you could say that we had a long shipboard romance, and as long as we were concerned with the fight against fascism and as long as we weren't in competition in her mind, other things didn't get in the way. She found us the Finca. That was the one best thing she did for me. And we went off to the Far East and some of what we saw in each other there caused some trouble, or probably I should say just brought it to the surface. Maybe if we hadn't gone, we'd have lasted longer together.

She had the sense of herself as competent and tough and able to get beneath the surface of things. But in China she saw me as I was in such situations—picking up enough language to get by, picking up what not to do to not get sick, gathering impressions on little data and turning intuition into journalism. It all made her less in her own mind, and she couldn't stand that. So she looked harder and longer at my many imperfections in her mind—and they kept growing in size and in number and importance.

She worked hard—she had to, she was making it strictly on hard work and talent—and to her it didn't look like I did. That's why later she didn't think the Q-boat work was real. I had my fun as I went along, and it looked like the work did itself. She hated that, and she started to think I was superficial—especially when I started picking apart her politics. She was consistent and I was consistent, but it was a different kind of consistent. She was always on the left, always for the people against the rich, against the fascists, all that, and so far so good. But that meant that she wound up in a cheering-box. The only time I was tempted into doing that, I wound up excusing Stalin's murder of Andres Nin and others, and it cost me the friendship of John dos Passos, and I'd have been better off keeping him and letting The Revolution go. My consistency was to honesty, not politics or ideology. When my head cleared again, I couldn't sign on to a one-party view of things. You should know, it's the same in your times. It's the same always, probably.

Well, anyway, I was finished with Marty before I even got to England. No point in saying it was all over but the shouting, because we already done all that. It was all over but the pretending, and the lawyers.

≈ 11 ≈

War without Illusion

What I'm trying to show you is that I didn't get to England in such great shape. It wasn't 1918 and I wasn't a kid thinking I couldn't be hurt. I had already been hurt, and I don't mean just in Italy in 1918. I went there [in 1944] under a cloud of foreboding, feeling the loss ahead of time, and I didn't confuse our gallant allies with angels. If England had let France do *anything* for Spain! If France had done it by itself! If Roosevelt hadn't been so worried about the 1936 election! So—I knew what they were, and just how far they couldn't be trusted, so it was hard to pretend (and I didn't pretend) it was a great crusade. It was just what had to be done. And maybe J. Edgar Hoover thought I couldn't see what Stalin was, but if he'd read *For Whom the Bell Tolls*, it was there clear enough. So it wasn't a matter of believing in our side, so much as believing in the need to destroy the other side. I wasn't under the illusion that the war was going to bring anything better than we had had. It was just going to remove one particularly bad and dangerous thing that had sprung up. You'll notice that Richard Cantwell [the hero of Hemingway's 1950 novel *Across the River and Into the Trees*] in his last days still hopes and assumes that Franco will get his, and the Civil War's results will be overturned.

≈12≈

Part of the Army

Okay, Papa, here we go again if you're so inclined.

Coffee in hand, eh? What would you have done if you'd lived before coffee?

I'd have never known the difference, I presume. Yesterday we set out to talk about your state after the war, but didn't get that far. So—

I had my only experiences of actual combat in France with Buck Lanham. In Spain, I knew which side I was on, and I was doing what little I could, but mostly I was *being there* and learning and absorbing. I was *observing*. In France I was with my own country's army, and I was living with officers, and I was in terrain vastly more familiar to me than to them, plus I had old friends and friends of friends and people who knew of me from friends of friends—so I was able to be of real service. You know the story; you know how the Army and I had to lie our way out of trouble, and you know more or less how I felt about it. But the bitterness about it—aimed partly at the correspondents who blew the whistle on me and partly at the objective situation—didn't ruin or overshadow the experience. I was part of the Army, finally, for the only time in my life.

Granted, I wasn't an organized official part of the Army, but so much the better. I just wish I'd have been able to serve in the same way and get recognition for it. If I hadn't been over there as a correspondent, but as some sort of adjunct to the Army, the value of what I did would have been obvious enough and there wouldn't have been any need to conceal it. But that's crying for the moon. If I hadn't been there as a correspondent, I couldn't have gotten there at all. And maybe I wouldn't have been with a sympathetic commander. And maybe even [Col.] Buck [Lanham] would have had to be different if he'd technically had me as an official subordinate.

Anyway, I got enough of combat. Didn't need any more, ever, and was glad to be able to leave with honor without having to stay for the end. I had more time in France than in Spain, actually.

When I came home in 1918, I came home as a wounded veteran (even though I hadn't been in the Army), but my experience of combat was secondhand, being mainly, almost entirely, the stories I had heard the soldiers tell each other. When I came home in 1945, I came home as *apparently* unwounded and *apparently* not a veteran (because I hadn't been officially a soldier), but my experience of combat was firsthand. You didn't have to have a rifle in your hand to be involved in combat in the Hurtgen Forest, and if you knew men who got killed, it didn't matter that you weren't an infantryman, if you were there and not hiding in the rear somewhere. And although untreated concussions are not the same as war wounds, they aren't free, either.

I *knew* combat. I *knew* the soldiers and the officers. I understood what I saw and I could discuss it professionally with professionals. I had the respect of men like Buck not because they were writers or I was a writer but because they saw that I was not a bluff or a *poseur*. But I was 45, and that's too old to be at war. It's just too old. Men do, of course. The officers of senior rank were pretty much all in their 40s and 50s. But it's too damned old to be accompanying boys of 18 and 20 across northern France in winter. I was plenty glad to be done with it, and glad to know it was going to be my last taste of it. You didn't see me volunteering to go to Korea, for instance.

～13～

Recuperation

So I came home, and I was bone tired. I wasn't elated, I wasn't in some exalted state of mind, and I certainly didn't think our "crusade" was something to give parades for. It was just a dirty brutal job that had to be done, and it was getting done, and I wouldn't be any help in Germany and I didn't want to see any more kids get killed and I didn't have any duty holding me there. I just wanted to go home and silently lick my wounds—and home wasn't even in the US, but in Cuba. Home was all different too, of course. Marty had found the place and had made it our nest, but she was gone and Mary was on her way. And the war had run over the old life the way it ran over everything else. You couldn't expect any part of life to stand still, any more than part of Spain could resist the 20th century. Didn't mean you had to like it, but there it was.

Were you in a black mood, then?

Not actively. It was more like recuperating from a fever. You sort of inch your way back into life, and you see that life has been going on without you, and there are a lot of big and mostly small adjustments you have to make. But there is a gray haze of fatigue you are pushing through, and it works as a cushion and at the same time it muffles things, making everything harder and less worthwhile-seeming.

I had lost five years of my writing life. Ten percent if I lived to be 70. All right, what you draw is what you get. I had a lot of new material, and I had a big canvas to paint if I could proportion it. And, after all, I hadn't been killed or obviously wounded, and perhaps I wouldn't be seen as too pre-war if I got something out soon enough. But I was tired, bone tired not even so much in my body as in my soul, and that's hard on a writer, for you don't just write from what you know, but from how you know it, and from what part of you knows it. That's a matter of emotion. If you can't touch the part of yourself that experienced certain things, there's no use trying to just talk about them, that's just a laundry list. And yet you can't just wait until you feel like writing. Amateurs may wait until they're in the mood, but professionals don't, because they know they can't.

That's one reason why *Islands in the Stream* begins with that long pre-war section. I could afford to go back into that place in myself, and that's also why it is so sad, because it was all lost. Thomas Hudson lost wives, love, children, way of living, use of his talents, and then finally his life. It didn't work out quite that way for me, but I could imagine Jack being killed—and, in fact, did for a good while [Jack Hemingway was wounded and captured, his fate unknown for months]—and the rest came easily enough.

≈ 14 ≈

Land, Sea, and Air

(10:50 a.m.) You had it in mind, I gather, to have a vast novel of land, sea, and air warfare?

That had been in my mind, but I couldn't get enough air experience to really know the subject. I'd left that too late in life. If you've spent a good deal of time hunting and fishing, you've absorbed the feel of the land and sea, and you can use it as background for your stories. But if you haven't been a flyer—and of course especially if you haven't been a combat pilot or haven't even had any equivalent to flight school or the special military training given to future pilots and mechanics and navigators and bombardiers—how are you going to write about it knowledgeably? You could write about men's reactions to [aerial] combat, or to prolonged strain, or to the effects of bombing, and you might be able to describe the experience of combat in the air—but it would take you a while to acquire the vocabulary, the unnoticed background that is the equivalent of knowing what the role of the pelican is in the life of a Key West fisherman. I didn't have it and couldn't get it, so the air component dropped out.

The sea component was there, but I had to untangle it from the Crook Factory of real life—and I had to consider how much of certain things I wanted to, or felt I could, say. But the two sections—Cuba and At Sea—that Mary and Charlie attached to the pre-war section they called Bimini is not entirely a natural fit. It needed a transitional section I didn't get to write. Where I went wrong was in the very final part of the Bimini piece. It rounded it off emotionally, but too abruptly and too cursorily. It needed to be expanded and done more carefully, or it needed to precede a section that would have gotten Thomas Hudson into the war. As it is, people who aren't familiar with the 20th century—as, soon, they won't be—will be unable to fill in the blanks. But, as a patchwork solution that saved all three pieces from oblivion, it served. I'm not criticizing their decisions, just saying this isn't what I would have done.

And I chose to do the land piece in a way that seems to have pleased nobody. Instead of set pieces, I had Richard Cantwell remember things glancingly, touching memories with his emotions and then backing away. All right, the romance doesn't work in the way it is, and I can see that now. I can only plead that I was involved in heavy wish fulfillment. If I'd made her [Renata, the love interest] a middle-aged woman, or even a woman in her late 20s, probably it would have been all right. Or if nobody had known of [19-year-old] Adriana [Ivancich, with whom for a while he was hopelessly enamored]. But the excellent material that is in that book gets passed over. I wanted to leave the impression of a man sick of war, sick at heart, sick of stupidity and suffering, even somewhat sick of himself. Painting scenes of warfare wouldn't have accomplished that.

Not even in conversation with fellow officers, or thoughts sparked by his chauffeur or by anyone?

Any story can be taken in many directions, but only in any one of them, not in all. The more you try to hedge your bets, the less chance that you will accomplish any one solid thing.

Do you think that Across The River pushed your idea of leaving out everything you could too far?

Well, maybe. It shouldn't have been too far. Readers should have been able to get it, and, after all, many of them did, and do. But I guess I should have thought that fewer people can do trigonometry than can add columns of figures. But even so—it was worth doing for its own sake.

≈15≈

Postwar Isolation

So—what was your life after 1945?

It wasn't as good as the 1930s, that's sure. Accumulation of the side effects of years of endurance, for one thing. Too well known for the wrong things, for another. Unable to get myself settled back within myself, mostly—and this I didn't ever consciously realize. People talk about my getting trapped in the Papa myth, but I wonder if they know what they really mean to say. It isn't that I was fooling myself, or that I was lost, or that I was trying to fool others. It's a little more difficult than any of those, or all of them.

When I came home from war for the last time, I came home from other things, too. It was no longer the 1930s, and neither the political stuff I'd gotten lured into nor the sense of one particular menace to be overcome—fascism—still existed. But what had we gained, and where were we going, and what were we going to do and become? I didn't feel a part of any of that. I was a writer, not a politician or a political hanger-on. But everything had moved to politics. The life I had lived was getting ever less possible for anybody to live, and even if you could, it was as an exception rather than as one among many. Once the times have moved on to a place you don't want to be, you are stuck writing elegies, or fantasy, or reminiscences. I didn't much like the postwar world, and I didn't particularly belong in it, and I didn't have all that much to say to it. Plus my friends kept dying, like Max Perkins and then Charlie Scribner, and it isolates you.

And you were living on an island away from your changing country.

I did get to Montana every so often, but that's right—my ordinary life didn't have anything to do with the ordinary life of Americans in cities or small towns, even. I started to lose touch. Even when my life had been conspicuously different—sea fishing, hunting, attending the corridas—it was different in a way that let people tag along with it and add to their life. But now, they didn't understand me or my life and I didn't much understand them or theirs. You ought to relate to that, too!

Oh yes. Television is a great divider depending on whether you watch it or not.

It isn't just television, it's everyday experience, and what people make of it. If you read all the time—and I did—and you had had unusual experiences and unusual friends and enemies, and you had had a certain prominence, and so had access to certain facts—you weren't living in the same world as most people.

Now, I am not talking about conspiracies. I'm talking about common experience, common understanding. The rich don't understand other parts of society very well, because they live isolated from other people. That had happened to me. It wasn't like Key West in the 30s, or Paris in the 20s, when I could hang around fisherman or workers as well as educated and artistic people. After the war, I was too famous and too pre-war for that to be possible. I was el viejo not just in years (and in being beat up) and not even particularly in wisdom, but in experience, which to a degree is the same as saying—he's past his time. And if you don't particularly like or believe in the times you're in—well, you are past your time, in a way.

And so?

And so it had its effect on my writing, because it had its effect on my life, on my experiences. How could I write about life in Levittown, even if I wanted to? How could I write about anything I didn't have a feel for? That isn't quite saying, if I didn't live it I couldn't write it, but if I couldn't find my way into it, certainly I couldn't write it.

I wish you'd done a better job of integrating the Harry Morgan book, before the war. I know it was the temptation to use "One Trip Across" and "The Tradesman's Return" both, but one being in the first person and one in third person breaks it up. And there's too much of a break in the action too, and the relevance of contrasting his life and the professor's life isn't nearly as clear as it should be. And that book couldn't have been put off until after the war.

Oh, I know. Don't think I didn't. But I had to get to Spain, and it all was starting to look over and done with. (I thought the war would get to us a little sooner than it did.) I needed a book and I didn't have the patience with myself that I usually had. Perhaps I wasn't thinking all that well.

Martha Gellhorn?

Can't really blame it on her. It is true, politics was the rock that book broke on. And yet, it was politics I was trying to show. So what could you do? I wanted to bring that hurricane in, but I couldn't bring myself to do it. It would be like using people's deaths for my own profit. Besides, what would Harry do? His opinion of it would have been harsh enough but could he have helped? And what would be the good of his traveling there and seeing things and not really doing anything? So I left it. But I started off thinking I'd show the effects of politics on a simple self-sufficient man. And when I botched it, it couldn't be fixed.

⇒16⇐

The Old Man and the Sea, and Perkins

(3:45 p.m.) Reading *The Old Man and the Sea*, I come to where the old fisherman prays a Hail Mary and then adds, "Blessed Virgin, pray for the death of this fish. Wonderful though he is." And I think, the Virgin is company for him (for those who believe) in the way that all my deceased friends, including those I did not know in life, are to be for me. The continued reality of non-physical beings is as real to them as that. This is what unbelievers do not understand, because it is something they have not experienced, and their unbelief in anything they cannot see or justify makes them think is impossible.

This afternoon I reread The Old Man and the Sea. What a fine achievement. Papa, did Max Perkins [who had died before Hemingway began writing it] read it over your shoulder?

Well, ask him.

Consider it asked.

[MP] Don't think that keeping an eye on earth through the lens of our old personality is the only thing we have to do—but we do it often enough. And don't think that because I am remembered via Hemingway and Fitzgerald and Wolfe and Scribner's and my other authors, that this or any of them or all of them together were the center of what you might call my soul-life. That would be like being a popular singer and having people think your life's purpose and significance *to you yourself* was encompassed in one hit song you sang. It *could* be, in theory—but it wouldn't be. The things one is remembered for are not necessarily the things closest to one's heart.

That's clear enough. Should I ask what was the center of your life?

It would depend on what you focused on. The emotional center of my life was my family, of course, especially my daughters. But suppose you want to look at what was most critical for my growth—again, it would depend on what you concentrated on. Editing people might one day challenge my intellect, another day, my patience. Being a part of Scribner's might lead me into uncomfortable situations as you noticed a while ago, talking with Ernest—divided loyalties. And life day by day has its own recorded challenges. "Unrecorded" doesn't mean unimportant; it just means, perhaps, private, or perhaps not easily categorized.

So, looking over your shoulder at the world that continues without you, what draws your attention?

[MP] It would be slightly easier to explain if we were on a particular subject, so let's take your original question. As time proceeded, my connection with my authors drew more and more people's attention to me, little though they realized that we here feel it! It's like the steady drag of a fishing line in the mouth, "Papa"!

[EH] Yes, that isn't a bad way to put it.

[MP] And when Ernest was working on the story that he had told me long before, he had me somewhat in mind—not front and center, of course, but there—and I felt it. Then when he dedicated the book to young Charlie and me—that brought more attention, reminding people, you might say. Reminding them that I existed. All during that time that Ernest was writing the book, he was actually dragging his pencil behind his imagination. So it was as though he was painting us a movie. You see? Or—probably you don't. It was a stretch of time during which his mind was occupied with one thing, sometimes consciously, sometimes not, but always there.

≈ 17 ≈

Hemingway's Fiction

Sunday, May 9, 2010

A lot of communicating yesterday—23 journal pages. I don't really know where to go with this today, but I have the sense, still, that you do, Papa. I have the continuing sense that you have your own point of view, of your life from the inside, that you want to get over.

That's right. And it isn't just vanity, or scratching an itch. Those things *can* motivate over here, don't let anybody tell you they can't, for people are people whether they have a body or not. But I am working with you on another level, as you would put it, to bring forward another project. You see that [Bob Friedman] sees this work a little differently than before. The outline of its possibility is beginning to be clearer to him. Not just a series of talks with dead people who might really be just the result of the author's imagination, but investigations into the nature of things.

Well, I did set out, in November 2005, to write about guidance and healing.

And you haven't left that path. In fact, you continue to whittle down your interests until those two activities are central. You don't even obsess over writing fiction much anymore!

Yeah, well, let's talk about fiction. Yours.

The first thing to remember is that I had to be practical. If I didn't want to be stuck writing for newspapers, I had to be able to sell what I wrote. But if I wanted to be happy with what I wrote, I had to keep writing the best I could, not like Fitzgerald did later, whoring for easy money. If I'd done that it would have destroyed me. If I could even have done it.

Now, in those days there were the magazines, and that was where the money was that would keep me going, and it was where I could keep my name in front of the public—publicizing myself and getting paid for it. The things I wrote that had no market, I sold or more or less gave away and considered to be writing exercises, developing my skill. Not everything that I wrote had to sell, just enough to keep me going and hopefully to get a little ahead. As you know, I did my stint at journalism, and that paid the bills for a while and helped me to hone my skills. *In Our Time* wasn't straight fact, but it certainly owed its existence to reportage. But nonfiction couldn't get at what I wanted to get at, and if it could have, there would have been no market for it.

Let's look at that. What you are doing, right here, is not fiction, but it depends upon the existence of facts not universally admitted even in your day. You are pioneering something, you see. Could I have done something similar in the 1920s or 30s or 40s or 50s? Even if I'd wanted to, if I'd known how, if I'd believed in it, could I have done anything similar and had it accepted as anything but fiction? And, there would have been no market for it as fiction, and I had to have an income. Nonfiction in my day depended upon what everyone could accept as fact. It's always that way, it's just that different times accept different kinds of facts. In my day, the market for exploration beyond the physical was very small and not at all respectable. Notice, I am saying *exploration*. Sensationalization is another thing. I'm talking about sincere attempts to get it down into print.

I wrote fiction, mainly, because it had a market and so I could afford to use it. But I wrote it in order to portray life, as deeply and carefully and importantly as I could see. You *can't* see inside someone in any way that can be verified or accepted as factual, so if you're going to do that, you do it as fiction, and you try to help people see what they might never see without your efforts.

As you're giving me that, I do see it, and it seems clear and obvious enough, though I don't know that I ever happened to see it before.

That's what I mean. You take "My Old Man," for instance. Why do you think you love that story? And why did you think it was autobiographical until you realized that it couldn't be? Think of "Soldier's Home" or "In Another Country." Short, both of them. Why do you love them?

I guess because they set out an emotion so clearly.

That's exactly what they do. Nothing else matters to any of them but that. And why did you find others of my stories so inexplicable?

Yes, I think I see. If I didn't emotionally understand the story, it just left me puzzled or irritated, or both.

And there you have in a nutshell the history of the literary criticism of Ernest Hemingway's works! If they didn't get it, they assumed the fault was in me. They'd have liked to fault my craftsmanship but the stories they *could* get showed that I knew what I was doing. So instead they faulted *me*. My values. My pretensions. My posing. My being out of touch with the real world of politics or whatever trend they believed in and clung to.

And if they didn't believe in the emotion—

Then they assumed I was faking, or was imagining something that couldn't exist. And if the story and characters would have brought them to an emotional understanding they didn't want to come to, they said the characters and situations couldn't be real. Harry Morgan half nature myth!

You must have gotten awfully tired of people misunderstanding or rejecting what you were doing, and having platforms to announce that misunderstanding on, and convince others.

A man has to go his own way, you know that, but he likes to have a sense that he isn't alone; that there are others who at least sympathize with what he's doing. I didn't even have my own family, most of them. I especially would have wanted my father to see what I was doing and approve of it, but maybe if he had, I couldn't have developed the same way. Maybe I would have become vulnerable to criticism. Or maybe it would have made things easier, who knows? Maybe I wouldn't have had so prickly a relationship with anybody who might criticize me and misunderstand me where I needed support.

Would you have admitted that you needed support?

Depends on who, when, where and why. Might as well throw in what and how, I suppose. On Times Square to a crowd of people, no. To a woman, indirectly, maybe. To myself in the middle of the night, never.

Now, to go back to what it was that I was doing. I was showing emotion by *not* talking about it. I was bringing it in between the lines, forcing the reader to get into a certain place if he was going to get the point. And I was doing it, at the same time, in a new way because it couldn't be done in the old way. (I don't mean to say that I'd thought this through; I was following the scent.) All the hearts and flowers wouldn't have helped the reader see what had been said. They would have *prevented* it. So, I stripped it down. Got rid of the ornamentals. Streamlined it. And the result looked different according to the eyes you brought to it. If you were wedded to the literary traditions and social conventions of the previous century, it looked crude, rough, deliberately uncivilized. Looked like a stunt, or a publicity stunt, or an attempt to shock for the sake of shocking. If you were my father, it looked like deliberately choosing to concentrate on the seamy side of life—like a boy in Sunday clothes deliberately stomping through a mud puddle.

But if you were open to new forms, it could be exciting. Then it was a question of how the subject matter took you. If you didn't like it, I was misusing my talents. If you did, I was telling the truth. And then, when I'd made my name and the form wasn't strange anymore, then if you still didn't like it, I was imitating myself, or was caught in my own mythology, or was unable to break into new ground, or was deaf to the new social consciousness that had rendered my concerns quaint and obsolete. And if you did like it, I was still telling truth.

I thought Maxwell Perkins made a good point when he explained your use of four-letter words—to Owen Wister, I think—as entirely congruent with your style, in that you rarely used a simile.

Max always understood me. We came into this world to work together. Not our only reasons, but that was one, for each of us. That's why people think of us together.

Thanks, Papa. Enough for now, I think.

Keep at it, a little at a time every day, and you'll get there.

≈18≈
Paying

Monday, May 10, 2010

Papa, as you probably know, I'm re-reading The Sun Also Rises. Can we talk about Jake's philosophy that you paid in some way for anything that was any good?

You paid some way for anything that was any good. But, if you were willing to pay, you could get good value for your payment. I didn't see much point in being a tragic figure or an accident, so I tried to turn to account anything that happened to me. First there was the mortar shell, the war wound. I parlayed that into a writing career, and a love story even if Agnes threw me over, and a lot of second-hand experience, stories I heard in the hospital, that was all the more concentrated because second-hand. I'd paid in pain, and in illusions, and in a continuing disability that I had to consider, though I didn't let it slow me down. And I paid my innocence, too.

Let's do more later when you are more awake and are less interested in reading more. I'm not going away!

≈19≈

Cripples

(8:40 p.m.) Okay.

You having finished the book and fulminated against the characters in it—

That's about it.

Well, I know your feelings and your questions, and as you have learned, there is no use for tact here—no possibility of it—so that simplifies things.

Robert Cohn. What was so bad about him, and why did it matter that he was Jewish? What does that have to do with anything? I don't understand your anti-Semitism, or Jake's or Bill's. And I don't see what it means, that Jake and Bill like Mike, an obvious pig, despite anything he does.

You must remember, first last and always, Jacob loves Brett and he sees her go off with one man after another. Is it so strange that he would sympathize with Mike, who is in the same position?

What does Cohn being Jewish have to do with it?

They felt that he felt he was superior to them, and of course they resented it.

That isn't good enough. Jake repeatedly says that Cohn was a nice boy and a nice man, though progressively less so. How did he show that he thought he was superior? Seems to me he just wanted to be liked.

Maybe they just disliked him, his Jewish mannerisms and everything that went with the package.

It doesn't make sense to me. I can see if you wanted to portray an anti-Semitic narrator with whom you didn't agree, but that isn't it. Your writing shows that strain in it, in the same way you use the word "nigger" in writing and in your own letters.

Don't judge me by the standards and the language of a later day.

Fair enough—but where are you now about your attitudes then?

How soon after you die do you expect that you will become in favor of slavery?

All right, touché. What we are is what we are. But—why?

Look, I had experiences with Jews, the same as I did with fairies and intellectuals and fascists and lefties, and experience forms your attitudes—well, over the ones you inherit.

So if you're saying that you grew up in an anti-Semitic culture and your own experiences confirmed you in those attitudes, all right, I can understand that. We're the product of our times and our place and our chosen attitudes. But then why weren't you anti-Catholic?

That doesn't seem to me to be the same kind of thing at all. It wasn't ever a question of being Jewish in attitude or emotion or, let's say, allegiance. You couldn't choose to *become* Jewish, and anyway there weren't any particularly Jewish traits I was ever attempted to imitate or acquire. Intelligence, maybe, but I had that. I sure didn't need that kind of clannish attitude. Being Catholic was something you could do on a personal level. It was the ceremony and the emotional intensity and the feeling of rightness. You could be a WASP who became Catholic a lot easier—a lot less of a total change—than becoming Jewish.

So what was your intent about Cohn?

You mean, why did I make the villain of the piece somebody who wasn't a villain at all?

Well, sort of, yes.

I don't think I did. If you look closely at the book, it didn't have any villains, just a bunch of cripples and a couple of relatively sound characters like Harris and Bill and the people of Spain.

Cohn was devastated to find that living with Brent Ashley—fucking her, to put it baldly—hadn't meant anything to her. But wasn't this the story of his first marriage? She left him while he was hesitating to leave her lest it destroy her. But when he found out it hadn't meant anything to her [Brett], *he couldn't bring himself to leave her and be miserable on his own.* He didn't follow the code, you see! He didn't have a stiff upper lip, and they despised him for it, and called it his Jewish suffering. And he wasn't a coward, because he could defend himself physically, but he couldn't act like a man, and they despised him for that too. He made them see how he was suffering and they hated him for it. He knew he was acting badly, but he couldn't help himself. Maybe he had lost self-respect, trolling like a male dog after a bitch in heat. It didn't make him any more pleasant.

And—again—his function in the story?

He was one form of cripple, the analogy to Brett. She was a cripple too. And she wasn't very different from him. The only thing was, she was a woman, and women weren't expected to act like a man, and men were.

I get so impatient with her and her stupid crippled vocabulary and her lack of any form of self-control, and her icy habitual using of the men who were infatuated with her. And her drinking incessantly. Ridiculous to be so judgmental of someone who is only a character in a story, I know.

Not so ridiculous. It shows you took it seriously—and anyway there were plenty of real-life Brett Ashleys. Nobody ever accused me of making up *that* type! But you aren't giving her much of a break. She is in love with Jake—or thinks she is, anyway. At any rate she is in love with somebody she can't have, and that's as close as she ever gets, maybe, from lust to love. And I said she had a hard background, including two bad marriages. Sure she drinks. What else does she have? Without lust and drink, what's in it for her? Sightseeing? Using her 35 words to become a writer?

All right, she's unhappy, but she doesn't go off by herself to be unhappy any more than Robert Cohn does, and nobody blames her for it.

Don't they? Ask the *toreros* who watch her take up with Romero. Ask Montoya.

I see. That's another contrast, isn't it? The healthy responses of the Spanish against the diseased responses of the English, Scottish, Americans, French, Greeks—

That's it. In Spain, real values prevailed—at least, until a certain point in the festival!

And Jake cuts himself off from them by pimping her to Romero, because that's what she wanted.

Yes he does. It's an irretrievably irreversible step, and it costs him something infinitely precious to him.

Seems to me like Jake lost, Cohn lost, Brett lost—and gained, because at least for once she didn't do what she wanted even if it would destroy someone—and Mike didn't lose because he had not much farther to fall, and Bill didn't lose because he wasn't all that involved. But all of them are sort of unsound.

Wounded. There is more excuse for that "wounded hero" stuff here than in most places. You could say, if you wanted to be more charitable than you care to be at the moment, that they were all wounded by their lives—maybe even by their times. Jake wouldn't have been wounded if he had been in a crash because of the war, but maybe the others wouldn't have been what they became, either, if they had been raised in another civilization. Spain, for instance.

≈ 20 ≈

Hemingway's Values

Tuesday, May 11, 2010

So, did you have a particular way you wanted to go, today?

Let's stay with that section you read out into your machine yesterday. (And wouldn't that have made my life easier! If it hadn't come with all the things that come with it.) There was a reason you were moved to do that. It was my credo.

Is that one reason you killed yourself ultimately, Papa? You'd run out of ways to buy anything?

No, we've talked about that. It isn't like I cut anything short. I could have continued to exist, hating every day of it and lashing out on all sides (or sinking into intolerable depression) or I could just bring it to an end. Mary knew that, and she helped me, but of course she couldn't admit it, any more than I could admit what I was doing in France [in 1944], and for the same reason: legal consequences. But she then, and I before, did what was *right* instead of what was legal. Harry Morgan would have approved.

All right, I see that. I knew and I suppose everybody knew that her reasoning was lame in leaving the keys where you could find them. I have supposed you made her life unendurable and this was her only means of self-defense, finally. And the fact that you killed yourself where you did, rather than in the basement, tells me you held her at least partially responsible for what they'd done to you.

That's right. And I wasn't even quite wrong in my reasoning about it, but I couldn't really realize, in the state I was in, that she had acted from the best motives. It seemed to me that she had acted with my enemies to destroy me, and really she had, only not—I see now—deliberately or knowingly.

Well, it isn't every biographer who can ask his subject about his suicide. If people catch on to this—and find a way to verify their results—that will be one more window into life, won't it?

To continue about my values—. I didn't care what was the meaning of life in any metaphysical way. I wanted to know, not in any abstract fashion, but concretely, day by day, action by action, *how to live*. And I trusted that if you lived right, maybe you'd learn the meaning as you went along, or maybe at the end. But the meaning of life can't be some abstract thing different from your day-to-day living of it. What kind of sense would that make? And I didn't for a moment believe that life didn't have a meaning just because I didn't know what it was. So—it meant that I had to have a code, and had to live by that code unless I found a better one, and for the moment the best I found was, live the life that's available to you. That's why I *planned* my fun, you know? That's why when I learned something, I *learned* it. That's why I was so fiercely intolerant of so many things and so many types of people that were phony or empty or just words or pretending, or dead at the core.

Now, people looking at my life from the outside, I can see they thought it was just pointless roistering interrupted by tossing off some bit of writing to pay for more pointless roistering, but that just shows that they didn't understand what they were seeing. My life was the *living* of life as it came, and as I could steer it or was steered, and I was living as best I could on my terms that I had set and accepted.

Work was the basis for it all. You will notice that Jake works, and Bill works off-scene, but the worthless lost ones—Mike, Brett, Cohn, the Count—have no work to do, and have no work they ever could do. Mike had been a soldier and, I don't know if you could tell, a good one. But he didn't have any work when there wasn't a war. Cohn had written a novel but he was crippled by having enough money that he wasn't forced to do anything to make a living, and he didn't have enough self-discipline to make himself work at being at least a better author of lousy novels. And it never even occurred to Brett that her emptiness had less to do with men than with the fact that she was useless and knew she was useless and didn't have any anchor in her life. Sex and liquor are well and good, but nobody ever called them anchors.

I worked, all the time, the way I read, all the time, unless I had declared a certain time no-work days or I was prevented from working by illness or injury or some specific circumstance. Without work I would have been lost, for I wouldn't have had anything to pay with except money, which is empty unless it is the fruit of something specific.

I mean—if you've paid out of yourself, that's one thing. If you've only paid money and spending that money doesn't mean anything to you because there's so much more, it isn't the same. As long as I could work, I could enjoy life as it came to me, and not just as raw material for future writing—though it was that—but as life. If I enjoyed breakfast, did that mean I enjoyed it because someday I might need to describe somebody enjoying breakfast? And yet, if I did need it, it was there. But that isn't why I ate breakfast. I didn't go fishing so that I could write about going fishing, either.

That's all very clear. And the meaning of life?

That was something very different. I said, as a young man, that maybe if you lived paying as you went you'd eventually figure out if life had purpose beyond itself. My times were against me there. What I knew wasn't in fashion, and those who knew it with me weren't the kind of people to provide me with that kind of support. Take Santiago, fishing alone in the Gulf Stream at the end of his life. He takes for granted the things he was raised to believe, the things simple people believe—God, Jesus, Virgin, the Saints—and also various superstitions, and they are all as real and as natural to him as newspaper reports of Joe DiMaggio and the *gran ligas*. He hadn't ever seen DiMaggio either, but he didn't doubt that he existed.

So I had my beliefs, sort of leftover beliefs, and my superstitions that seemed valid enough to me, and were anyway a comfort and a support, but none of it was anything I could put forth except as speculation. And I had none of your repeated systematic testing of boundaries between one world and another. Didn't know it could be done, wouldn't have known how to do it. Would have, though, if I'd known how. It wouldn't be any different from the rest of my life. One more skill to learn. But I was left sort of clinging to an inadequate life raft made of bits and pieces. At the end, I still believed as I did when I was a young man, only I didn't have anything left to buy, and nothing to buy it with.

Admirable man, Papa, and maybe your continuing education of people, through so much undying literature, is a continuing filling of the well so that you may buy things over there.

Or next time.

Yes, or next time.

≈21≈

The Revolutionary Features of A Farewell to Arms

Thursday, May 13, 2010

All right, Papa. As you will know from tuning into this station, I found A Farewell to Arms *different this time. Perhaps because I had just come from your later works, I found this one disappointing in the love story, riveting in the war story, for a total effect that was much less than* The Sun Also Rises, *which had been written earlier, or, of course,* Bell *or* The Old Man.

You are reading with the benefit and disadvantage of hindsight. You can see how the work falls down, but it is much harder for you to see how revolutionary it is, how hard-edged, next to the novels that were being published at the same time. This is not the same thing as pleading for mercy. It says, in itself it succeeded so well that its very revolutionary features have become a part of the culture, and so they blend into the landscape.

Those features are mostly the description of the war, I suppose.

No, the romance too. If you knew the conventions of the time you would know that the very casual assumption of the romance was a revolution. She didn't feel guilty! They didn't bother with forms! Their relationship proceeded more or less without reference to society except occasionally. Ferguson showed them (and reminded the reader) from time to time, and Catherine felt it acutely for a few minutes in the transit hotel when she said it was the first time she felt like a whore—but mostly they proceeded innocently and without reference to religious rules or social mores or even, strictly speaking, legalities. And the narrator took it all for granted, you see, rather than moralizing about it. Nor did she die because she had sinned. She died because life handed out meaningless death—to her, to Aymo, to how many millions of soldiers, animals, civilians, trees, buildings—

You state that very clearly. As so often, it is a curious feeling to not know, then have my pen explain, and then know.

Now maybe you can see that A Farewell ought to be looked at in two ways. It is an enduring work of an author, yes, but as time passes it will be seen as a less and less important work, because it was mainly a shot in a battle, or a battle in a war, and the battle or war won, the shot or battle is less important. It is more a means to an end, you might say, than an end in itself. So its flaws of composition don't matter. Yes, it seems shapeless for those who don't notice that a journey in each case separates out the books, and yes, if you are most interested in the war, the romance is a sort of interruption and their subsequent married life—call it that—a long irrelevance tacked on for no particular reason. But this is only for those who don't understand. Those who see it clearly see why. Max did.

I see that. Interestingly, though, I still can't help seeing it through your later work and of The Sun, too, and feeling that it fights against itself somehow.

Yes, it does, and in its way that was revolutionary too. It wasn't lack of skill. He was immersed in Army life, and she came to him as a puzzle to solve so that he could get sexual satisfaction. He was used to getting it by telling the necessary lies, and he never expected anything more than a chess game until he got it. The fact that she was so suddenly in love with him showed him there was something wrong with her—she was crazy, for reasons stemming (as he eventually found out) from her own romantic history, in which she had behaved conventionally *and bitterly regretted it*; knew that she had made the wrong choice. She had no support in conventional morality after that, and never had had any firm religion, and so she was adrift, you could say. She had to make up her own rules as she went along, and this before he did, for at first and for a long time he just was a soldier among soldiers, a man among men, even if a foreigner. It wasn't until he was almost shot that he wound up in the same predicament she was in: He had followed the rules and it had worked out badly, so he had to start making his own rules.

Frederick Henry isn't as far along as Jake Barnes, you see. By the time of *Sun*, it's several years later and Jake has had several years of being crippled. He has had time to experience prolonged consequences. He has worked out his own rules of conduct and his terms of being in the world. He bought his way and had his fun as best he could, and mostly had a satisfactory life—in the daytime. Jake is what Frederick would become in a few years: wounded but whole, whole but irretrievably wounded.

Frederick Henry sought a sexual conquest, and to his surprise found love. Found that he could *feel* love, and *give* love, and in this sense *live in* love. That changed him. It made him vulnerable in a whole new way, and he had to learn to live with that. Until then he had been floating with the tide, cut off emotionally from his family at home for reasons never explained (because they don't matter) and cut off yet connected to his army friends because he was in another country's army, yet he was sharing the experience. He had Rinaldi, and the priest, and the others were acquaintances, even if very close and long-term acquaintances. The wound separated him from them—and brought him to Catherine—and when he returned to the Army, he did not really return to them. He was a part of the Army when he was wounded. He was a part of Catherine when he returned from the hospital.

So the whole book is his progression from emotional isolation while in an Army and in a cause he more or less still believed in, to emotional involvement with one specific woman, to separation from the Army and (by the manner in which the separation occurred) emotional divorce from the Army and the cause, to physical separation from the cause, the Army, the war, the country—his whole past life as far as the reader had been told that life. And then, when it was just him and her—she too was taken. The baby was never central in his thought, except as a potential danger, and a potential wedge between him and her in the life they would have after the birth. The book is an expression of one state of mind—life takes everything, sooner or later. I didn't have being dead to remember, or maybe it would've had a different tone! When enough people make it clear that death *really* isn't the end except as the end of a chapter, which it certainly is, then everything about life and death will change again, as you well know.

Whew. Less than an hour, but I'm tired. Always an amazing, reward-ing process, but not so different from ordinary life when we ponder things and let wisdom percolate up.

No, not so different. Not different at all. That's what it is.

~22~

Hunting, Fishing and Our Primitive Selves

(4:20 p.m.) Okay Papa, this may provide a test for us, a discussion on a subject we disagree about. I've picked up Green Hills of Africa *and re-read nearly the first 100 pages. What is it with you (or anyone) and hunting? I don't get it.*

You want to make your case against hunting?

I don't have a case against hunting; I just don't see where the fun comes in, killing something. Tracking it, out-thinking it, sure. Seeing the game close up—with a camera, say—absolutely. It had to be a thrill. But why kill it? I'm not talking about shooting for the table. I wouldn't enjoy it, but I'm willing to admit that if I eat meat, it is merely a luxury for me that I don't have to kill it. Two things I can't get about you: the eagerness to kill for sport, and the competitiveness in everything.

We may need to agree to disagree.

Well, sure—but if you could explain how you saw it, I'd be glad to know.

Hunting and fishing are like bullfighting, in a way. They go back way before our civilization, so they put us into contact with parts of ourselves we might never know otherwise. Civilization stifles; you must have felt that. Hunting, fishing, puts us back to the old days when it was us against the physical world, but does it in a modern way. The modern part can be overdone, and of course each year it's a little more overdone, because each year you get a little softer, a little more used to things the same civilization you're escaping provides. You want books, and liquor, and gaslight, and baths, and then you wind up wanting GPS and satellite uplinks and laptops and photos from Mount Everest. Still, the idea underneath it all is the same. It's like they say about women, so you could say about civilization: You can't live with it and you can't live without it. Hunting and fishing provide that compromise that stops you from losing your last link with our earlier selves.

I suppose you could get something of the same thing hunting with a camera. Don't know how fishing with the camera would go—it would have to be under water, and there wouldn't be any question of a three-hour battle, or even a three-minute encounter, once the fish was spooked and took off from you. But, with hunting I suppose you could do it with a camera, except the danger to you wouldn't amount to much. After all, if you miss a shot with your Nikon, or catch him out of focus or something, he isn't going to charge you in a rage. (Well, maybe if he was vain enough–.) Joking aside, I don't see where the danger would come in, or the drama. It seems to me it would be pretty tame.

Well, that touches on the second question, always shooting to best someone else (and your own record, of course).

If you don't understand competition, you can't understand me. I know that you've puzzled over my turning even my writing into a contest against the greats, and it seems silly to you. But what else do you have, but competition, to show you how you're doing?

What if you don't care how you're doing?

Then you aren't ever going to be champion. And if that doesn't interest you or concern you, fine—but if it does, you're going to have to compete—against others, against your own best, against the record books, against the clock.

It seems to argue an insecurity, to me.

And an unwillingness to measure yourself against others seems to me to argue an insecurity, plus if you don't compete, you'll never know.

You couldn't ever switch that competitive instinct off, could you?

It's like my temper. I couldn't ever switch that off—reliably—either. I didn't pretend to be perfect. But I was what I was, and how do you like what I was in 1960, when they [had] burned the competition out of me?

I see your point. And I don't hear you saying that everybody else had to be like you. But you'd have thought less of Max Perkins if he couldn't have hunted or fished.

No, more if he hadn't been willing to. I knew his was mostly a city life; I made allowances. But when we did go hunting and fishing he liked it.

My parents and my aunt and uncle used to listen to the prize fights, and I couldn't—and still can't—see how anyone can enjoy a sport, no matter what level of skill it involves, where the object is to beat up the other guy and hopefully not get beat up yourself. Even if it weren't usually crooked—I can't understand the draw, and I know you liked it too; doing it, and watching it.

You just pay too much attention to people getting hurt, or the animal getting killed, or the fish getting caught and killed. You couldn't enjoy a bullfight if you obsessed over the horses—and still less if you identified with the bull. You're taking your eye off the ball, which is—the effort, the skill, the risk, the stakes. It is us in touch with the most primitive thing in us—and that primitive part of us has its rights! It can't be denied without breaking out somewhere else, like it or not. Maybe more hunters and fewer commuters adds up to less neuroses and piled up tension that leads to crazy wars and senseless violence in the streets and against the helpless. It's going to come out someplace.

Well, you always make interesting arguments from an unusual point of view. Thanks.

≈23≈

The Code

Saturday, May 15, 2010

From *Green Hills of Africa,* nearly the final page:

"We have very primitive emotions," he said. "It's impossible not to be competitive. Spoils everything, though."
"I'm all through with that," I said. "I'm all right again."

One thing I have noticed, Papa, is that you don't use books to make yourself look better. You portray yourself as you remember yourself. That isn't the same as saying that you remember yourself or even experienced yourself as other people would describe you—whoever does that, or could do it?—

but it certainly shows an honest man. Shows me an honest man, anyway. Doesn't show a poseur.

I remind you of your father.

Yes indeed. Dad didn't have any Anglo-Saxon reticence about bragging but he didn't exaggerate what he had done, as far as I know. It was more like he was so delighted, he told you so you'd be delighted on his behalf. My mother disapproved, and made the disapproval clear.

I know how that is! But if you can't ever blow your own horn, you lose something. People get tired of hearing it, so you have to keep it to a minimum if you can, but if you've done something excellent, why shouldn't you be able to boast of it? Or even describe it honestly?

And the people who are criticizing you for boasting about what you did couldn't do it themselves—

Exactly. Because I don't care who it is, British reserve or whatever, if you've done something excellent, sooner or later you're going to find a way to talk about it. Not all the time—maybe it will take a drink or two to loosen your tongue—maybe you just figure out a way to have people drag it out of you. But if you care about the people's opinion that you're with, you're going to want them to know—and if you don't tell them and nobody else does either, how are they going to know? That doesn't mean you're going to brag about everything in your life to everybody. But if you're with fishermen, you talk fish, not books you've written or boxing you've done or anything else you might be secretly proud of. And with another crowd you don't talk about fish but about whatever their interest is. It's normal, it just gets disguised a lot of the time.

Now, it's one thing to brag about things and never have done them—that's just being a fake and a blowhard. It's another thing to shut up because you don't have anything to say that you're proud of talking about. And it's true, I knew people who lived so much inside themselves, they never seemed to talk at all about anything they had done—but I knew, and I noticed that others knew, and we weren't all eyewitnesses, so how did we know? It stands to reason that they told somebody!

The reason it's worth talking about this is that it's just one of the conventions I didn't follow. It's like people go to a school and they learn what "is" or "isn't" done, and they judge everybody else, for the rest of their lives, on whether they follow the code or not. If you know the code and don't follow it, you're a bounder. If you don't know the code and you seem to follow it anyway, you're one of "nature's gentlemen." If you don't know the code and don't follow it, or follow it in some things and not in others, then you are either someone who can be dismissed from consideration, or you are a "find," someone to be taken up, or you're a natural phenomenon who follows his own rules, a sort of professional eccentric.

I didn't have this so clearly when I was alive. I could see how people acted, but I couldn't quite see the underlying mainsprings. It's pack behavior, with a complication that one pack's rules are extended as if they applied to everybody, whether they naturally belonged to the pack or not.

This explains so many things, you see. You can't use rich and poor as a divider, you can't use educated or uneducated. You can't use culture or uncultured, though it can often look like that. What I experienced was pack behavior. The pack versus the outsider or at least the outlier explains a lot about my relation to the critics and essayists and other authors and reviewers and academics. All my objections to them center on their pack behavior or my fear of it. All their objections to me center on the things I did, said, and wrote that sounded to them to be either deliberate or unknowing violations of what was proper, or fitting, or couth, or genuine, or civilized. This proceeded to their denial of the very quality of my writing that made it impossible for them to ignore me, and impossible for them to destroy me, though they could and did prevent my receiving professional recognition or prizes until I was safely past it.

What could have prevented it?

Nothing, probably. For me to conform to their expectations would have required my giving up the qualities I valued, in writing, in living. I wasn't "one of the boys" in that sense, and never could have been unless I or they had been willing or able to change.

Writing is a solitary occupation anyway. It means seeing, judging, understanding, weighing, balancing—and how are you going to do that as part of a committee? It means expressing whatever you can find of the truth, and how are you going to do that and stay a member in good standing of a political group, or a "movement," or of any association tighter than good fellowship and the comradeship of fellow strugglers? Writing is hard enough, without trying to write while staying within someone's fixed limits, or your own fixed limits. The ones who write as part of a "literary movement" are as bad as the ones who write as part of a political movement. As soon as you hook up with a group, the word compromise is right there in the middle of things—and when did compromise ever produce greater literature than political manifestoes, or party platforms? Find a group of writers who define themselves as part of a group, and you'll find a group of very mediocre writers. (Groups defined by what other people call them are another matter. That may be just similar striving seen to be similar.)

Now, in the 1920s, the "official" literary establishment huddled around the word "propriety." They wanted you to be decorous—to not use vivid Anglo-Saxon words, to not describe unpleasant realities, to not exceed the grasp of the genteel reader of the *Saturday Evening Post*. My novels and short stories offended, and seemed aimed at shocking for the sake of shocking. The critics were so busy assuring their public that they disapproved of my characters that it didn't occur to them that I sometimes drew what I saw regardless of whether I approved.

In the 30s, it was leftist politics. You could pretty much say that the mainstream of American literature in the 1930s was leftist politics. There wasn't much that was written of serious literature that didn't try to describe the social situation or call for the revolution. (Of course, some of those guys would have been the first ones shot if a revolution had actually come.) So there I was. *Death in the Afternoon* was about bullfighting. *Green Hills of Africa* was about safari hunting. Both took place on different continents from America and took place in another world from the social concerns that were New York's literary world. And, both were nonfiction, both experimental, and both dealt seriously with subjects that the political-literary establishment couldn't care less about and, if it gave them any thought, hated and despised.

To Have and Have Not could have been my big political book and should have been, but I didn't put in the extensive time and energy it needed past a certain stage to solve its central problem and produce a unity out of several parts. I had to get to Spain. I felt I had a stake in the Republic and its resistance to fascism. I sacrificed art to politics, or to world affairs, or to resistance to fascism, or something, and in the end the result for the world was a botched book that couldn't be fixed but could have been a classic. I hope the establishment was satisfied—except, of course, it wasn't, because it had to see the book as my trying unsuccessfully to jump onto the social-consciousness bandwagon. And the rest of the decade was war and politics and then the long silent creation of *For Whom the Bell Tolls*.

By then it was the 1940s, which started off as a war on fascism and ended as a war on a vastly strengthened communism, with individual liberty that much further behind. But throughout the decade, the literary establishment was cheerleading. It didn't like the fact that Bell was balanced, although the people did. It disregarded *Men at War* because it didn't notice it; didn't see the work that had gone into it, couldn't see that it could have had any significance for me or by me as a writer. And then for the rest of the decade I published journalism and worked silently and published nothing.

The 1950s was the most conformist decade of all, probably, and the worn-out soldier Richard Cantwell was not anybody's idea of a hero, except maybe the soldiers. *The Old Man and the Sea* was a major hit because it was upbeat, timeless, nonpolitical, had no love interest to make them wonder what I was indiscreetly revealing, and had a protagonist who couldn't possibly be autobiographical. Plus it had the unity and compression that make a classic. But then they gave me a Nobel Prize and wrote me off, and in fact except for *The Dangerous Summer*— pseudo-journalism, pseudo-autobiography—and reportage on Spain that Hotchner had to get into shape, I was finished. Even *Movable Feast* was a time capsule. As I said earlier, I had no contact with the times I was living in, and then I was finished.

If you look at my career in this light, you can see how I was never going to be the establishment's fair-haired boy. What did any of those grand themes have to do with anything that mattered to me?

That's very clear. Why isn't it clear to history and literature?

Perspective. You have to be able to see it in perspective. Besides, who had any incentive to produce a fair assessment?

Well, your biographers, for instance. You have been blessed with some seriously good biographers—Carlos Baker, for instance, or the man who wrote the five-volume bio that I learned so much [from], whose name I am blanking out at the moment.

Reynolds.

That's right, Michael Reynolds. Seems to me they took you seriously, respecting your work and your intention.

You can see the limitations of the genre, now.

Can I not! The biographer doesn't have the benefit of the inside view that you are giving me. Everything they do is based on secondhand evidence at best.

Of course. But within those limitations, they did as well as they could, I suppose. But trying to get to something reasonably accurate by using dead evidence isn't the way to get to the truth. They don't realize it, but they do their best work less by accumulating evidence than by using that evidence as a springboard for their intuition. That is when they get the idea of my life (or anybody's life) and its meaning. Their judgments of the externals are usually so partial (that is, so fragmentary in the evidence they base them on) as to become more fiction than fact. Yet despite being wrong so often and so thoroughly in detail, an honest biographer paints his subject as he sees him, which is realer than the evidence unless he dislikes him. It is the empathy that carries the portrait from evidence (much of it mistaken or misleading or false) to impression. Reynolds certainly did that. Baker did it. Hotchner did it, though his was as much a portrait of himself as it was of me—which is how I would have done it. There are others, of course. Meyers. But no need to list them. The point we started at is that if you can't see my mainspring, you can't sum up my career in the way I would, not [that is, rather than] in the way some survey of American literature would. And you can't assemble my mainspring by assembling evidence, because you don't manufacture machines by using items you find on a treasure hunt, and you don't breed animals by—well, that's enough of that analogy.

Going to stop for now. Thanks for this very interesting discussion.

≈24≈

A Boy's Perspective

A friend of mine, a retired teacher of literature in Denmark, followed these conversations as I sent them around on the Internet, and one day wrote me that her students never could decide which was the point of "Indian Camp," that Uncle George was really the father of the baby and so the Indian killed himself, or that the Indian couldn't stand her pain, and so he killed himself. So I asked which it was.

Neither. When you read my stories, look at every element in them. You may not know why, but every element is there for a reason. And, remember, you are to get an emotion from it. Look at the last line.

Nick knew that he would never die.

List the elements in "Indian Camp."

["Indian Camp" is only three pages long, but I listed many thing, including: the rowboat with two waiting Indians; Nick, his father, Uncle George; two rowboats, each with an Indian rowing; George smoking a cigar and giving the Indians cigars; a dog barking, then more dogs; an old Indian woman holding a lamp; the young Indian woman who had been trying to give birth for two days; her husband, who had cut his foot badly three days earlier; Nick's father explaining that her screams were not important; no anesthetic; hot water, coffee, and sterilization; the doctor washing hands carefully and thoroughly, explaining why; the woman biting Uncle George during the operation; Nick's father showing Nick, and Nick looking away; Nick's curiosity had been gone for a long time; Uncle George looked at his arm. The young Indian smiled reminiscently; Nick's father excited and talkative afterwards. "One for the medical journal"; "oh you're a great man all right." The proud father dead with throat cut. "Sorry I brought you, Nick. Awful mess"; always such a hard time? Exceptional"; "Why did he kill himself? Couldn't stand things, I guess"; do many kill themselves? Not very many; do many women? Hardly ever; "is dying hard?" "I think pretty easy. Depends"; the sun coming up. Bass jumped. Hand in water; quite sure he would never die.]

So compressed; hard to summarize more than it already was.

All right. Now, try to relax and we'll get it through. Can you see how sex and death are interwoven in the boy's experience?

I guess it was his first sight of a woman's sex organs, and in a gory con-text. I guess that's why "he looked away, his curiosity gone for a long time."

And he asks if many men kill themselves, if many women do, and why, and is dying hard. And the physical surroundings—the morning, the warmer water, the fish, his father rowing—makes him "quite sure that he would never die." Going forward in the dark it had been first the three white men, or the two and the boy, then they met the Indians and divided, then they were all together, then George went off by himself, then it was Nick and his father returning in the daytime.

I'm afraid I am still too dense to get the full intent.

The doctor intended to begin Nick's education, but he got more than he had bargained for. He was not an evil or cruel man, but he turned off his emotional response to do the job he was there to do. Coming back he told Nick he was sorry he had gotten him involved, but he wasn't sorry for anything else—not his lack of sympathy for the mother, not his own unawareness of the effect of someone's pain on someone else. He didn't realize. He didn't realize that the Indian—who couldn't get away because of his foot—would be affected by the pain that he himself had disre-garded—not the pain but the evidence of pain, the screams.

I don't understand the Indian smiling reminiscently. Just to bring the connection to sex back?

The same action in different contexts has different meanings, and it can suggest connections. As it did.

Nick was a boy and he didn't really understand a lot about what he was seeing, did he?

That's the point exactly. That's exactly it. He was quite sure he would never die. He would also never get involved in messy situations, would never be callous or unimaginative, would never cause pain and certainly would never kill himself. That's why the last line. He recorded, he remembered, he observed, but he didn't really understand—and the reader who did understand got the point. It wasn't designed to teach obstetrics or fishing, and it wasn't a detective story. It was to feel that state of observing but not understanding.

And Uncle George?

He showed sympathy in contrast to his brother's (or could be his brother in-law's; didn't matter) businesslike manner-of-fact attitude. George shared cigars; George helped, though it is mentioned only in the doctor asking him to move the blanket; George was a little disgusted by the doctor's slight bragging and his self-satisfaction; George was upset by the suicide and didn't want to be around the doctor's matter-of-fact attitude about it, even though the doctor *was* upset. The two men were upset about it in different ways. The doctor was upset that Nick had seen it, that it was senseless and unnecessary. George could imagine the man's cumulative state—for he had been unable to get away, remember. He had badly cut his foot the day before she had started going into labor two days before. He'd stood it all. The doctor *abstractly* understood, but he didn't necessarily let himself feel it. His concern was for Nick. Where did Uncle George go? He'll turn up all right. In other words, nothing happened to him; he's safe. But he's not in sight. So you see, George was there to bring out certain aspects that couldn't have come out if the doctor and Nick had been there alone among the Indians. George was *hurt*, he was *injured*, by the woman's pain, as the doctor was not. But there's no need to make George the baby's father—if I'd had that in mind, you'd have known, and if I'd had that in mind and you hadn't known, I'd have failed (assuming perception on your part).

Another strand to the story was good intentions going astray, wasn't it?

Yes. The doctor saved the baby and the mother but never thought of the father; he wanted to give Nick experience but gave him more than he wanted to. George was there in sympathy but never realized who needed it, and wasn't able to do anything except help in the operation.

Other elements in the story?

Well, reread it again and see if it looks different now.

I see that it is a description as a young boy would see it. The objects that stood out to him. And I noticed, this time, the line about the men having moved off up the road to be out of the range of her screaming. Her husband is smoking a pipe, like them, but he is right there. As you say, he couldn't get away.

When the doctor says the screams are not important is when the husband rolls over against the wall. And you will notice, the young Indian woman after the operation "did not know what had become of the baby or anything." Nick's perception, you see. Sensory inputs still wide open, regardless of what he did or didn't understand.

I can see how the stories were aimed: you wanted people to react to them as they reacted to life. The stories affect you as life comes at you, and they affect you but you may not know why or how.

That's it exactly. Does this say anything about how far off the critics were? If you criticize the facts of the story but don't absorb the atmosphere of it, you can't see the reason for the facts. So you don't know what you're talking about. You wind up trying to make George the father because of the cigars, or you ask about the wrong things. But the reason for the story is right there in the final line: "In the early morning on the lake sitting in the stern of the boat with his father rowing, he felt quite sure that he would never die."

That's as much as I can do for now. Thank you. I'm learning something.

≈ 25 ≈

Helping People to Feel

May 18, 2010

Papa, I suppose that "The Doctor and the Doctor's Wife" is built upon your life but is no word-for-word autobiography, even necessarily disguised autobiography—and critics who approach your work go wrong to think so.

That's right. A writer takes what he knows and tries to render it so that it's truer than the real thing, so that people who weren't there can get it even though they weren't there. So you have to intensify and magnify and simplify and clarify—and you have to do all that without distorting the subject! It's like Georgia O'Keeffe painting her tiny subjects huge, so you can't help seeing. Now, this is not a blanket endorsement for Georgia O'Keeffe's painting style or subject matter. It's an illustration. She painted tiny things in proportion but huge, so if you glance at it, you have a chance of getting something of what she had seen, and if you looked longer, she had done it so carefully that you couldn't keep seeing more and more closely into it. My writing, the same idea: The real thing has to be portrayed larger than life, starker, changed in so many ways, if it is going to have the effect on you that the original emotion had on me.

So how do you do that? You invent, but what do you invent *from*? It has to be, from who you are and what you know—it comes out of *you*. If I had told the story of the Cuban fisherman who hooked a really big fish and stayed with it for several days, and killed it finally but lost the meat of it to sharks on his way home—and told just the facts, as if I were writing copy for the *Herald-Tribune*—and had all the facts right, biographical and piscatorial and climatic and geographical—do you think I could have gotten across any of the meaning of it?

The *plot* is one thing. The *story* is another, different, thing.

So the material for the stories came from what I knew regardless how I knew it. Maybe I observed it first-hand. Maybe I was told stories and something jumped from the storyteller to me. Maybe I did research, the way I learned things specific like skills. Maybe my life was research as it went along, picking up background of what it was like to walk down a dirt road in early morning, say, or the streets of Paris in the fall. You understand.

But whatever the material was, and however I'd accumulated it, it couldn't ever be the final thing until I had worked it. It was always raw material until I invented. Had to be. It always is. It is, even if people think they are just reporting—but in that case they are working without knowing it, and if they are blessed with something the way Scott Fitzgerald was, the magic comes through (as long as it *does* come through) even though they don't really know what they're doing or how it is happening. A lot of journalists work that way and don't even know it.

So, you invent. But you can't invent without any consideration of what you're inventing from. If you're going to start with the [Gerald] Murphys [socialite friends of his from his Paris days, used by Fitzgerald in a novel], you can't do just anything you like; you can only do what Gerald or Sara *would* do, or *might* do; you can't do what they never would do. Now, if you want them to do something they never would have done, you have to have them be only partly the model you are inventing for. You see? You can't have, oh say a star athlete, maybe a specific star athlete, acting in ways no star athlete possibly could, *unless* that is the point of the story, in which case you had better know exactly what you are doing and why and how it could happen. When you invent, you have to know what you are inventing from, and what you are inventing toward, or you won't know what you're doing.

All of this, of course, is meant to apply to sincere writing that tries to express one thing (or many things, with great good luck) truly. It doesn't apply to whoring. Whoring may be learned—Scott certainly learned it—but has the disadvantage of requiring you to bring yourself back to a sense of innocence if you wish to be anything but a whore in the future—and how can you deliberately do that? You can, maybe, if you have some real shock that reminds you that you were real, once. But not commonly, even then.

All right, so, you *know* something, and you invent. You invent toward a certain effect. Now maybe you can do this by just feeling your way toward it, and if so that's a gift, but even there you have to know how to recognize what you have been given once you have received it, or how are you going to edit and revise what you wind up with? And if you don't feel for it as you go along, the only other way I can think of that there could possibly be is to know ahead of time what you want to produce as an effect. You may not know how to produce it, so you may do just as much trial and error as the guy who just keeps trolling until he hooks something, but you do know what you're trying for. You see? Either you start by knowing what effect you're going to try to achieve with certain material, or you start with the material and see what kind of effect suggests itself, but either way there's the work of going from material to effect by way of invention, and the invention is bounded by what is possible while sticking within the limits of the material.

So I could take my parents' lives and tell a dozen stories, and each story might express one aspect of something I'd seen or could imagine. To get to the emotional effect I wanted, starting from that same material, I might have to change the "facts" a dozen times, to let the raw material let something happen that did what I needed. If I'd been writing auto-biography, or biography, or history, I'd have said so. And if I had been writing fantasy, I'd have announced it by publishing in the *Saturday Evening Post*. To write truly, I had to take what I knew and say it in such a structure, with such words, that let you see it too, that sometimes all but *forced* you to see it too. And if I failed at that, or you the reader did, there was nothing. Now—having said all that, you tell me—what is the effect I aimed for in "The Doctor and the Doctor's Wife"? What is the *point* of it?

I'm going to need to feel my way to it. The doctor is a good judge. He saw what Dick Boulton was doing and knew why. He was smarter than to fight him when that's what Boulton wanted, though it made him mad enough that he half-fantasized killing him. His wife, a Christian Scientist, thought she understood things and clearly didn't, and she was either ignorant or stu-pid or both. There was war between them but he tried to keep the peace, even knowing better. I don't see why the unopened medical journals irritated him unless it meant he wasn't keeping up with his profession. When he went out and found Nick reading, Nick chose him over his mother. I guess the final effect I get is of the doctor living his impossible situation, with an invalid wife who was certain of things she had no clue to, and a man cheating him because he could, and a sense of time leaving him behind, and only his son as a clean, innocent accepting (in fact eager) presence in his life.

Well? Was that so hard?

It's an amazing amount to compress into a few pages, and without say-ing anything much to the reader. Little touches like Billy looking grave, and taking the time to shut the gate that Dick had left open, showing that it wasn't the doctor who was wrong or even was contemptible, but Dick who was callous. You truly were a master.

Thank you. I'm very pleased that you can see into the story now.

Most people already knew how to do that, I suppose, or you wouldn't have been published.

You'd be surprised. Think of the misinterpretations of "Indian Camp." But people *felt* something even if they didn't quite know what they were feeling, or why.

Amazing achievement, anyway. That's it for now, I think. Thank you.

─*26*─

How to Work and What to Work For

Thursday, May 20, 2010

Okay, Papa, what shall we talk about today? Started Death in the Afternoon again, as you no doubt know.

Let's talk about work and working and work schedules.

Everything in life is alternation. Things wax and wane in importance. Too much of anything is not a good thing, but too much of anything *in the wrong time* is even worse. So, scheduling helps you keep things in balance; it reduces the impact on you of the things you can't help.

I got up early and worked then, for several reasons that ought to be obvious. You're fresh in the morning—provided that you didn't abuse your body too much the night before. You're clear, too—you don't have things of the day hanging over you, or distracting you. And you are not plagued with company or with people's demands early in the day. Most people sleep later, plus they take time to get themselves organized, plus they have their own lives to deal with. It's very convenient in many ways, and when you're done for the day, you're done. You can—and ought to, almost *must*—turn your mind to other things.

But when you work, *work*. Bring to it a single-minded intensity, don't just work at half speed, or with half your mind. The very intensity with which you work will be a reward: it will increase your energy, and your enjoyment, in a way that going through the motions never can. If you don't work hard, how can you know the difference between work and play? How can you live? Existing is not the same as living, in the same way that dusk is not the same as high noon. Living without intensity is living with much more boredom, with a lack of savor. Why do you think I wanted out when I could no longer live with intensity?

People think my life was a frantic progression from one time-filling thing to another—bullfights, sea fishing, partying, drinking—and fewer people remember that the work that underlay all that, and financed it, is not something that can be made into dramatic stories, so is unreported, leaving a very distorted picture of the balance of my life. But even when they realize that my life had careful alternations of work and play, they usually don't realize that the play wasn't frantic, wasn't purposeless, wasn't self-destructive.

Deep-sea fishing isn't purposeless and isn't destructive. It is a different application of discipline and intensity. Big game hunting, the same. Hunting small game requires intelligence and sharp instinct and reflex, even if it doesn't involve personal danger. Observing *corridas* is different the more knowledge you acquire, and how different is it to appreciate a bullfight than to appreciate an opera, say, or a symphony, or a baseball game, or any intricate performance conducted within strictly understood and observed rules?

Parties, all right, that's relaxation. A lot of people, a lot of food and drink, that's a balance to all those hours working alone. It isn't what it would be if the parties weren't a balance to work, you see. Same parties, same amount of wine or liquor, but the total effect is entirely different.

So, *work*! It isn't a matter of earning your pleasure, as much as it is of making the pleasure possible. There aren't any people more sad than those who don't have any real work, unless maybe it's those who have *only* work, or only meaningless work. Your day-to-day schedule is going to be a certain amount of work, a certain amount relaxing from the intensity of work, and then either a certain amount of play or the same time spent quietly refilling the reserves for the next day's work. Your week-by-week schedule ought to have the same alternation. Don't work Sundays, or if not Sunday, some day you choose. Or if you wish, maybe don't work two days in the week, or three, or whatever suits you. But the alternation is the important thing. Some days must break the routine, or else the routine will become unsustainable. You'll be draining your batteries all the time, and at some point you're going to have to refill them, either by some time off like a prolonged vacation or probably by some form of illness. And in the course of a year, too, there ought to be some extra time that

breaks the schedule, some Sunday of the year. It is only when you deliberately break up your schedule that you can keep the schedule up for a long
time without you breaking down or just grinding down.

Beyond the span of a year, that is, breaking your life into larger
chunks the way a month is a chunk of weeks, and a week a chunk of days,
and a day a chunk of hours—well, here you're into astrology, or into anything that looks at the ages in a man's life. It ought to be clear enough that
there are some things you *can* do and *can't* do at any stage of life. Try to
stay with the rhythm of it.

So, let's assume you are able to work on your own schedule, and aren't
just putting in time for somebody. How do you work best? The first thing
is to know what suits you. Do you do better in short spurts, then a pause,
then another spurt? Do you like steady-as-she-goes? Do you prefer to
orchestrate things so you do some easy things first, move toward harder
or more intense things, then taper off? I don't know that there's any right
or wrong about it, but you want to know what kind of routine suits you.
You fit into it better. You aren't chafing against the harness.

All of this has been just clearing away the shrubbery. The big question is, what are you working *for*? What are you working *towards*? If you
are doing some job you don't care about one way or another and you're
just putting in time because you have to feed your family, that's one thing.
But even there, you should know *why* you're doing what you're doing. If
it's just a job and you know it, you won't hesitate to change for something
better that pays better or is better somehow. But if you're doing the only
thing there is for you, the work equivalent of the only girl for you, then
you you've got to stick to it and be true to it, and God help you if you
throw it over to do something that pays more or is steadier, or for any reason. If you have to, all right: There's no telling what our lives really mean.
But you'd better be sure you really have to, and you aren't just settling.
Things that settle can wind up in quicksand.

And if you don't really know what you want to do?

Then you have to find it.

And how do you go about finding it?

How did *you* do it?

I floundered around, working at various jobs and reading all the time.

That's one way to see it. But you could also say, you floundered around because you had a *fixed idea* about what you were going to do, and you had blankness as to how to do what really called you, and you didn't see a path because you hadn't done the research and couldn't have done it. You would never have found your way along "the path without a path" by following logic or any form of matter-of-fact common sense way of going about things. But the path found you. All you had to do was listen when the promptings got loud enough. Do you have any reason at all to think that this wouldn't hold true for everyone?

No I don't.

All right. So—the simple rule is, to find your right work, you have to keep your eyes and ears open to the promptings of the inner self. It knows. Call it your higher self, if you like, or your soul, or your hunches. Otherwise you're on your own, and the world's clues might mislead you. Or maybe not; I don't know that you can make rules about it.

And there's one more thing to say about work, and it's important. Not everybody's life centers on their work, and not everybody's should. There's many a guy whose life is making money to feed his family, and his *family* is his life, and his job is just a sort of social interaction. And of course in your time that's true of women as much as men.

~27~

Understanding Your World

Friday, May 21, 2010

Okay, Papa, much good discussion yesterday of how to work. It makes me aware that I do not work nearly enough, and that I am habitually lost as to what to do or how to proceed. I'd prefer to do much more.

Yes—except that you read all the time, out of lifelong habit and a sense that there is so much out there to be read, far exceeding your ability to keep up with even the small area that interests you. Don't I know the feeling!

*Callaghan said "Hemingway read everything." And your omnivorous
reading of newspapers, magazines, books, is well known.*

Yes, and I re-read a lot, too, though not like you. But in all that reading, I didn't get lost in other people's worlds. I had my own. It served as
a balance between my world of action and an inner world of a different
kind of action. And this is something that biographers ought to spend
more time on than they do—what did the subject of their biographies
read? What did he get out of it? How did he fill his inner world? Because
if he is a big reader, that's a big part of his inner world, a big part of his
inner life, and to pass it over by saying "he read a lot" is the same as saying
"he sat around a lot with his nose in a book," or a newspaper, or whatever,
as if it were an inert activity. It misses that part of him.

But the biographers can't capture that aspect of anybody, and I'll tell
you why. They'd have to read the same things, and the same mixture of
things, and they'd have to do it while the same kind of things were going
on around them, and they'd have to be associating what they were reading with a million things from the person's past life and past reading.
It can't really be done. That's why somebody writing your biography is
a waste of time to cooperate with. It'll be like a newspaper story, never
quite right in the detail, and therefore misleading at best.

Biographies are important, as histories are important, or news stories are important—but you can see why people sometimes get lost in a
different world, relying too much on what they read and not enough on
what they experienced firsthand. You go to a book, or to a news story, as
a resource, not as the final word. Could I have understood Spain by reading books about it? Could anyone? You can catch a certain fascination
that can lead you to experience, but that's about all.

You've seen the letter I wrote to one of my biographers [Charles
Fenton], objecting to the whole enterprise, and you've seen Lindbergh's
letter to somebody pointing out the huge number of errors in a biography of him that he had read at the other person's request. Reporting
on someone else's life is always going to be a secondhand kind of thing;
would be even if they could get the detail right, which they never could.
So—don't over-invest in them. Nonetheless, even though nothing you
read can be the truth the whole truth and nothing but the truth, you
need it. It's your window on the world. How else are you going to know
anything about who Coleridge was or what he wrote or what it meant to

him or to his contemporaries? How else—to speak about newspapers—
are you going to know what everybody else is also reading?

All I'm pointing out is something that ought to be obvious to everybody anyway. You can't trust the news media to tell you the truth, but you
can't live unaffected by them. And it isn't any different in principle about
books. The things that drive them will be different, and the way they go
about things will be different, because they're asking a higher upfront
economic investment than an Internet site, say, but ultimately they're
going to want an audience and a profit, and that is a pretty big common
denominator. It's true, you can find individual books that tell the truth,
but you can find individual new stories that are true, too. But the overall
mass of things is going to be falsified by the same pressures. No matter
how true and fine an individual book or news story or Internet site, the
great mass of it is going to be horseshit and lies.

You have to know that, if you're going to understand your world!
Doesn't matter when you live, or where, I am confident that if you really
look, you'll see it's true.

So—if you can't rely upon anything you read being true and accurate, but you need to rely on it for general grounding, where does that
leave you? (And when I say read, I mean watch and listen, too—every
way in which you get "the news" day by day.) You'd better have a grounding in direct personal experience. But, personal experience of what? Do
I mean go out and see for yourself what's behind all those news stories?
Obviously not. Even to chase down any one of them would make you
into a researcher, and you'd wind up like Carlos Baker or any biographer,
trying to fix in their mind something that is always fluid and mostly
intangible.

So—personal experience of what? Of the things closest to your
life, of course. If you are a woodworker, that's it. If you are a writer, it's
the writing process. If you fish, maybe it's that. Something *real* to you.
Psychic exploration, why not? Collecting things. Gardening. It could be
anything, provided that it is real to you. Yes, even reading biographies
and histories and collecting a sense of how things were that may or may
not have anything to do with how they really were in truth.

You often see people going off the deep end with their theories and
their ungrounded certainties and their fears, their fears in all directions.
All this is because your times really are changing faster and faster, at an

unsustainably fast rate of fastness! Not only do things change fast, but the rate at which they change is changing too, and it's always faster. It disorients people. Plus, everybody has a sense of things being out of control. The only counter to that is the hope and fear that somebody somewhere *is* controlling things, but, given that the world gets continually stranger, and harder to grasp, the natural assumption is that the person or people or group behind the change are malicious or at least self-interested, and so, in effect, hostile to the larger interest. People look at where you are, and where you're headed, and think that since more rational, more livable alternative routes weren't taken, there must have been a conscious subterranean force that consistently skewed things. But those same people would regain their balance if they would just hold to that one thing in their life that is important but doesn't need to be reported by anybody. There is no substitute for personal first-hand knowing.

Reading can be a form of first-hand knowing, but what can that knowing be, but recognition? That is my fiction.

≈ 28 ≈

Learning

Saturday, May 22, 2010

Still reading *Death in the Afternoon*. If I had my way, I'd put out an edited addition—mutilated, people would think it at first—that showcased the truly wonderful learning there is to be had in it, merely by removing what sets up the narrator as querulous distraction. As it is, it is occasionally like listening to a great violinist wisecracking as he plays, or complaining about his hotel. And it's a shame, because it is great playing!

Papa, how did you come to learn so much about things you came to care for? In short order, as they occur to me, writing, appreciating painting, hunting, fishing, shooting (as opposed to hunting), bullfighting, military science, wines and foods, and intangible things like the interactions in nature, and the likely responses of fish.

How do you learn anything? You pay attention, you ask, you try to get the experience yourself, and when you can't get it—painting, the fish—you try to get inside the mind of the person who *did* paint, or the fish that took the hook. But having the experience doesn't mean just doing something and checking it off your list. It means watching somebody do it, and doing it, and remembering doing it, and analyzing what you saw somebody do and what you remember doing, and then doing it again with what you have learned, and analyzing it again, and so on. There's always more to learn, if you keep it an *active* process. But it has to be active; it can't just be doing it and not thinking about it, not learning from it. You can learn from any shot you take, any fish you bring in, any painting you see. But *it* doesn't come to *you*. *You* have to go to *it*. That's the only way to master anything.

Now, you've read about how I would analyze what specific detail evoked an emotion in me. That was my way; there are others. But the critical part is putting your *attention* on it. You've got to work it with your mind. That doesn't exactly mean *thinking* about it, though that has its place too. It means connecting with what you just did, what you just saw or felt or even heard. You're fond of saying that sometimes something is easier done than said. This is a case of easier done than described—but it isn't all that easy to do, either, until you know what it is you're doing, and why. It is the difference between somebody who sees something and a trained observer seeing it; it's the difference between a tourist watching a bullfight and an experienced viewer. At first you don't know *what* to see, or *how* to position yourself to see it, or *why* it's being done. You have to learn how to know all these things, if you're going to understand how to learn it.

Notice what I just said. You've got to have the what, how, and why just to learn how to learn. They aren't even the first step, but the step toward the first step. You've got to be a reporter writing for yourself, and always on the job, or ready to be on the job. It takes energy, it takes attention, it takes disciplined intelligence and perseverance and a lot of other qualities that aren't ladled out in bucketfuls, and anyway it takes work and the habit of work. And you have to find a teacher. That will save you the time you need to save if you're going to learn more than one thing in a lifetime. And that means you have to come to it in a certain attitude, or a good teacher won't bother with you. But if you're a good pupil and he's a good teacher, you should be able to surpass him, finally, because he has heaved you over his shoulders, giving you what it took him long years to learn.

But remember, there is a huge difference between a teacher showing you how to catch a specific fish at a specific time, walking you through each step, and your being able to do it when he isn't there, even in your mind. I could walk Max through catching a big marlin, but for him to know how to do it first to last, he would have had to put in concentrated time learning, and it would have had to be important to him, and he would have had to have the aptitude not just to be okay but to want to be expert.

It was a very noticeable quality of yours, that you became expert in so many areas that interested you.

I notice you didn't mention history and great literature, but I had my footing in both of those, too. It's just, there isn't much call to exhibit those, or teach them to anybody, and how can you teach a mental arrangement in the way you can teach a physical skill? You can't. Or I couldn't, anyway. "Hemingway read everything," Morley said, and I did. But I didn't read things just to give myself something to do. I was learning all the time, and by the way, you ought to understand my irritable reaction to so much that I read if you remember your own reaction to insincere plays: They made you livid with their insincerity and their facile bandwagon-riding.

Yes. I do remember, and I see.

What's the purpose of reading? It brings you into other worlds, right? You experience what you can't experience any other way. It's a time machine, and a window into other worlds, and sometimes it brings you into whole new parts of yourself that grow from that, to your amazement. So *why* waste any of that kind of magical opportunity writing bullshit? And why waste it *reading* it? And to get tricked into wasting time on something that is just a fake is annoying. I read history because I liked reading it. Why else? But like you I used the books to put together a picture in my mind—a roadmap. We say it is so we can understand the present, but really does it have to have a use? What use is it to look at an Utrillo, to really look?

I think you are often underrated out of the assumption that you are under-educated. Of course that requires great stupidity in the face of the evi-

dence, or an entire ignorance of the existence of the evidence, but there are plenty of people who fill that bill.

There always are. But if people would look at who my friends were, and what I actually included in my novels, where it fit, they'd get another idea.

The kingdom of the mind is impossible to dramatize, though.

Yes it is, and the hell with them. The real problem was, I was never in uniform.

I understand that. They were always trying to find a slot for you as peg, and you never fit.

Broke a few pegboards, though.

Yes. And maybe ultimately split the peg?

Life did that. It always does. It's just a pleasant surprise afterwards to find out that the end of the story is more like the end of a certain way of *writing* the story.

≈ 29 ≈

Life and Interpretation

Sunday, May 23, 2010

All right, Papa, here we go again. Before I ask the questions my friends have suggested, let me ask if you have something specific in mind for this session.

Don't forget the thoughts that have come up as you have continued to read *Death in the Afternoon.*

Mostly my thoughts have been, what great serious thinking and careful analysis. The other thought that has come to mind repeatedly is how much good thinking is contained in your books that, for some reason, makes no impression on The Hemingway Myth. That myth is not really larger than life. It is distorted, with certain elements exaggerated and others ignored—suppressed, I sometimes think. The result misses you entirely.

And so does biography based on external fact, as I've said. What we do is only part of our life, only part of what we are. Why we do it—in what internal and external circumstances—is rarely obvious. That's why these professors keep coming up with their theories, trying to explain everything. But nobody's life can be explained, just explained *away*. And I never could persuade anybody of the fact.

Yes, I've been thinking of that professor you worked with—or worked against, sort of—whose name I can't dredge up. Hanson or something. [Charles Fenton. A year and a half later I read his book, The Literary Apprenticeship of Ernest Hemingway, and liked it a lot.] He kept trying to persuade you that what he was doing in rummaging through your life was important to the world, and I guess you felt that all the rummaging (that he thought of a serious research) couldn't come to anything because the job couldn't be done by anybody.

Well, it's clearer when you see them trying to practice biography on *you*, and you see that everything they're concluding is wrong because of what they don't know, or don't believe, or even what they do know or do believe but don't put together with stuff they might never think of. Now, of course, I see the value in biography—up to a point. But I think that point has long since been passed, because people are trying to get an outside view of the inside using evidence that is only on the outside.

A white whale may be many things, but what writer of fiction would be dumb enough to try to pin a symbol to one specific meaning? Why would he even think it was a symbol? Why would he expect to know what his unconscious mind was telling him anyway? *Moby-Dick* came to Melville, and he worked and worked to find what was in it and bring it out. He went way beyond his depth as a craftsman and when he struggled back to shore, he'd caught a whale! But the whale wasn't just blubber and spermaceti oil. It was the boredom and calm and routine and incidents of a four-years' voyage to the South Seas and back, captured in a hundred chapters of material about whales. Now, you years ago realized that. And you saw Melville's humor, how funny his temper was, how he saw things with a satirical eye even if a sympathetic one. "Heed it well, ye pantheists!" But the reason you didn't make Moby-Dick into a Symbol of Evil, or Symbol of Vast Impersonal Nature, or Symbol of The Unattainable Goal or any of that is because you were shown that the academic game is limited and the academics don't always realize it. Until you came to this table today, you didn't realize why you got the impulse to read *Moby-Dick* while you were in your year of graduate school. Now you do.

Huh! I'd never connected the two, no.

And you weren't intended to connect the two. But *Moby-Dick* reminded you, on an unconscious level, that the academic trick of associating one thing with another, comparing one thing to another, understanding one thing in terms of another, has the drawback of obscuring the thing itself! If something is always seen as being more or less related to something else, it becomes an endless contest, a wrestling match. Nobody can look at a symbol and tell you what it "means"—so, if the professors and the critics try doing it, in the first place they're going to fail, because they're going to miss the thing in itself. In the second place, they're going to wind up ascribing motives and associations and complexes to you that are just things they're making up as they go along. They may not realize it, because the beauty of their brilliant insight blinds them, but *they* are making up the connections they think they're seeing. And of course in the process (assuming you take them seriously) they're making you look like a pathetic mess instead of a careful craftsman. Scholarly analysis has its place, but that place is not, repeat not, in interpreting symbols. If anybody is going to do that, it had better be another artist—and he's going to know better than to do it!

Take Santiago, fishing alone and having his daydreams and memories, and using his skills and fighting his flight, and dreaming of lions. There's plenty of symbolism in that story, but the symbols were put in by life, not by me. And so they can only be interpreted by life, not by me—or you either. Santiago could symbolize many things, and I'm not going to start to list them. So could the fish, and the boy, and beisbol and the gran ligas and Joe DiMaggio. We've been through all that. But my job—the only job I could do or should do—was to choose the symbols to start with, the story of the old man's great catch, and follow it as it led me. What work of art—as opposed to hackwork or whoring—can ever be designed and produced to order? It is the artist's job to go fishing in the unconscious and bring back a fish and describe the fish (the story, I mean) so that others can recognize it.

If the artist is describing his fish of a story, that's all he can do. It's all he *should* do. If he starts putting in symbolism from the conscious mind, he's going to cripple the effect of the story. He's going to mutilate the fish. That isn't the proper use of his skill as a writer. The writer's function is to fish and to bring all his life to the process of fishing. If he properly lands the fish, he and the reader will both have something neither one could have had otherwise, because it was created out of the unconscious, normally not a part of their world. But if he tries to get cute, or tries for a consciously chosen effect, or tries to be "meaningful" he is going to botch the job.

It takes all a writer's skill and all his life and preparation to catch a fish and describe it properly. He reaches out, and he keeps reaching out as he works at it, taking out all the wrong words, turning back at all the wrong turnings, holding to the indescribable *feel* of the right thread. He doesn't have time or effort or disengaged ability to spend on consciously putting in symbolism! If he sees it as he's working, it's as much as he can do to stop it from getting out of control. And I don't mean out of *his* control, I mean to stop it from taking an unwarranted importance.

If that isn't clear enough, it's going to have to do anyway.

Well, it's clear to me, and I think it will be clear to anybody who ever tried to write a novel.

I can see that the professors are used to doing things their way, and I guess if they'd stick to saying, "Hemingway's characters and plots suggest this about life" instead of, "they show this and that about his deeply rooted complexes and his ambivalent feelings about his hunting dog and the geese," I wouldn't have anything to object to. In fact, maybe they'd actually make something clear. But to do that, they'd have to do the same thing the author has to do—the thing you say I didn't do in *Death in the Afternoon*—and that is, get the author out of the way! Don't waste your time saying, "This proves Hemingway was ambivalent about drinking." Say, "This could be looked at as a message from life meaning whatever, that used Hemingway to put words around the message."

Yes, I agree. Parlor psychiatry—what I call psychiatry-without-a-license—has a lot to answer for.

～30～

Men and Women

Monday, May 24, 2010

All right, Papa, here we go again. Should I ask one of my friends' questions, or do you have a preferred topic?

Let's talk about men and women, as your friend asked. You want to put his question in here, as it is the specific nudge, the loosening of the rock to start this particular landslide, if that's what it turns out to be.

Michael said: "Can you ask him what are some major emotional and spiritual differences he noticed between women and men now that he has passed, compared to his worldly view." That's the first part of it.

He is asking, how much of what I thought in life has turned out to be just wrong, now that I have a larger perspective.

That's the sense of it I got, yes. I'm sure it has you smiling.

Those are pretty broad brushes. Major emotional and spiritual differences. I don't think the question can be answered in the form he has asked it. What makes him (or anybody) think there is only one kind of woman or one kind of man? And what would make anyone think that broad generalities could be applied to either one, *as such*? I mean, when you cross over you realize those things that were part of you while you were in the body that didn't manifest directly. You are half your father's genetic makeup and half your mother's—but each of them was half and half too, after all. The main differences between men and women are physical and social, not so much emotional and spiritual. So really, as far as I can see, it's a question of how much anybody's society teaches him—or her—about the rules he or she should play.

Let me try to narrow that down.

On the spiritual side, do you think there are two strands of spiritual inheritance, male and female? And if there were, do you think anyone could inherit only the one parent's inheritance and not the other's? And if the "you" that comes into the world, and takes up a body and an identity, has previously had lives in which the opposite sex was experienced, do you suppose that that experience goes into abeyance until the life is over? No, if there is a gender-based reason for differences in spirituality, it is beyond me how it could be expressed, or what its function would be.

And, since we just said that everybody inherits from father *and* mother, each of whom inherited from father and mother, and on back forever, how likely is it that there would be emotional differences based in sex? Except, of course, there are—but let's take a look at the situation before we jump to conclusions.

A woman's life is affected by the hormonal changes that dictate the body's rhythms. Estrogen and testosterone produced different environments for the two sexes to live in. But everybody who has lived in the world knows effeminate men and masculine women. In other words, proportions vary. It ought to be obvious. And besides, what of boys and girls? Even when they are children with none of the chemicals of adolescence running through them, they behave differently, think differently, are interested in different things, and act (usually) pretty predictably as representatives of one sex rather than the other. So it isn't just a matter of chemicals.

I don't even think it is a matter of society's expectations, particularly. Yes, any society will channel the differences into what it considers gender-appropriate roles, to the extent that it can, and the more rigid the roles, the more you'll have people like Gertrude Stein, exaggerating their non-compliance. But the fact that it has to channel the difference shows that there is something to channel! Your society has been loosening the rules and changing the expectations to such an extent, in such a short time (as a society goes) that you now [in effect] have several countries with different unspoken rules. Has that, or any of it, eliminated the difference between men and women? Do you think it is likely to?

I think if you will look at my writing, you will find that I didn't write so much about how women were as about how men lived or tried to live with women, and that isn't quite the same thing. To show how hard a man can find it to live with a woman—how disruptive to his own idea of his life she can be—is not the same thing as saying that it is the woman's fault. Of course the man is going to experience it that way. Women experience living with men as just as exasperating.

Men and women also experience each other as divinity in bodies, and not just for the sex act but in the very same interactions that drive them crazy. You have to remember that, when you try to do some thinking on the subject. That phenomenal attraction, that periodic repulsion, it all goes on regardless of anybody's conscious intent. Then you add conscious personalities to it! Of course it's going to be difficult.

Look at it in layers. At the most basic is the physical conditioning for male or female mammals. You don't have anything to say about that. What you draw is what you get, as I used to say.

On top of that is your specific physical inheritance. Your ancestors, living in you.

On top of that, the rules and clues your family lays down, the ideas you absorb about who you are and how the world works.

Then society itself, with what you might call the petrified expectations of millions of people. It all has weight, and even if you move somewhere else, you were shaped by what shaped you. The rest is your attempt at re-shaping.

Not much room, after all this, to talk about major emotional and spiritual differences between men and women! You have to add so many qualifiers and "yes, but" statements that you wind up not saying very much.

The same with his second question, which is really about his own situation specifically. If he will expand his view to several women he has been closely connected to, he'll see easily enough that generalizations about differences between the way men work and women work are likely to fall down as soon as you get more than one example of each! Now, what we could talk about more profitably is men and women trying to live with and without each other. *That*, I wrote about a lot. And I certainly experienced it.

Of course, first there's the sex drive, and it *does* drive! It drives through everything. And the funny thing is, I don't think anybody really knows what it's about. When you think about it, don't think in generalities, which will be pretty useless, and not in stories about other people, which will be second-hand invitations to generalization. Think in terms of your *own* experiences, and not in terms of what he or she did, said, etc., but in terms of how *you* felt. Who was the "you" who was so head-over-heels in love, and where did that person go when you weren't any more? What was the basis for that obsession to have sex with somebody, and where did it go? Yes, of course there's the physical explanation, but— *what is it?* Elk experience the same thing. Dogs, cats, you name it. They may be monogamous or not, domestic in nature or not, herd animals or solitaries, it doesn't matter—they all have that instinct. Why? Or rather, how? We know what it's there for. It preserves life in bodies. But isn't it strange when you actually look at it?

And I am not talking about the sex act itself, either. You know that Dr. Johnson said "the expense is damnable, the pleasure fleeting, the position ridiculous"—but the fact didn't slow him down any. It couldn't. Those were just intellectual judgments; they didn't weigh anything against that drive. Think of how sex drives you, and how strange it is when you come to look at it. Sure it's pleasure, but there are so *many* pleasures in the world! Sure, it leads to children and families and the continuation of the world—but once somebody has done his duty by the race, he doesn't just lose interest. Don't you think it's something a little bit stranger than just physical attraction? And what's physical attraction's basis, for that matter? Why does one set of characteristics attract and another set leave you cold when for somebody else it would be the other way around? It isn't like there's some absolute scale of beauty or attractiveness—*except individually*, one by one. Each person brings his own set of scales.

I have said for years that sex is a matter of energy more than of physical bodies alone. I feel the attraction not to a body part but to some emanation of energy that I can't describe. It isn't as simple as Rub A against Slot B, or whatever.

Maybe not in your experience. It certainly *can* be. And there, in the question of sex without acquaintance, is another whole subject.

Maybe another time.

Oh, I wasn't going to talk about that now. For one thing, we're running out of time before you will have to stop for a while. And there's something else I want to say anyway. The whole point of talking about sex *as sex* is merely to demonstrate that it isn't there that the problems between men and women arise.

Bad pun.

Thank you. Sex between a man and a woman can be good or bad or in between, and of course it's going to fluctuate as they fluctuate day by day. It isn't the thing that *causes* trouble; it's the thing that *shows* trouble.

It's a barometer.

Pretty damn good one, too. If the sex is no good, there's something wrong with the relationship. If the sex is great—and the relationship isn't just about sex, because of course some are—then things are probably pretty good elsewhere.
But . . . .

Papa, I'm sorry, but I'm pretty worn out. It's 7:30 and we've been going an hour and a half. I hope you can hold that thought till we come back.

Sure, why not? Tell your friend he started a good topic here, one we could explore for quite a while and never get to the end of—and never get much agreement about, either.

Okay. Thanks for all this.

≈31≈

Hemingway and Jung on Sex

Tuesday, May 25, 2010

All right, Papa, I am ready if you are. Michael thanks you for your reading on things. I take it you had more to say about sex, as opposed to the relations between the sexes.

Huge subject. If I were trying to write my autobiography from this perspective—which I am not—I'd have a lot I'd need to say about sex and my lifetime, for of course it was an important thing for me, but—as you might ask yourself about yourself, or ask anybody about themselves—*why*? I know it seems like a schoolboy howler, but if you take the question seriously, you may find that it is more complicated, more intermixed with other things, than first appears. The only thing I know about Carl Jung's work is what you know, of course—

We could ask him to join us. (It would ramp up my own anxiety, naturally, but that isn't necessarily a reason not to do it.)

Go ahead, then.

Dr. Jung?

[CGJ, to EH] You have not read Jung, but *I* read Hemingway, and with some interest. It was more than practicing my English.

I never happened to think of it before, but you died within a month of each other—June 6 and July 2, 1961. Not that it necessarily means anything, but it's striking. So, Papa, you started to say that all you know of Jung is what I think I know.

[EH] Everybody talked about Freud, and to me it sounded like a lot of horseshit built around something that might or might not be true or useful—but where you, Dr. Jung, wrote (and Frank read) that in other, more primitive, cultures, sex is taken for granted and may not be very important, whereas they might have an enormous appetite for, and interest in, food—that struck home. I can't see it clearly but I can *feel* that it applies to what I've been trying to say here, and sometimes tried to say in my writings.

[CGJ] Yes. You had a firm but vague grasp of the fact that sex is not what it seems, and is not in any way under the control of the conscious personality, and has its own demands and channels. What people *do* may be under their control, to a greater or lesser extent depending upon the integration of their personalities, but what they are *urged* to do, or *impelled* to do, or perhaps *compelled* to do, is not. And the autonomy of the sex drive—its direction, its preferred manifestation, it's waxing and waning according to its own laws—all of this cuts against the materialistic, reductionist view of the world that would maintain that we are soulless automatons, or, at best, are the creatures of chance, with no particular destiny and only a future shaped by further chance.

This is why Freud's theories—or rather, the popular understanding of them—*revolutionized European culture.* In the wake of the de-Christianization of European culture by the cult of scientism and the assumptions of what one might call spiritual autism, the spirit had only a desert to inhabit (among the educated and lost) or an unconnected faith (among the faithful, who were, by that faith, cut off from Europe's main cultural mainstream).

If you believed, however, that Freud had proved that all higher and lower impulses proceeded from the sex drive as it interacted with society's needs and restrictions, suddenly you were free to be "modern" and yet (or should I perhaps say therefore?) liberated. That is, you could follow primitive instincts and express uninhibited behavior without in that way betraying or countering your membership in the "modern, civilized" world.

This was not enough, because it left out too much. Still, it was an advance. And Freud's advocacy of taking dreams seriously cannot be overrated, for this in one bound took Western civilization over the barrier that it had raised against its own development. If you think that the individual and the individual's consciousness are autonomous and sufficient unto themselves, you may proceed to think that your world of physical matter is all there is. But once admit that dreams are worthy of study—even if you think they are only clues to what your conscious mind does not wish to know—then you have opened the gates!

I'm a little lost as to where we're going, here.

[CGJ] Ernest—"Papa"—was a physically oriented man, but he had strong intuition and although his thinking function was more developed than his feeling function (which is why the periodic explosions), he was a dramatically well-balanced man. That was one source of his tremendous attractiveness—people are drawn to wholeness. *Because* he was well-balanced (however little it may appear upon reading superficial biography) he did not accept anything at its surface manifestation. You touched on this in the discussion of learning, the reiterative immersion until he was satisfied that he *knew* every important relationship between every important element of whatever it was that he was studying. *But he did not confine himself to reading and writing.* He lived, as actively as he could, and therefore had life as a counterweight to theory.

So, sex for him was not theory, but neither was it only practice. He *thought about* everything that he experienced. You must always keep this in mind, in considering him. Life for him was not a one-off event, but a continual reinvestment in past experience, and an enrichment of the present. If you do not see where this leads, I am confident that he does.

[EH] I wouldn't have thought of it that way, but I see it. I was seeing that none of the easy answers were enough, but I didn't have the basis for constructing any new theories about it. And I *did* construct theories.

[CGJ] Consider your lifelong connection to Catholicism, even when the politics of the church alienated you and even though you lived outside its rules. Pretty disreputable to connect with the Catholic Church when you weren't born into it. Chesterton found it hard enough. Let me suggest that Catholicism and superstition and intuition are closely connected, and are therefore often to be found in the same personality types. I do *not* mean that Catholicism *is* a superstition, nor that it is the result (or cause, for that matter) of intuition. But those attracted to one are likely to be so constructed as to be tempted by the others. Were you not in fact somewhat proud of your superstitious nature, rather than ashamed of it or apologetic about it?

[EH] I wouldn't have drawn the connection. Upton Sinclair connected Catholicism to Latin countries to bedbugs.

[CGJ] But he wasn't in sympathy. That warped his discernment, as strong mental prejudices always do.

So to return to the question of sex—

[EH] I see the point. Sex was something stronger than anybody, and so I treated it as one of the more important things in life, particularly since society—and literature in English-speaking countries!—had so downgraded and simplified and prettified it, and lied about it, and in fact couldn't even talk straight about it, so that the very word "fuck" shocked and derailed people in print when they heard it every day, or, if they didn't, didn't because it was being avoided by circumlocutions.

People asked why I was so hard on fairies, and assumed that it was because I secretly feared I was one, and repressed the attraction and all. It doesn't seem to occur to them that *I was describing what was all around us*, and doing so in an unsentimental way, and a non-hysterical way. And as to what some people call my locker-room talk in real life—that is, not in print—I admit, I did have a strong inclination to be the bull in the china shop. I found this pseudo-gentility so stifling! Why couldn't people just be what they were, and admit what was, and live with it? I tried to help things along in my writing, no reason for my life to be any different.

Now, if I remember rightly, we began this with the idea of exploring the fact that sex is one drive among many, but has exaggerated importance in the West because it had been so systematically repressed.

[EH] Well, think about that, though. *Sex* wasn't suppressed (how could it be) so much as *discussion* of sex, and *expression* of sex. So you had this huge boiler with the safety valve tied down. If you can't turn down the heat, you can regulate the flow by tying down the safety valve, but not forever. And once it blows, it blows, and you are not going to be reconstructing that particular boiler any time soon.

In my time, as you both know from being within my mind, sex is everywhere, almost tiresomely so. It sells everything, it is conceded to be important in and of itself, and the stupidest people's sex lives are assumed to be of interest to people, and evidently are.

[CGJ] Yes, and in your time Jung grows in attractiveness and Freud declines. I say this as fact; there is a conclusion to be drawn from it.

I suppose Freud opened the safety valve and the pressure is being lessened by the steam proceeding to fill every space? And when the pressure of sex declines, other things will assume greater importance?

[CGJ] Let's say that other aspects of life will be seen to be fascinating and productive, in the place of sex, for the coming into contact with new forces is always numinous in itself. Think of your friends, coming to The Monroe Institute because there they can be among others who are equally interested, and can learn to control transpersonal powers. Is that about sex?

No, and in fact it makes sex look sort of humdrum by comparison. Or, not humdrum, not routine, but—ordinary, or, I don't know—

It makes sex into one of the facts of life like coffee or lunch or creation or the enjoyment of a sunset or a novel. And this is as it should be. It puts it in perspective not as the only thing that counts or as the transcendent experience, but as *one* aspect of life. And of course a life built around the assumption that contact with the other side was the only thing that counted would be equally one-sided, distorted. Balance is all, except that sometimes we reach balance only through progressive excess.

Well, this went off in a direction that surprised me. Thank you both.

≈32≈

Reputation as Non-Physical Heredity

Thursday, May 27, 2010

Did you have a preferred topic this morning?

Let's take one of your friend Bob Friedman's questions, why is what we are doing important to me and to you?

Shall I take a stab at it first, or do you want to go ahead?

What I have to say about it won't take all that long, maybe. For you, it's interesting material in itself, and it's good practice the way talking to Joseph Smallwood was good practice. The way to become a writer is to write. The way to learn to talk is to talk. The way to learn any new skill is to practice it extensively and as regularly as possible, and in connection with the rest of life, not in a vacuum. And beyond the learning of it, in your case there is the teaching of it, if only by example.

In my case, there's the helping to bridge the gap. It isn't as if this is the only such process or dialogue going on. Think of millions of people learning this, quietly, one by one, unknown to one another, each with all the assistance from the other side that can be asked or needed. As Lincoln said, everybody helps—those who can't skin can hold a leg. And in my own case, beyond the satisfaction of helping the process, I can get into the conscious mind of your time some truths about me that could help change the way you think about me, which helps me here. That's one of the drags that being a public figure creates; one I didn't count on when I was alive there! If I had known, I might have taken some care to correct my reputation, if I could have.

I looked up the professor I thought was Hanson and it turned out to be Charles Fenton, but we both knew who I was referring to. Do you mean helping people like him get your life straight?

No, I mean living with an eye toward a different kind of non-physical heredity.

I don't quite understand that.

I'd be surprised if you did. Let's see if we can clarify it.

When you're in life, you realize that what you do isn't necessarily known to others, and certainly the reasons for what you do are often enough entirely obscure and misinterpreted. But you have to live with (and within) your reputation. The smaller the neighborhood, the firmer the reputation and the more it hems you in. As your neighborhood gets larger, or as you change localities, you get to reinvent yourself to those around you, if you care to, or if new surroundings bring out different sides of you. But there's such a thing as bursting the bounds, and becoming a transcendent figure, standing for something in people's minds, and everybody having heard of you and thinking they know you. Look at Lincoln, for instance.

Well, Papa Hemingway became my myth, and I helped create it, and went along with it, and it took on a life of its own, because it sort of fit my life. But it isn't the only way the mythmaking could have gone, and if it had gone in other directions, I would have had different dimensions of freedom. I never appreciated, even at the end of my life, how Scott Fitzgerald had been warped and crippled and distorted not just by his own ideas but by the pressure of expectations from people he didn't know.

I'm a little hesitant here, but I think we need to call in Carl Jung. He can explain what was going on, I think.

[CGJ] But you are afraid you are making me up, and making up the data, and thus exposing yourself to the danger of being exposed as a fraud! This is no improvement from where we began.

Well, I do it regardless.

Yes. But you will do it more easily without the exaggerated respect for facts and data and verification and criticism. Such things must be risked and dealt with, or even disregarded, if one is to accomplish the clearing of any new trails.

Yes, I know. It just happens to be my particular obstacle.

If it were not this, perhaps it would be lack of access, or lack of anything to say, or inability to say it. But—continue to overcome it. Work at it. Nothing worth your while comes without obstacles, however talented or lucky you may be, or however perfectly fashioned for a particular line of work.

≈ 33 ≈

The Hidden Pressure of Expectations

[CGJ continues] Now. Ernest experienced the hidden pressure of people's expectations. *This is a real and not a metaphorical force.* It has real effects that may be used, well or badly, but will in any case be experienced. As with anything else in life, the more consciously used, the better, as conscious control puts the conscious personality where it should be, deciding. Surely this is obvious.

Lincoln became president of the United States, and his very election brought to a head a crisis that had been building nearly his entire adult life. He found himself at the center of the storm from the first moment, and had to grow into acceptance of the role fate had in mind. By his depth of character, by the human qualities that gradually became evident to people, by his ability to articulate what his people felt but could not express, he came to mean more and more. By his identification with Emancipation, he moved from partisan to statesman to iconic figure. And of course by his martyrdom he perfectly fulfilled the savior archetype in modern guise, and this—combined with the success of his twin causes of Union and Emancipation—assured that his reputation would continue to grow. People's affection grew. People's hatred or incomprehension lessened, with time. But all the time his cultural effect grew. He became more central to the myth of the American experiment; not merely the political but the social experiment.

As he lived he was the recipient of people's prayers and curses. After he had finished living, still he was the recipient of prayers and curses. *This did not and does not leave him untouched.* There is no such thing as an electric current that flows without flowing. There is no such thing as nonphysical connections among people of similar vibrations flowing without flowing. Lincoln limits and channels and also frees and directs people's energies to the degree that they allow themselves to be affected. *But those in bodies can easily choose* whether to be consciously affected. Those not in bodies cannot.

You will notice that my [Jung's] work was done in the most sheltered part of Europe that was yet central. Portugal, for instance, was equally sheltered, but was a backwater. Austria, Germany, England were all central but not sheltered. My work had to be done quietly, steadily, without distraction but without isolation. In short, my life's circumstances were an alchemical retort, within which life proceeded to experiment and produce new combinations.

When my work came to be carried on, one strand of it came to be Robert Clarke, living an entirely obscure, humble existence in an English backwater. Externally he had no credentials but experience; no connections, no way to make his work known. But when he was ready, how easily the way opened. A letter to Colin Wilson, a referral to you, and the publication of two books. Then, when he was safely dying, the entrusting of three more books to you. None of this, you see, was produced or affected by the pressure of other people's expectations. His alchemical retort was entire privacy through obscurity. Thus three examples of how fame, or constricted specialized fame, or entire obscurity may shape a life's work.

Hemingway is an example of a life lived itself as an example of wholeness, of gusto. The image, however, became increasingly skewed *and skewed his life accordingly.* And continues to do so 50 years after his death.

Friday, May 28, 2010

Yesterday Dr. Jung said, "Hemingway is an example of wholeness, of gusto. The image, however, became increasingly skewed and skewed his life accordingly. And continues to do so 50 years after his death." Papa, you heard that, presumably. Do you understand what Dr. Jung means here, and do you agree?

I brought up the subject, remember.

So—either of you—how does an image reduce someone's options, or, as it was put, skew his life, after he's no longer in a body to have his life skewed?

You might as well ask how mind control works, or if somebody can be hypnotized, or if you can call spirits from the vast deep. It's all the same thing. You are treating people as if they were unconnected, or as if death disconnected them. You know better in another part of your mind. Apply what you know.

In other words, we are all one thing, so of course we affect each other.

Even the grammar of the language makes it nearly impossible to make a clear statement in that direction, doesn't it?

Well—I'm getting the idea, I think. But I never thought that the pressure of people's expectations continues after we're gone.

Well, think about it a little. What is the pressure of people's expectations, except psychic pressure? It isn't like anybody is physically pressuring you. (Of course they might—putting on economic pressure, or threats to your safety or your family's, but these are just means by which to exert the real pressure, which is *psychic* pressure.) It's actually easier to resist such pressure, if you are aware that it exists, when you have a body and a physical set of surroundings and circumstances to help you do it. "The body and its stupidity," as Yeats said. Once you're out of that particular buffer, the pressure exists and your means of resistance to it are greatly lessened. Fortunately, as soon as you're dead, most people don't realize there's more they can do [to you] than write obituaries and biographies and lying articles, so they leave you alone more. But those who do know don't let up, unless it costs them more than it gains them.

Now don't go getting the idea that we are defenseless on the side, exactly, and of course don't get the idea that influence is a one-way street. But that's the question you asked: How can we still be affected 50 years later.

Not sure I've got the answer yet. I'm getting an idea of it.

≈34≈

A Path Less Skewed

Dr. Jung, what would have been a path less skewed for Hemingway?

[CGJ] As I said, his life was a pattern of wholeness, of gusto. In many ways he showed how "modern life" might be lived in a satisfactory, fulfilling way. But the access to too much money led him into things that somewhat disconnected him from the source of his strength, which was his connection to the people. His second wife's Uncle Gus, although generous and well-intentioned, in this way provided irresistible temptation.

Financing the 1934 safari.

Deep-sea fishing is one thing, and game hunting with it. Those were out of the reach of the wage-earning man, but not impossibly out of sight. But a safari was a different order of magnitude. A safari was too different from ordinary people's life. And here we enter a complicated discussion that we must take slowly, must plod through, if you will, if we are to disentangle several interwoven threads. You will bear with me, as I am a German by language and heredity, if I am ponderous.

Not sure if that's the first joke I've heard you tell, but anyway I have the patience if you do.

Do you? It's not an obvious characteristic at all times.

And there's one on me.

Yes. Now, let us look at various aspects of things which may look similar or identical. You will remember that I was part of an expedition to East Africa not that many years before Hemingway's safari. Not many people could have done that either, and I had a physician's income and my wife's family's resources to draw on. What were the differences between my expedition and Hemingway's safari?

First, his was centered on animals and mine on humans. In both cases we shot for the pot, but in my case it wasn't about trophy heads or personal danger or exhibition of, trial of, skill.

Second, although neither expedition was publicized in advance, and both were written about later, in my case it was to illustrate what I learned of internal differences in people at different levels of development, and in Ernest's it was to produce and sell another book—a somewhat daring and original book—in the course of building his public reputation.

A third point of comparison—I was 50, and unaccompanied by my wife. He was in his 30s, accompanied by his wife and her reminders of another life.

Fourth, he brought all those books! That is, he was careful to immerse himself only so far; he never lost sight of land. Not that this wasn't wise of him, but it was a point of difference. It wasn't Ernest who was in danger of going native!

Remember, in all this we are to explore how the Hemingway myth began to obscure a better version of the myth that gradually became overlaid, then lost sight of.

A safari was a step too far.

This doesn't mean it was "right" or "wrong" for him to follow so strong an urge, but an urge may be followed in a productive, organic way, or in a forced, artificial way, and the difference is not trivial.

When he wanted a deep-sea-fishing boat, he paid for it by writing for a magazine. That was an imaginative way to obtain what he wanted without going impossibly into debt for it. Because it wasn't a gift from Uncle Gus, it was his in a way that the safari was not. This showed, in his writing and in its effect on his career and more on his public persona. Everyman could imagine himself, with a little financial change of circumstances, deep-sea fishing at least for a week or two. He could see himself as a novice *aficionado* at bullfights in Spain—for if travel to Europe was mostly for the well off, it was not nearly as prohibitively expensive as a safari. Everyman could not imagine himself on a safari, could not imagine himself caring about hunting trophy heads in quite the way Hemingway did, and could not help feeling somewhat cast off, like a poor relation watching a brother get rich and move to a better neighborhood.

Not that any of this was conscious, either on Ernest's end or on that of the public. They were still interested in *him*, but they now began to be interested in him as a different species of being, not as one of them. The intellectuals, meanwhile, who were already critical of the mystical elements in him, and his seeming indifference to politics and social injustice and ideology (which I must say was mostly his distrust in panaceas and in government) now became convinced that he was merely one of the idle rich. Yes, Hemingway, idle! Or perhaps they regarded him as, you would say, a wanna-be. In any case, as an irrelevance or perhaps an obstacle to their self-defined mission of social elevation.

I can see all this, though I'd never thought it through.

Well, if you see this much, then you see the germ of all his problems later. Is it merely coincidence—do you believe in the word—that his attempt to repeat the safari 20 years later ended so disastrously? That it physically damaged him to a degree from which he never recovered? He was trying to go back—to retrace his steps and find the right path that he had missed, perhaps—and what he found was only confirmation that he had lost the way.

Papa, do you agree with all that?

[EH] Like you, I hadn't put it together in that way. I know that surprises you: You still assume that as soon as your body starts cooling, you suddenly know everything and you can do anything, but life on this side isn't any simpler or more straightforward than on your side; it's just that the rules are different. You could put it, gravity functions differently here, but we still have to figure out which end is up. I suppose this is why you read both versions of my second African journal. [*Under Kilimanjaro* and *True at First Light*] It showed you where I was, in a way that even my sons didn't get the sense of. If I hadn't gone on that safari—. Well, I was in Key West, and liking it. I was learning the lay of the land, and the feel of the sea. There was something in me that responded to the sea. It wasn't a bad life. But Africa!

I know, shades of The Last Good Country.

Yes, there was some of that. And we would be *experiencing* it, not settling there and changing it and ruining it.

I got the impression that you got bored at Key West. I was struck by Reynolds' statement that after you left Paris, you would never again live in a big city.

Think of your own experience. Cities are for the young and for those who need a city's resources.

But—should you perhaps have lived sometimes in big cities?

No, you have to have your center of gravity in one world or the other. If you are mainly in cities, the world of nature is going to become more and more foreign to you, no matter how many times you go to it. If you live mainly close in nature, you will lose the rhythm and pace of the city. They don't go together.

And if you'd have been doing your writing in the city, it would have disturbed the balance in your life!

Exactly. I had heavy reading, disciplined writing, extensive correspondence. That was a very vigorous life of the mind. If I had lived in the city, I would have had to exercise in some artificial way, some city way, like boxing or even exercise machines and treadmills. What would be the advantage of trading the Gulf Stream for somebody's gym?

So it was Pauline—not being Hadley, I mean—that was the problem?

Life isn't that simple, and *I* wasn't that simple. But I can see where you are going with that, and we can explore it if you wish.

But another time.

Yes. You can see that you've been at this a while.

It's a little after 6:30. Long enough, I guess. All right, thank you both.

≈ 35 ≈

Hemingway's Reaction to Jung

Saturday, May 29, 2010

Papa, now that I have re-read what came yesterday, do you want to give your reaction to Dr. Jung's analysis of the effect on you of the results of that safari?

You know, it's one thing to react to a new idea, and another thing to think about it. The first is instant and usually emotionally charged, because emotionally driven. The second is slower, because it involves a long chemical process of analysis; weighing this against that, looking at this in light of that, readjusting the balance—in fact, that's a better analogy. First you have to weigh the new elements, then you have to shift the cargo to keep your boat trimmed. Okay, that's two analogies, and they don't work very well together. The point is, when you actually consider a new way of looking at something—especially if it's something close to you, so that every aspect of it is connected to many other strands of yourself and your interests—it is going to take you some time to readjust things. That's a bit of work, too, sometimes, so it's one reason why people usually just shrug off the new viewpoint as wrong or not relevant. When you get someone like Carl Jung looking at your life and talking to you about it, you've got to listen. You'd be crazy not to—especially here, where it's so hard to change. So—I've been thinking about it.

That sounds sort of funny, since it only came up yesterday morning.

Your time. I sure wish somebody would come up with a way to make it clear to you, and believable, the differences in time between the two sides. But we aren't going to do that today, that's for sure, so let's just leave it that I've been giving Jung's words some serious thought. And, of course, he and I are in direct communication now.

"Of course"?

Links are established by way of the physical world; that doesn't mean they then rely on a physical link to stay established. It depends on how much the two on this side have in common. Besides, he had read Hemingway; that makes a difference. And it would have been easier if I had read Jung.

All right. It's a funny thing to look back on your life—this particular version of my life, anyway—and realize that it can be seen differently in a way that makes sense of things I hadn't ever considered in connection to each other. That doesn't mean the way I always saw it was wrong—what would wrong mean in the circumstances?—but that it gives another insight into it.

To me, the difference between deep-sea fishing and the safari was mainly that I could do the first any time, and without a lot of planning and preparation, and with just a few friends or a hired crew if need be, and it was on the sea, and although there is always more to learn about the sea, still, by now it was familiar enough. Africa and all that would have to go into making a safari was new, and intricate and exciting. The other factors didn't occur to me, even afterwards. I was used to living my life for my own reasons, in my own way, by whatever rules I accepted, which amounts to saying "by my own rules" almost. So I never thought to think about how it would look to others, or what it might do.

Now, I realize that Carl didn't mean, "the safari changed your image," as much as, "the safari changed your life, which gradually changed your image." And even that is too simplified a version of what he said and meant, but after all, it is right there, you can always re-read it. I think he's right, but at the time it was too subtle for me to see it.

You have to realize, I was used to the rich, and although I wasn't in awe of them, I did envy them their command of things. In those days I thought that having enough money meant you could buy whatever you needed and wanted badly enough, and the idea of "useless money" hadn't yet occurred to me. I knew that I had talent, and maybe genius, and had the discipline and energy enough to develop it. So, if I got rich I didn't figure that it would ruin me *as long as I held tight to writing* as my center—my vocation, you might say. Because, it is lack of something you have to do by your nature, as much as anything else, that guts you if you have too much money. And it isn't just, too much money, I suppose. It's more like, no external reason to exert yourself. You've got a nation full of people who retired too early because they didn't have jobs that meant anything to them, or because they thought that money without work was a good thing in itself. Well, it's better than no work and no money, that's for sure, but it isn't enough.

Anyway, it isn't that the safari got me used to living among the rich, or living like the rich. And it isn't anything like my feeling like a poor relation to Uncle Gus. I like him and he liked me (while I was still married to his niece, anyway). There wasn't any flavor of dependency in the relationship.

You will remember, we started this by asking what effect the pressure of my reputation had on me and has on me. And we haven't even begun to talk about that, but all this preamble is necessary. If you can understand one example, it will give you the model you need to understand things more in general. And if you can understand somebody who is famous, it helps because there are so many data points out there, as you'd say. And it helps that it's somebody at my level of fame and not Abraham Lincoln's, for example, because the level of stuff projected onto him would be overwhelming. And, it helps that I left my life in writing for you to latch onto and work your way toward me.

In other words, it was a set-up. I say it with a smile, but I knew it. I had the sense of you, or something, or someone, choosing me. There was no obvious reason why I should start buying and reading everything you'd written and then start communicating with you.

You were willing to do the work, I was willing, Carl and others were willing—do you think it could all come together by accident?

I don't believe in accidents.

Well, that may be carrying things too far, but mostly it's a matter of definition. There are plans, and then there are all those free wills in action, and then what you draw is what you get.

Yes. The guys—the other guys?—always say, "we're always on Plan B."

The thing to remember is that this isn't just about *me* and not just about *you* and not even just about the process. It's about everybody who ever reads this, early or late. We aren't going to the trouble of having these conversations just because there's nothing to read over here, and nothing on the radio.

I figured that much. Shall we go on?

All right, let's try to finish this one topic. And you might ask yourself, what is important about whether Hemingway's life went off in the wrong direction? Why should you care what happened so long ago?

Well, the impression I had was that it concerned the interaction between this side and your side.

You could look at it more like this: Your lives are not divorced from this side. Not now, not ever. That may be easy enough for you to accept, but the converse is equally true: When you get onto this side, you are still not divorced from the other side, which at that point is the physical.

It's a dicho, one of your reversible statements.

It isn't even that. Wherever you are, you are intimately connected to the other side. Always were, always are, always will be, like it or not, believe it or not. Suppose you don't believe in the air, since you can't see it or taste it or feel it. Doesn't matter, you're still living in it and can't help living in it, because there isn't any other place to live. It's the same here. We talk about the physical and nonphysical as though they were separate, but that's just the effect of language. The two sides are like two sides of a coin. Can you have a coin with only one side?

≈ 36 ≈

The Image Machine

Sunday, May 30, 2010

[I started re-reading Reynolds' fourth volume, *The Thirties*, and it is interesting how much clearer it is and how my viewpoint seems to have changed, so that I am easily seeing a difference between fact and attribution, between description and attribution of motive, or judgment of state of mind.]

Where we wound up yesterday, Papa, was more or less centered on one of Bob Friedman's questions he suggested I ask you: Why is this dialogue important to you, and to me? Okay, your move.

Again I return to the question of how people's expectations and reactions to somebody or somebody's reputation affects a person. As I know *my* life, that's what I can talk about.

Carl's point is that people began projecting their own internal makeup onto an image of me that they created as they read my books and read about me—supposedly true things about me and my life—in the lying press. The more they projected stuff onto me, the more that image gained power, and the more it gained power, the more the press and everybody seized on it to make money by blowing the balloon bigger, and so on. It wasn't a limited process—it was the Hollywood image machine, relentlessly and ruthlessly turned on to me for their own economic benefit (I became "news") because the demand was there and could be fed and increased.

You'll notice, this didn't have anything to do with the content of my novels, or of the two nonfiction experiments that really deserved serious attention if I do say so, *Green Hills* and *Death*. What happened is that anything in those books—or any books, or short stories—or anything in my life, that fit into the emerging myth, that fed it, got magnified and got attention paid to it, and got twisted if need be to fit better. Anything that didn't fit got ignored, and anything that cut against it was apt to be attacked and derided as phony or affected or dishonest.

Now, I am going to say this all a second time, to try to avoid misunderstanding, because not everybody who comes to this is going to come to it with sympathy and knowledge of the facts and understanding of my life from the inside. And a fast reading can lead people to the wrong idea. The Hemingway Myth was created because something in people responded to something in me and my life and my values that they sensed. In your way of seeing the world, you'd say something like "their threads vibrated to my threads," though that isn't right, really. Just like John F. Kennedy, I radiated something that excited and energized people, and regardless of what they *thought* it was, they were responding to a perception of wholeness, that lent us an air of glamour.

I am *not* saying I was glamorous. I *am* saying, people saw me through a glamorous haze, because of what they had within them that responded to it. And plenty of people *didn't* respond that way; my image didn't match that something within them. (And of course, close up anybody becomes less image and more real individual, which is why people are so often disappointed when they meet their heroes in real life. It isn't necessarily that the person is a fraud, or even that the image is wrong, but it's because no human matches any god, and those are the energies we're talking about here—the magical, beyond-human energies that borrow individuals and attach to them.)

Once that glamour process began, and at first it was easily confused with merely becoming famous for what I'd written, it began to become profitable to people to feed it and feed off of it. At first it was mild and even benign, like a paragraph about "lunch with a visiting author" in a newspaper or magazine, or a profile piece in connection with the book. But it grew, and it grew, and *it had nothing to do with my work*. And this means that it had nothing to do with *me*. It was grinding for its own purposes, some conscious (cashing in on the publicity that might attend my name, say), and some, an increasing amount, not. In other words, after a while, no matter how consciously the press was using me—not to mention Hollywood!—they were also being used in turn by forces that had their own agenda.

I'm not talking about conspiracies, by the way, or anyway not the kind of conspiracy people invent where conscious people plot behind the scenes to direct every little thing. If it's any kind of conspiracy, it is a conspiracy of *forces*, not of people. The psychic energies that latched onto my name and a mostly-imagined image were not being directed by anybody in the body. They were more like shock waves, or electrical waves, or, I don't know, I'm out of my depth here. Maybe try Carl.

Dr. Jung?

[CGJ] The understanding is correct, if the conceptualization is not quite.

First off, you must understand that I came to understand more than I felt comfortable expressing, during my lifetime. We have discussed this before. I had to preserve a certain respectability in my time, or lose the ability to serve as a bridge for the time coming. Besides that consideration, which was not inconsiderable, there was another of equal weight— although I might feel that I had begun to understand, I could not yet formulate my understanding to my satisfaction. Anyone who thinks and observes is likely to die with unfinished mental business!

Here is the way I have come to see the process Ernest describes.

Begin with the fact that all minds are part of one greater all-encompassing mind. That mind in effect is divided into specialties. *In effect, remember*. So, a part for planets, say, and within each planet a part for geology and a part for what we call living matter and within that a part for animals (animals as opposed to vegetables and minerals, you understand, staying with conventional systems of taxonomy), and within animals is a section of that mind for mankind, and within that, races, etc. down to individual families and at last you, the individual.

This is the reality that I described from the other end, beginning at the individual level, moving to the community of beings at ever-higher levels and remaining entirely silent about portions of the mind beyond humanity-as-a-whole. Even at that my scheme was described as mystical. Now realize before we go any farther that this way of categorizing the one mind is only one convenient way of looking at it. There are others. Life is never so simple as our categorizations. How could it be? To use the analogy you like, it would be the goldfish creating the fishbowl. Nonetheless, we can profitably continue with the analogy. The mind is the nonphysical aspect of being, the underlying pattern upon which the physical is constructed. *Everything physical is invisibly connected* to everything else physical, because everything physical is out of the one creating mind. This is not theology, nor philosophy, but fact.

From this fact you can see that it must follow that people are moved by invisible strings. They are not puppets, and their free will is not illusion—but their freedom exists only as one among many. No one lives on a desert island. Every individual's life has its yearnings, which stem from some incompleteness pulling toward wholeness. What that yearning is depends on what the person has to begin with, but of course no one is whole or can be whole and still remain human. *The closer one approaches to wholeness, the greater the attractiveness*, because the larger the range of people that are pulled into that field.

For instance—returning to Hemingway as example—

Intellectuals saw him as the thinker who could act, and live with gusto.

Sportsmen saw him as the fisherman or hunter who wrote books and enjoyed a wide success.

You see? The list could easily be expanded, but to do so would itself become so interesting as to blur the point. Those who can identify with something in a famous man or woman can thus in a vicarious way identify not merely with his or her fame or achievement or success, but with his or her *wholeness*, or approach to wholeness rather. And the more well rounded the person—the more intellectually and emotionally whole—the more handles for people to grasp.

Let me illustrate that for clarity. If someone becomes famous for a very narrowly defined achievement or quality, only a few will identify with him, or her, and so the level of fame will have nothing to do with the glamorizing process. After [Jonas] Salk invented the polio vaccine he was famous. Everybody knew his name and had an idea of what he had done. Did you see any Salk Myth arise? Monet became enormously successful in his lifetime, his paintings worth a fortune. There are many Monet admirers: Is there a Monet Myth? C.S. Forester's Hornblower novels made him into a worldwide name, as did for a time so many authors' works. Where are their myths? It is not achievement that creates glamour.

Nor is attractiveness as a personality enough. Has anyone mentioned Richard Halliburton to you lately? Is there an active Halliburton myth? It faded, as his reputation faded, because there was not ultimately enough satisfying content to sustain those who would grasp it. Swimming the Hellespont appeals to escapism, yes, and it has a splendid boyish enthusiasm that people may find refreshing—but then what follows? Halliburton couldn't find it and neither could those who for a while were enthralled by his reflected glamour. And his books didn't have Byron's genius, so dying mysteriously and young wasn't enough to perpetuate the myth. He faded into the Western sunset, appropriately. And the very fact that few of your readers will have heard of him makes the point. There is a difference between notoriety and fame, and between fame and glamour, and between glamour and a human life.

≈37≈

Paranoia

Monday, May 31, 2010

In the middle of the night, I realized that we should talk, Papa, about temper and paranoia and what people call mental illness. I felt a real reluctance to bring up the subject, and yet a real urge—possibly not coming from me so much as from you—to do so. From whatever source, then, let's discuss it, if you are willing.

Oh, I'm willing enough. But explaining it isn't going to be so easy, and we're going to need Carl and we're going to need the tools you got from what you call the guys upstairs—in other words, concepts you have been given without knowing just who provided them.

You're talking about screens and filters and movies and all that. Well, sure, let's see what we can do. Dr. Jung, you are in agreement, I take it.

[CGJ] As you already realize, this is an attempt on all our parts to bring forth a set of concepts, a way of understanding the world, by means of cooperation between those out of, and [those] still within, a body. So, your part is more than the willingness to do the work of receiving and rebroadcasting the information: It involves the absorption, over decades, of massive amounts of history so that you would be ready. "Massive amounts" means, not that you have read enormously widely or deeply— you have not, as you know—but that an enormous percentage of your psychic energy have been channeled into that reading, and the associated construction of a mental picture of the times. This began when you were ten years old, and it has not yet reached its culmination, but you are now in the full flow of internal events.

All right. Papa, it pains me on your behalf to read of the explosions of temper, the needless suspicion, the damaging things said or done, the inability to apologize or make amends, the progressive alienation from those to whom you had been so close. I recognize all these things from my own life, of course, and I wonder if it has not been for you as it has been for me—an assumption of an inability to ever get your point of view, or your motivations, understood, as one strand of it.

[EH] Yes, but that isn't what we are after here. You know what it is to be at the mercy of reactions beyond your control, doing things and saying things that you get blamed for—because they were done with your body, after all—but that you feel like *you* didn't have much to do with it all.

Yes, I have read of multiple personalities in which one will get into trouble and leave another to deal with the consequences, and I have thought, that's more or less what I have experienced sometimes.

And there's no way back.

No, no way back, because we are supposed to take responsibility for our actions, including our words.

Even if *we* aren't especially the ones who did or said it! That's part of the problem. Also, it makes us unpredictable to others, and puts them always on edge, and we don't feel like that's fair—and it *wouldn't* be, if they were always dealing with us and not this other personality that pops in unpredictably. But it isn't as simple as multiple-personality disorder, either. That's a label they are using but it's misleading because they have the wrong model for what people are, as you know. They're treating something that *is* multiple as though it were individual.

Well—Dr. Jung? You can phrase it better.

[CGJ] I have the background to understand it better, now that I am safely outside of a body! But my present understanding will not fit entirely comfortably within what I wrote or understood prior to 1961, of course. I would be very disappointed if it did!

The subject is the influence on the conscious functioning mind that may result in paranoia or suspicion or ungovernable temper or selective amnesia. All of these may stem from an individual's finding himself in the position of having to rely entirely upon his own judgment, in situations in which that judgment is clearly inadequate as a reliable guide. One floundering in quicksand quickly loses perspective, and may become dangerous to himself and others *because* of that floundering, which of course stems from the quicksand—so that it becomes a self-reinforcing process. Rather than describe examples of people being caught in the quicksand, and rather than passing strictures on their behavior while enmeshed, it may be more profitable to describe the warning signs, and send out precautions to take, to avoid setting foot into similar quagmires oneself.

Regardless of the model we use for consciousness, we may say this: Humans in society function most frictionlessly when they share common understandings of the nature of the world. Thus, the simpler the society, the more harmonious, because there are fewer causes for discordant perceptions. And—regardless of how simple or complex the society—each society evolves rules for perception and therefore rules for permissible and impermissible actions. If the pig is taboo, you don't barbecue it with vinegar sauce! And therefore, the closer an individual is to the common understanding (which has nothing to do with an intellectual exercise, but has to do with the assumptions he shares with his fellow society-members) the smoother and more harmonious his path in life.

But what is an artist? [Or a] scholar? What is anyone who delves deeply into specific or general matters normally left at the edge of consciousness? He is someone who is attenuating his ties to the mass of his fellow men (or women, of course, but I find these circumlocutions cumbersome and unnecessary, so will continue to omit them).

Now, if someone is stepping away from the common understanding or if his life *leads him away*, whether or not he intends to go or even consents to go, he to some degree loses a part of the certainty that accompanies the man surrounded by his flock, and he by being forced to rely more upon what seem like his internal resources develops a new, less stable, source of guidance. One might rephrase this to say: Inner direction both precedes and follows separation from society's more or less invisible guidance by commonly shared perception.

I realize that this isn't the way it is commonly looked at, but it will repay thought. If you prefer or are forced to think for yourself, to become your own judge, you cannot without doing violence to your own nature retrace your steps and rejoin the herd. In a sense, *this* is individuation. But what [is it that] is being made into an individual? The original mixture of elements that were *not* individual, surely. Do you see how the wrong model of the human consciousness distorts the reality? And that wrong model stems from a wrong model of the human position in the physical and nonphysical worlds. So, although it may seem that we strayed from the theme of Ernest's mental problems, in fact we are not yet even to where we can profitably use them as examples, which is our intent. If you have not quite seen it yet, this process intends using one life to illustrate certain aspects of everybody's life, and this for a reason.

All right. It has been just an hour; I can go on a little, if we're not at a natural place to pause.

Perhaps you might sketch briefly the influences on human consciousness you were given over many sessions by unnamed friends.

Of whom, I begin to suspect, you were one! All right. [Although I am the source of what follows, I take it out of italics to make it easier to read.]

Between the real world as it exists and our perception of it, we have *screens* through which we watch the show, and *filters* that prevent us from seeing certain things, and *scripts* that kick in automatically when triggered, and *robots* that deliver pre-programmed responses to certain stimuli or in certain situations. Seems like there are more, but this is what comes to mind at the moment.

Screens and *filters* are, some of them, cultural, some connected with a particular group belief, some individual. What they have in common is that they are between us and what really *is*. They color our ideas of reality, more or less invisibly to us. Racism may be an example of a screen that interprets the world, and a filter that rejects contradictory information.

Scripts kick in when triggered. They are totally automatic in nature, and while they are being played back—either aloud or within us—we are really not very conscious. They are like commercials interrupting the program, and, like commercials, they are rarely noticed consciously and so are highly effective because unjudged.

Robots are whatever they are—I haven't been given that information, and don't really have a guess beyond that they are an integral part of us. They control more of our lives than we usually realize, for better or worse. At first I thought of them as always dysfunctional, if not malign, but I have come to realize that they are functioning exactly as designed. In one way or another they acquire their programming and they continue to do what they were programmed to do, until we consciously contact them, update their files, and either bring them off-line, or reprogram them to meet the same situations with a more constructive response—according to our needs and understanding as of when we reprogram. One nice thing is that they may be reprogrammed as many times as we desire (as far as I know).

I know that there are more things that have been identified, but this is what comes to mind at this moment.

[CGJ] And thus we have prepared the ground for the next discussion.

Later today, maybe. I am curious to see where this is going. It certainly didn't go where I thought it would when I had the thought of Papa Hemingway's increasing mental problems, a few hours ago.

≈38≈

Spiritual Causes of Mental Disorder

(7:30 p.m.) It's good to read your biography, Papa, to reinstate some distance between the portrait we are painting and anything seen from outside. The biography of your final sixteen years paints you all too often in an unflattering light, particularly in relation to your women. It certainly looks like you had serious issues that you never did resolve. I don't mean that as criticism, but as observation. We all have issues.

It is to talk about issues and how they skew our lives (or how they define our lives, if you prefer to look at it that way) that we are engaged in this work. Let's talk about my robots, and screens, and filters, and scripts.

All right. How?

We'll ask Carl to do it.

[CGJ] Ernest could be analyzed according to conventional schemes—and he has been, although of course not by a qualified professional dealing with him in person—

Not even at the Mayo Clinic?

He was examined and treated, but I would hardly say analyzed, and certainly not assisted! Working from too mechanical a model, they attempted to shock him into better health, as though he were a computer needing to be rebooted. They did not get to the causes of the symptoms they could so easily see. Instead, they thought to provide an amelioration by changing the symptoms. Of course they might not agree with this statement.

No, Ernest was never analyzed by competent professionals seeking the spiritual causes of his disorder; instead, he was chastised in the press and often enough in person by various people with various axes to grind. The result was always the same: admonitions to shape up. But they could not tell him *how* to shape up, because although they could see the symptoms, they totally misjudged the causes, or if they could see the cause, had no idea how to overcome its effects.

Thus, anyone who knew him knew that he talked of how he hated and despised his mother, and how he blamed her in immoderate amount for various misfortunes to himself, to his father, and to others. Yet the more perceptive of them must have observed that at the same time he longed for the express approval of this despised woman—and was not capable of receiving it even if she had been capable of offering it.

This was his pattern. It continued all his life from the summer he was denied the use of the cabin in the woods country until his last days. But *why*? And *how*? And what could he have done to escape the pattern, if he had known how? And what good *and bad* effects might have followed if he had done so? Psychology is not an experimental science, so no one can know the results of actions not taken. However, given that alternative lives are easily read from this side, you might say that here psychology can be an exact, not merely experimental, science. Of course it helps that we can see inside the head we are shrinking, and can see the view from inside the head looking outward. So, we take up the question of Ernest's relation to his mother, and we attempt your technique for the purpose of exhibition.

What was the *screen* through which he always saw her? This is a complicated mixture: We are dealing with reality, not sanitary examples.

- *respectability (she an example)*
- *dominance over father*
- *condemnation of Ernest's character*
- *inability to appreciate his genius or achievement*
- *self-centeredness—her art over the needs of her family*
- *she fit in with the "respectable" but Philistine element that his books exposed and condemned and sold to.*

And the filters that assured that he could not receive certain data?

- *any attempts at reconciliation*
- *the father's part in the marriage*
- *Ernest's own contribution to strife*
- *the artistic temperament and talent that was part of his inheritance from her*

The scripts that ran when she came up for discussion—

- she had taken his money that should have gone for education
- she killed her husband
- she tried to dominate Ernest
- he would support her financially but he would control the money
- she took every opportunity to denigrate his subject matter, and never appreciated his work

And the *robot* associated with the relationship assured that any inter-action would be monitored to detect and prevent any attempts on his independence. At the same time, it would assure that he *was a different person* in her presence than away from it, for her immediate presence somewhat overshadowed the constructed image. You might say that, in person, she interfered with screen and filter; although she did not in per-son disable or sidetrack the robot, her presence did derail the scripts and often leave the robot inactivated.

Now please understand, this is vastly oversimplified; still, it is some-times necessary to over-simplify in order to say anything meaningful. And, of course it is understood that if Ernest and I were still in the body, none of this could be said to a third party—not that I would have been given the opportunity to examine him in any case.

[EH] Well, if I'd had any idea who you are and how you are, I have been happy to put myself in your care.

[CGJ] Yes—if you [had been] someone entirely different! As you were, you could not even admit to yourself that you needed help.

So. This is how we might have used your "robot psychology" to get at the root of things. Of course (I keep repeating "of course" but I must say many things that I think must be obvious, because they may *not* be obvious) *telling* someone does nothing. They must be assisted to find it for themselves, or it is not only no assistance but is potentially harmful. So if we had been proceeding according to your scheme we would have been getting Ernest into the feelings that arose, and guiding him to learn when those feelings first got associated with that issue, and how those feelings came to be translated into a typical behavior.

Can a biographer do any of this? Can the literary critic who is attempting to pin down the specific meaning of a symbol, as though it were an advertising sign? You have been told many times, do not judge others, because you never have the data. You never *can* have the data. Yes, discern as best you can, but do not condemn. Nothing productive has ever come or ever could come by means of condemnation. Avoid judgment, and try to understand.

Well, this has been interesting, and it came fluently enough, but I'm not sure where we're going with it. More tomorrow, I hope.

"Righteous persistence brings reward."

Yes, my favorite line from the I Ching, honored more in the breach than in the observance—but not so much this month!

June 2010

Units and Rage

Tuesday, June 1, 2010

Well, that was quite a May, wasn't it?

Yesterday's entries involved just a sketch of just one issue in my life. You can imagine how many such issues arise in anybody's life, and they're all active, they all cause trouble or anyway they all *color* a life; they create complications, and that is what life is, complications.

That's very clear, but I don't see where we're going with it.

The hard thing for you would be to see it plain ahead of time; that would make the spelling-out of it nothing but drudgery. And besides, you'd miss the chance to record your reactions, because the odds are you'd never bother to go back and record even what you remember. Easier to do it as we go along.

All right.

So take my temper. You can relate.

Can I not!

You can see how it looks from the outside, and you've heard the suspicions that sometimes having a bad temper is a strategy. But anybody using it as a strategy is just pretending. We are talking here of sitting on a volcano. You don't know what you're going to do ahead of time—I mean, it isn't like you're *planning* to lose your temper. You know how sometimes after a particularly violent attack you feel *sick*?

Oh yes. Drained, shaking, and a sensation I've never thought to try to describe, but I'll bet you can.

It's almost like nausea, almost like a headache. You spent in a few minutes the energy you might normally have used for a week. It flowed through you so hot and so fast that sometimes it really did need physical release or it felt like your body would explode. That's when the physical danger would arise. You could kill somebody, easily, if the fit was still on you and a weapon was at hand. A chair, your fists, a gun, anything.

Well, who ever *wanted to* make himself sick, and maybe do damage he'd feel guilty about, and maybe kill somebody? Sure, plenty of times people are mad enough that they would want to hurt people, and sometimes they try, but I'm talking here about so fighting mad that you lose sight of limits, or if you keep yourself within limits, it's sometimes just barely. And the limits *you* keep yourself in, others say you already went way too far.

Oh yes, and they're criticizing you for not having enough self-control.

Yep. They're controlling a ten horsepower engine and you're control-ling a ten-horse team, and they figure if they can do it, you can do it.

But of course, we need self-control, and those around us do, and society in general does.

Sure, but what I am talking about is how much there is to be con-trolled sometimes for some people, and how it isn't as easy as it may look. And here is where we tie it to your robots and screens and all. It isn't like normal; everyday you are in charge of the rage-machine. And it isn't like you can do more than try to keep it from kicking in and try to pick up the pieces if it does kick in, and sometimes, if you're hanging onto con-trol, stop it from going hog-wild. But *you* and *it* aren't the same thing at all. And it's worth getting this clear, because the easy thing is for people to say, "you're just trying to evade responsibility for your own lack of self-control, and you're refusing to grow up," or something. That's great condemnation but as Carl says, it doesn't *help* anything. It doesn't under-stand, and that means all it's doing is putting distance between itself and behavior it disapproves of.

Hell, who *doesn't* disapprove of behavior like that? Who *isn't* ashamed of it? But—what about the fact that it wasn't us? What about the fact that we, who wouldn't ever do something like that, are being held responsible because it was done with our body? And what about the fact that when we come back—when we muscle ourselves back into control or, more likely, when the rage-machine lets us back in because it's done for the moment—then we have to live with the consequences and *don't even know what happened.* If you're treating people as if they were a unit, you say, "you have to take responsibility for your own actions." But this amounts to saying, "you're the commander of this outfit and you're responsible for anything it does, whether you yourself do it or not." And that isn't wrong; how else could society function? But *see* it that way, *say* it that way. It will clarify things.

If you were an officer commanding a company of men, and one of the men fucked up, it would be your responsibility, but nobody in his right mind would treat you as though you had done it personally. You have the responsibility to prevent it, or, if it happened, to clean up after it, but *you yourself didn't do it*, and if anybody treated you as if you did, all they'd do is muddy the waters. You'll wind up defending yourself for the wrong thing—not for failing to prevent something, but for *doing* the some-thing. And it won't do one thing to prevent the something from happen-ing again. It won't help you keep the rage-machine under control. In fact, it will identify you and it in your own mind, which will make it harder for you to keep control or to get control, because it's like thoughts—if we think they're "our" thoughts, we don't examine them the same way we'd examine them if we thought of them as coming from someplace else.

And of course in my day (but not much less in your day), people think you're *one* thing. They think each person is a unit, and they think so even though their own personal experience should tell them otherwise every day of their lives. But this is one of those screens you talk about: Society says we're each a unit, so that's how people see it until something goes around the screen and they see things differently.

I don't have it in mind to reinterpret my life this way, exactly. Anything I'd say would be seen as self-serving. But we can use it as an example. You see, it is important that people see the effects of that social screen that makes us inclined to see ourselves and each other as units. It's accurate enough that it will serve, but it's inaccurate enough that it is distorting our view, and as the times change, it is more dangerous all the time to confuse what we see through that screen with what really is. That's our theme here, remember: getting a better look at what really *is*.

≈2≈

Psychological Models

Shall we continue?

[The following felt like Hemingway and TGU blended, or alternat-ing.] Using temper as an example is convenient for several reasons. For one, anyone who knows The Hemingway Myth knows about explosions of temper. For another, it's something most people can imagine. Anybody who has ever gotten mad—and "mad" in the English way of using the word means "insane," remember—anybody with that experience knows what it feels like to be at least a little out of control. By sinking into that remembered feeling, they can get the sense of being more than one per-son, either one of which drives at any given moment.

If you can get a sense of it from *any* emotion or state of being, then you can generalize, for unless getting mad is different from every other mental and emotional state, once you've realized that there is a separate part of you living under the same roof, then you can't go on pretending or assuming that you are all of a piece.

Obviously I realize that people have experienced what they call moods and realize that they aren't the same when they're in one of their moods— but that doesn't mean that they realize what's going on. If the model is "we are all units," then any fluctuation of mood or habitual perception (the way you change as a commuter, for instance, as opposed to how you are either at home or at work) is shrugged off as a passing thing of no importance. There is no fact that can't be seen through the commonly accepted screening, or it wouldn't be so commonly accepted! But there are lots of things that would upset that model if thought of, so robots of one kind or another are set into motion to discourage you from thinking of one thing in association with another thing. The robots protect the model by preventing or at least discouraging re-examination in light of mutually contradictory evidence. Filters do the same thing, and may be indistinguishable from robots. Contradictory evidence may be suppressed or not, but even if not suppressed, any mental effort to realize the implications of that evidence will be blocked as much as possible. It isn't always possible, because there are always crosscurrents, but generally it is.

This is why sometimes a new idea may have a revolutionary effect, and also why they don't come along every day. If a new way of seeing things somehow gets by the filters and robots, there may be a host of previous perceptions that [had been] walled off from each other or ignored entirely, and suddenly there is an earthquake, because suddenly things make sense in a way they didn't before that one critical fact or idea or suggestion or association of ideas slipped in.

So if we can get the new model out into the world, some people are going to have their inner worlds lighted up like firecrackers. Get enough people like that and it doesn't much matter what happens in the world externally, there's going to be a change. But there's not much good setting out abstract ideas if you don't ground them in specific examples, and unless the examples are from life, they're going to be theoretical, abstract, lifeless. They won't convince in the way examples convince. What has more impact on people, a history of the Spanish Civil War that sets it all out, however accurately and sympathetically and justly, or *For Whom the Bell Tolls*? That isn't bragging, it's illustrating a point: Specific, emotionally linked examples make an impact. In your terms, they connect mental and emotional bodies.

[CG Jung] Psychiatry has identified, or rather we might say has defined, several specific variants of mental illness, all of which depend upon the model of the individual psyche being unitary except in pathological cases of dissociation. And here we may see what could be termed professional screens and filters reinforcing (conforming to) society's screens and filters, for if it were not for these screens, professionals could not possibly ignore the implications of what they observe every day in their practice. But instead they are like medieval astronomers, carefully and exactly measuring their epicycles, and confusing their precision in measurement with accuracy of concept. Epicycles did very well preserve the appearances; they "saved the data." They provided a theoretical underpinning for accurate prediction. Nonetheless, to paraphrase Galileo, the sun was the relative center of the solar system, not the earth.

So with psychiatry and psychology in my day and still in yours. The individual as unit saves the data, but the concept relies upon its own epicycles nonetheless. The individual functions as a unit *in certain ways*, and seen in a certain light, but hardly absolutely. It would be less inaccurate to say that what you call an individual is a temporarily cohering subset of some aspects of other subsets of the great mind that is all things. You can imagine how popular a definition this would be, or, at first blush, how useful. Yet it is the germ from which many useful things may emerge. Thus, the use of aspects of Ernest's life as specific examples from which may be understood greater principles of which they may serve as illustration.

Again, time for you to do other things for a while, and if we do not see you in this way until Thursday, all will be well.

As always, I thank you both for this. It feels like we are on an extremely interesting journey, and I don't even know where we're going or when I signed on. Rather like life itself, come to think of it.

Yes. Enjoy your voyages. This is said to you, and to all.

≈ 3 ≈

The Individual as a Society

Finished Reynolds' fifth volume, The Final Years. Reading of that long last act, Papa, the drinking, the drug cocktails they put you on, the accumulating injuries, most notably those received in Africa—

Looking at all that increasingly manic, increasingly depressive behavior—

Looking at self-pitying, and lashing out, and amazingly unconscious behavior (as with Adriana, for instance)—

It can't have been fun to be around you, and can't have been fun being you.

Does my suicide still seem like such a tragedy, such a dead end? The family exit was messy—it was designed to be, of course—but it *did* get me out of that situation.

But how did you (why did you) get into that situation in the first place?

If you will look at my life not as the life of one individual, acting in a unified manner according to thought-out plans for carefully considered objectives, but instead as a society of individuals—

Well, let's take your wagon train analogy. You've used it to describe short journeys where a group of people come together, they do the same thing at the same time, and they go their separate ways at the end. Let's apply it to a lifetime. When you look at your life as a group journey, a lot of things make more sense than they do if you think of it as one person being born, growing up, flourishing, getting old maybe, and dying. So many things look different.

Take inconsistencies, for instance. Well, you wouldn't expect a whole group of people to be consistent, would you? Take force of will or lack of it. It just makes sense that some wagon trains have strong leaders and are very disciplined, and others have weaker ones, or less demanding ones, and the train is less disciplined. Take range. Some wagon trains are going to be made up of mostly the same kind of people, maybe all from the same village, all from the same stock, maybe lots of them kin, and the range of difference among them isn't going to be very large. They'll have individual differences, but generally they'll see things the same way.

Others will have been slapped together in haste, maybe, or for whatever reason will contain people of all kinds, many of them not seeing eye to eye, maybe many of them even hating each other.

All this isn't just a flight of fancy. It's a metaphor for what life in a body really is, and not a bad one. Start seeing yourself as a society instead of a unit and some things will come clear. You are a society of people inherited from your parents and all their predecessors. And you are a society of all you've ever been in your history through the non-physical, too. You think of this as meaning "past lives" but that isn't exactly it, and we're not going to pursue it, because it doesn't lead us anywhere we want to go.

All of this is abstract. Pin it against my very public life—and the private aspects of it, too—and we'll flesh it out. You've already seen how the example of explosive temper illustrates that we are different people at different times. It's more accurate to say we *are* different people, or *express* different people, than to say we act *as if we were* different people. There isn't any "as if" about it, except, all those different people are traveling together (pulling and hauling against the harness often enough) so we are *one* person consisting of *many* people. It depends on how you look at it.

Suppose you get drunk. They say "in wine, there is truth," meaning that you say things you might not say otherwise, because alcohol reduces the inhibitions against saying it. But that isn't all it does! And here is a clue to your question about why I drank so much.

Go ahead. I'm very interested in that question.

Stick with the society idea. If you have a society of people, and only one or only a few get to run things, and the vast majority don't get much of a say—especially if you can imagine it that the few get to breathe fresh air and the many are crammed down in steerage, breathing and re-breathing stale, foul air all the time—you can see that anything that unbuttoned the hatchways and let the steerage passengers out would be risking a huge explosion, or call it a temporary revolution. And the people that came running up the ladders into the daylight are not likely to have had their manners improved by their confinement below.

Now, change metaphors. Go back to your wagon train. Maybe your wagon master goes off somewhere and people take turns being temporary wagon master. Some may be poets, tyrants, losers, can-do movers-and-shakers; could be anything. They are all part of the one wagon train, but they're all different individuals with their own histories and objectives and points of view. Now, who can predict what they'll do, or how they'll see things, while the wagon master is gone?

And—to carry that analogy one last step—during the process of drinking, the wagon master gradually loosens up; he feels himself going off duty; he's willing to share the reins with others when normally he wouldn't. *His* world expands; he feels freer and less burdened. While he's sharing the reins with others he may feel a part of something much bigger than himself, something more attractive, more important, the way Joseph Smallwood felt as part of the army at Gettysburg. But—then the wagon master gives over, and goes away, or goes to sleep, or whatever, and when he's back in charge maybe he remembers that sense of being bigger than his usual self, but maybe he doesn't remember *why* he felt that way, or maybe he thinks it was only a side effect of the drinking, not a real situation.

Now, as wagon master, you are responsible for the behavior of the people that make up the train. You have to be. If it weren't you, who could it be? But the thing I am trying to emphasize here is that you may be responsible for them all, but you aren't *the same* as them. Just like any officer of any unit, you're going to have to answer for things you yourself think are stupid or irresponsible or even reprehensible—but they are *your* responsibility. You can't escape the responsibility and there isn't any reason you should try to—but just remember that you don't have to identify with every member of your society just because you are going to be identified with him by others.

Let's continue this analogy. Suppose your wagon master gets killed, or gets lost, or loses his ability to be wagon master and nobody else steps up to be wagon master. Then you have a candidate for the lunatic asylum, because there's no stability, neither of purpose nor of point of view. Then you don't have a unit—a wagon train—except in so far as they share a body. In other respects they're just a bunch of wagons that happen to be in the same place or in close proximity. And maybe you call them a *disassociated* individual. Isn't that a telling phrase? An "individual" that is no longer a coherent society, a society that no longer functions as if it were an individual.

Now, you're thinking I'm poaching on Carl's territory, but doesn't all this have clear application to my life as illustration? And if I handed you off to Carl, even if he were talking about my life, wouldn't it create a separation in your mind? These things are *real*, and they are important, or you can't see things straight.

≈4≈

Disturbing Evidence

Good morning, Papa.

You have been reading my biography as reconstructed by Reynolds, who did a careful thorough job and paid perhaps a little more attention to me as a person than to me as an author, as opposed to Baker, for instance. Reynolds is showing you what I looked like, acted like, how I looked and acted to others, on the evidence. And you in your reading are finding it disturbing because you are wanting me to be better than the evidence shows. You can see that I always talked about despising phonies—and yet I did so much pretending. Sneered at imitators and thieves, and did both. Had rigid standards, and lived a life that often didn't have anything to do with them.

And the cruelty, Papa! The viciousness, the backbiting, the out-of-control crudity and grossness, the sexual innuendo and bragging that sounds to me like people with sexual problems who can't keep their minds or tongues off the subject. It makes me cringe to read of it all, not least because Reynolds like the other biographers I have read—Baker, Hotchner, Myers, Mary— admires you, likes you, sympathizes with you, but has to tell some ugly truths.

Yes, and it makes you worry because what you're bringing through doesn't match all that—so you wonder if you're creating a portrait that isn't real and doesn't have anything to do with anything. Well, some of the detail or the reconstruction may be skewed a little, the way you might not remember something quite right and even the details you're sure of might not be right. But the picture my biographers paint is accurate enough. It just isn't the underlying story, and now we're close enough to bringing in the connection, you can feel what it is.

Yes, I can see that the discussions of individuals as really communities is intended to tie in with your life—which is so much on the record—by way of mutual illustration.

It isn't as simple, understanding things, as looking at them from the inside view. You've got to have a third view, which is what we're working on now.

I'll show you. Say we were talking about some party where I blow up, or where I do some crude sexual talk that embarrasses everybody. And, as you see, the older I got, the more it happened. What's really happening there? Who's in control? Is it the writer, looking for copy? Hardly. The host, trying to make it a good experience for his guests? Clearly not. The war veteran (for I *was* a veteran even if I was never in the army in any formal way) or the careful craftsman or the loving husband or the thousand other roles I fit into? No, for the moment I was the *borracho*, the drunk. It's worthwhile to treat these different aspects of our lives as if they were different persons, because, basically they *are*. We are more like ringmasters, or teamsters, than anything else. It all makes dull reading, and puts you to sleep, if it's just left as theory. It's only when you put it together with real life that it means something, as opposed to being just an abstract idea. Distrust all abstract ideas until you see them with a human face. Communism looked good until they tried to put it into practice. But then, so did capitalism.

Who was "I"? And if "I" was only one thing, how did "I" show so many sides, and if not, where did "I" go when different sides emerged? More to the point, if I was one "I"—why did "I" do things "I" disapproved of? It's like St. Paul said, I did the things I didn't want to do, and I didn't do the things I wanted to do. You've read all this in Gurdjieff. Now you can make it real to yourself. Our job in the physical is, starting with a group of what you could call smaller "I"s, coordinating them and leading them to act as a team instead of a scrum. The better we do that, the more satisfactory a higher-level "I" we wind up with. You've heard this too: It's why nobody ought to be judging (that is, condemning) anybody. You don't know what they are trying to coordinate, or juggle, or even survive.

So, to look at my life as an example. I had one very clear, very important, very precious strain that was cold, clear, lucent idealism. It ran like a stream from my earliest boyhood, admiring and identifying with the same thing in Teddy Roosevelt. That boyish quality in me didn't disappear—wasn't submerged among other traits—for a very long time, but even when it was out of sight, it didn't cease to exist. If you cease to look at it as a "trait"—whatever that word is supposed to mean in substance rather than in its effect which is clear enough—and look at it as one sub-assembly of me, or as one of the lesser "I"s that I was juggling, or teamstering, you'll begin to see my life a little differently. That "I" didn't cease to exist temporarily when I did something like double-bill for dispatches sent. Neither did it approve. Neither could it stop the clever, worldly-wise, hard-bitten "I" that worked off some resentments by doing it. (Neither could Hadley, for that matter, whose idealism flowed with, reinforced, that particular "I".) So when that particular "I"—the clear idealistic "I"—came back to the surface at some point, it knew that "I" hadn't done that, and if the body (so to speak) had, it could react only with guilt (and confusion) or with denial.

Ever seen those reactions?

Understand, now—*I'm not excusing anything*; I'm not using *explanation* to show that I was right all the time. I'm *illustrating*. There's a difference.

≈5≈

A Model of Interaction

Saturday, June 5, 2010

I am still reading Reynolds, Papa, getting toward the end of The Paris Years, and while he is very good as a recorder of your life, and seems to be appreciative of your work as it changed our literature, I don't get the sense that he knows the kind of thing you've showed me here. The analysis of A Farewell to Arms, for one, though I haven't gone back to reread that session. It does show me the value of this, and the autonomy of the information source (that is, I'm not just making it up)—and shows me I need to index the material. On May 13th, not very long ago, in one short paragraph you summed up what it was about in a way I couldn't have done—and in other paragraphs you reminded me why it was revolutionary. I presume you have a reason for it—

Notice that our habit of cooperation, call it, has grown so dependable that I can haunt you while you're off duty with the idea of something, and you can recognize the difference between such communication and a "stray thought." It's another benefit of continued Intuitive Linked Communication (ILC), for those who wish to practice it.

As you were writing that—that's what it felt like, [even] if it was my hand and arm doing the writing—I suddenly got the sense that you and I connect along your idealistic thread, which is why the "you" I am experiencing is so different from the total you as expressed in your life.

Yes, and that is a first *experience* of something you've had as a *concept* for several years now. There's a difference, experiencing a thing, or hearing a concept, or experiencing the same thing in light of the concept. That's what this process is all about. *Frank* is experiencing this at first hand; anyone reading it, or reading of it via anyone who earlier read of it, may get enough of a sense of concept-as-experienced to serve as a bridge for their own first-hand practice. In other words, one person's experience makes it easier for another to have a similar experience, and perhaps carry it much farther. I'm going to ask Carl [Jung] to draw us a model, I think: This wouldn't be my strong point.

[CGJ] Yes. Consider this model a thought experiment, not dogma or even teaching.

In other words, you are going to present something to help us bridge over to a later concept.

Precisely. Concepts are scaffolding. It is no tragedy, no waste, and certainly no presumption of error, when scaffolding is taken down after the structure has been completed.

Your model of rings and threads has helped sketch the fact that relationships *within* individuals are as important and as meaningful and as full of consequences as relationships *between* individuals. Indeed, our point is that no one is "individual" in the way society assumes, even though the possession of separate bodies leads to the presumption that minds and other forms of energy are equally separate and distinct. Now we extend that concept in practice, at least a bit. Not so much Frank contacted Ernest, but a strand of Frank contacted a strand of Ernest (because the strand was shared, of course).

But see what results. The contact and the resultant interaction has the potential to change both! I don't have a diagram to illustrate the point, but the concept can be made clearer. Frank consists of strands ranging from 1 to 9, let us say. Ernest, let us say, extends from 9 to 18. In their connection, as they communicate beyond a superficial level, it can become as if both of them extended from 1 to 18, or as if either of them shared any one strand or combination of strands. This is important because it shows the bridge between imagination and manifestation. This will require some explanation.

Let us say that in life Ernest extended from 9 to 18. As he was created, he was incapable of extending beyond that range by himself. *But anyone with whom he interacted potentially extended his range.* Or take Frank's two favorite statesmen, John F. Kennedy and Abraham Lincoln. Kennedy radiated wholeness and versatility, Lincoln depth and compassion. In both cases, this showed an initial disposition *heavily modified* by extensive contact with others, absorbed and transformed by their ability to sympathetically comprehend the range of the others. And the example of ILC being practiced here shows another way in which instinctive sympathy may broaden one's range, quite as much as if experienced externally.

Given that such interaction occurs continually at levels far below and above consciousness, as well as a certain amount consciously, does this not somewhat redefine the concept of an individual a bit further? Initially the model was designed to show that you are not as much of a piece as you commonly think. This demonstration of how the model operates is designed to make the model a bit less static. There is nothing static about your life in time. *You* change continually, and those around you change continually, and you change each other, again continually. This is not chaos because each person has a core, and because people are not equally open to change, and because not all parts of a person are equally open to change. Not chaos, but never static.

[EH] And, to make the specific application clear, you might consider that everybody is functioning in a sort of closed-off, divided state. The idea that you're separate individuals leads society to do some insane things whose consequences would be perfectly predictable if the model were understood. Just as there isn't any "away" to throw stuff, there isn't any "individual" to be unaffected by what happens to everybody else. John Donne said it and I quoted it, but people take it only politically. The entry point was your getting a sense that your "feeling" for me didn't match the sense of me you got from reading about me. It progressed to your seeing that you and I connect along specific threads. (You've concentrated on the one thread, but there are more.) Now we've shown that not only do people *experience* each other differently depending on what they share; they change each other depending on what the other has that they find attractive. It is the finding attractive and being able to follow that thread that is the essence of free will, of choice, of life. And it is imagination that offers the key; is the door through which you enter.

Say a little more about that?

Your senses can only report what is there to be reported. Your thoughts can only process what is there to be processed. Those are valuable functions, but they are only half the story, and the mechanical half, at that. Your intuition reports what your senses cannot. Your imagination processes what your intuition reports. These two are valuable functions. Obviously, of most value is senses and intuition both respected and listened to; both thought and imagination used on the combined data returned by senses and intuition. Anything less is crippled. And how do you suppose I functioned as a writer?

Oh, I don't have any doubt about that, Papa! And I see, wholeness, again, is the source of that immense attractiveness that was powerful enough to influence the whole world.

Yes—and it was my disruptive negative traits that made me a lot of trouble, don't forget—and *The Paris Years* should be showing you that they existed in full measure long before fame.

I do see that. And I sense that we're going to discuss their significance some more, yes? But I think I should quit for the moment. As always, thanks to both of you, and to all others who participate.

And our thanks to you and to all who read this and participate.

～6～

Hemingway's Moods

All right. Where do we go specifically this morning?

[EH] We could go many ways, but let's stick with me for the moment. I watched, listened, felt, smelled, tasted everything going on. I read incessantly and I thought about things (although, from here, I must say, I did a hell of a lot more associating of thoughts than I did thinking things through). All of that was to the good. What I couldn't do, though, was put equal attention to my mental and spiritual environment, and this hurt me and those around me. And this is worth considerable exploration, because it isn't a matter of doing an extensive post-mortem on a famous writer, but of using pretty well-known facets of that writer's emotional life to illustrate *your* lives from a new perspective. We talked about screens and filters and scripts and robots. That was to to show the behind-the-scenes mechanisms. Because if you look closely at my life—or at yours—you'll see how so many crosscurrents kept the seas so choppy. Clumsy metaphor, but anyway.

If I could have observed my own inner weather with the skill and attention and detachment and deduction I brought to observing weather at sea, how different my life would have been! Or, another view, if I hadn't lived within a physical manic-depressive cycle, how much less turbulent it would have been. My life would have had problems—what good is a life without problems? It's a filled-in crossword puzzle—but they would have been an entirely different set of problems.

This is difficult to express clearly and twice as difficult to be *heard* clearly. I don't have time enough, you don't have paper enough, to list everything I *don't* mean and don't want to be heard as saying. So—reader—try to read this slowly enough to really hear me. The faster you read, the more you skate across the surface of what you're reading, and the less chance you have to absorb what always must remain between the lines.

As I aged, my mood-swings got more violent. If I was up, if I was down, either way I was in the middle of a mood *taking it as objectively, obviously*, an accurate reflection of the world. This shouldn't be news to anybody. Everybody has moods; everybody remembers the feeling, once out of a remembered mood, that it was really a different person living that mood. Well, using concepts like "moods" disguises and distorts what's really happening. It makes it sound like there's this one person, this unit, who goes into changing sets of feelings, either periodically (mania to depression and back again) or according to circumstance (in reaction to being in love, or because of a car accident, or anxiety over something or other). That's one way to see it, but look at it starting from the assumption that you are a community, and what does it look like?

Suppose we use numbers to describe emotional downs and ups. Let's say a one is when you're too depressed to get out of bed, and a 10 is when you're so revved up that you can't sleep. (There are other ways to cut the pie, but let's start with this one.) If you look at yourself as an individual, you say you *move* from 3 to 6, say. But if you start to see that you are a community, how does it look? You have certain subgroups that add up to three, others that add up to six. It isn't [so much] that you *moved* as that this or that group surfaced. Analogy, but a closer, more useful, analogy. Those subgroups may be ad hoc, a bunch of threads coming together (so to speak) from one specific cause and maybe never coming together in just that way ever again. Or they can be recurrent, even chronic, and this is what plagued me.

If you look at my life story, you will see that certain situations evoked a certain response. You could say—"they brought out his mean streak" or "they brought out his paranoia" and putting it that way gets the job done, in that it's a way of describing behavior and pinning it in a cause-effect matrix. But if you really look at these metaphors—because they *are* metaphors, it's just that common use has made them seem realer than they are—what does it mean to say someone has a *streak* or even a *complex*; what does it mean to say that an event *brings out* a recurrent character trait? We know what is meant, and we even think we know what the specific words mean, but when you really look at it—

If you see yourself as a loose (or tighter, but let's start where most people are, a loose) community, you can see that a perceived threat is likely to bring out the army, just as they would in the larger community that consists of "individuals." You don't speak of your external community responding to a perceived threat by getting into a mood—but you easily could. It shows you that the differences between internal community and external community aren't very large. There is more commonality there then there is difference between a "community" of individuals on the one hand and "individuals" in the body on the other.

Does that need to be made clearer?

Perhaps. As I understand it, you're saying that what we think of as our moods are actually the activation of certain groups within us.

Yes. And if the same groups keep showing up in similar circumstances, they might be called a mood. Now, there's plenty of work to do here, showing how robots and screens and filters affect to that community's perception of its environment, and maybe skew it terribly—but this is enough for a while.

Yes. I always regret when I run out of gas, but it's nearly 8 a.m.. Thanks Papa. More another time.

≈7≈

Hemingway as a Community

Monday, June 7, 2010

Good morning, Papa. And Dr. Jung and any others who are participating. Who's up?

[EH] Let's keep going while we are going well.

Okay with me, to put it mildly.

If you look at my life while considering me as a community of parts, you will read it differently. For one thing, you won't feel compelled to weigh and balance traits and actions and talent and work and insults and all and come to some sort of sum, some judgment of me and my life. Leave that to Anubis: You're not now and never were and never could be up to the task. And in the absence of a need to judge will come the space to experience, to weigh my life in a different manner. You've seen it written, perhaps: "Compassion liberates; condemnation imprisons."

That isn't referring to what[ever] is condemned or seen with compassion, but to the person doing the condemning, or extending the compassion.

The hardest thing to get across is that advising compassion is not asking forgiveness or indulgence or partisanship. It is saying that you cannot understand a thing, no matter what, whether it is an action, a political movement, a new way of painting, a life—anything—without putting yourself sympathetically *inside* of it. Any external view that is not balanced by an internal feel is going to be just that—external; superficial.

The way to know is simple enough. Do you feel self-righteous in thinking about whatever it is that you are considering? Well, if so, then you may as well resign yourself: It's a sign that you have not gotten inside what you are looking at. Yes, yes, a lot of poor jokes there, waiting, but the point remains: To understand everything would be to forgive everything. Or, as your friend pointed out to you years ago—Everybody's doing their best. That, along with All Is Well; All Is Always Well, will take you far.

≈ 8 ≈

Hemingway Writing

[This entry came as a wonderful gift. I was moved to sit down and write in my journal, and as soon as I put pen to paper, this came through spontaneously.]

(12:45 p.m.) Day after day I wrote, and this is how it is. You've experienced something like it. You wake up early in the morning and you get up and you get going. You're sitting there and maybe it's coffee like you use or tea—I liked tea—and it's paper and pencil and a pencil sharpener, and you're living in your mind for all those hours.

It isn't like you don't know you're in a room, writing. It's more like a kid who's sitting in a cardboard box and he knows it's a cardboard box but he also knows it's a boat, or an airplane, or a stagecoach. You're sitting there, writing, or staring at the wall or out the window—and at the same time you're someplace else, living another life, feeling a different season's sun, maybe out in the Gulf fishing with Santiago, or just driving down an old road you loved, or one you'd made up. And you loved that bilocation feeling, without even thinking about it. In fact, if you did think about it, you'd probably think about it wrong, because you'd be wishing you were really there—wherever you were writing about—when what you really wanted was what you had—being here *and* there, living it, writing it.

And then there was a whole different set of exercises, and satisfactions, when you looked at the way you'd described something you remembered, or something you'd made up and experienced in your mind, or something that was remembered and then reworked, or something that started out looking like it was made up but then got hooked into something from the life you'd lived. And you'd look at the words, feeling for the soft spots that had to be taken out, looking for the blank places where the words had gone dead on you, looking for the things that you'd said that were good in themselves but didn't quite belong. And you'd cross out, or you'd move, or you'd reword, and maybe you'd re-read it and it still wouldn't be right and you have to do it again, more probing, more moving around, more listening to the echoes, listening for the dull thud instead of the bell-metal ringing. And all this exercising of skill from another dimension—because it couldn't be done by logic—left you just as cold-gloating satisfied as anything you could do in life.

And you'd come out from there at noon, or whenever your schedule called for, or maybe earlier or later depending on how your work was going, and it was turning the key on that part of your life, and you were free to be with another person, and to enjoy pleasures simple and complicated, expensive and cheap and free, pleasures strenuous or contemplative, athletic or aesthetic or gastronomic or piscatory or *anything*. And underneath all the pleasure—even just reading, if that's what you were doing, even just a mid-day nap, if that's what you wanted—underneath it all was the morning's writing, the long immersion into that active-receptive country that only another artist could experience. And the days went by, silent, providing no anecdotes or additions to The Hemingway Myth, not memorable in any way except perhaps eventually in whatever manuscript they produced—and they were incomparably, indescribably sweet.

Biographers don't really convey that. They may sense it—after all, they are artists themselves—but it doesn't lend itself to long description, because nothing much happens externally, and if they put in a few paragraphs like these, indicating the flavor and texture of such a part of a life, after all they can't keep repeating it every so often chapter by chapter, but the artist experiences it, day by incomparable routine day, and his life is a delight in those times no matter how his art makes him sweat.

And then, there's another thing to be said. To have that deeply satisfying routine interrupted, or threatened, is almost more than you can bear, especially if for stupid reasons but even if for the best. What movie-rights deal is going to make up for costing you that quiet ecstasy, even if only for a few days? What's it worth to have to trade living in two worlds for business dealings, or politics, or family troubles, or your own illness or incapacity to work for some reason? It's awful, and there's no way around it.

They say, "he's in a good mood, because his writing is going well," and they just don't really have any idea what they're talking about. Even if they've experienced something like it, it doesn't occur to them in such a way that they can translate it to others. Writing as an out-of-body experience! That's what you should call it.

Another aspect, come to think of it. When you're spending time in that invented world, that land of imagination, of imaging, you don't want to leave it and return to the single-vision world. That's like leaving the world of alcohol-induced gaiety or clarity or let's just say sparkle and living in a dishwater-flat emotional nothing. But if you stay drunk you lose it all, and if you were to stay in that double-image land your mind half created, half entered, it would go dead on you and you couldn't write out of it and then you couldn't even visit. There's a cruelty to the way life is organized. You can get by on the level easily enough, maybe—"life at half speed," Conrad's character says—but if you get highs you're going to get lows, and an artist gets highs. First he gets them from that territory he goes to while he is practicing his art, and then maybe he gets his highs from alcohol or cocaine, and he doesn't realize maybe that what he's doing is trying to drink away or drug away his loneliness for that for country. And of course I don't know about women artists but it's common enough for men to find that same echo in sex, especially sex with women he loves. There's a lot of crap written about sex—I wrote my share of it—but there's something there regardless, and if you haven't experienced it there's no telling you, and if you have, there's no telling you. All I can say is what I'm talking about is entirely involved in romance, not just fornication. So—but, enough.

In the mornings, I wrote and for the rest of the day, and in the evenings, and in the night, I did other things, and so I kept the balance, and in those times, whenever and wherever they came, life was clear satisfying contentment. Biographers miss all that, because it isn't easily communicated, and would need to be repeated every chapter.

≈ 9 ≈

Individuals and Communities

Tuesday, June 8, 2010

Yesterday mid-day I was sitting at the kitchen counter, reading the end of [Reynolds'] The Homecoming, when an impulse to pick up journal and pen resulted in the day's second entry—to my delight. A nice gift, Papa—thank you. And of course it has not escaped me that this time you came unbidden, and that the content delivery and style of your message was less me and more you. I'm very glad to serve as conduit, and not because you were famous but because we were friends.

You heard your hesitation, there? Before you wrote "were friends" you began to write "are friends" with a different meaning.

Yes, and I had the sense, too, that this is one reason why we are able to communicate—but whenever we were friends, it wasn't when you were Ernest Hemingway.

Questions like that aren't meaningless and they aren't necessarily frivolous (that is, they may be or may not be, depending on what you're going to do with the information) but they aren't going to help what we're doing here. If you start talking about "past lives" you immediately wind up thinking about people (including yourself) in their *individual* aspect, and it's easy to lose sight of their *community* aspect, which is the thread we're following at the moment.

Yes, I have found it hard to put the two together. I figure it is because we don't have the right concept.

That's *exactly* the problem. And in that problem of contradictory observations and contradictory analogies lies the germ of the solution, because if it didn't *nag* at you, maybe you wouldn't ever put your attention to it.

I went wandering somewhere, just now, and I feel the loss of connection not so much to you as to where we were going.

Your perception is gaining in clarity and intensity as we do this. Practice makes perfect. Earlier you would have thought you'd lost contact with me; earlier than that, you might have thought *I'd* withdrawn contact from you. Now you feel (but in the absence of an explaining concept) that you somehow didn't lose contact with *me* but with the topic of the moment; with the *point*. Let me suggest a different figure of speech. You and I are together on a street corner, talking, looking at a bird in a window. For a moment you get distracted by a glimpse of movement from the side of your eye—you glance over to see what it is, instinctively as we do, and for that moment you aren't anywhere different, you and I aren't separated, you haven't changed location relative to me or to anything. It's just that your attention wandered and *you followed it*, distracting yourself from the bird you were looking at. If you then were to forget that you and I were on that street corner, you might forget that you and I were even talking.

That is a very close analogy to what it's like over here, except that we don't have the body to hold us in one place, but also don't have the body to drag us away from a place. It's less stable here, in terms of "external" forces. You bring your own stability or lack of stability with you when you've given up the body, and if you were really such a thing as a disconnected individual, you'd be in hell of a mess.

That felt at the very end like a hand-over from Hemingway to Dr. Jung.

And you were able to allow yourself to perceive it despite the problem that logic would pose.

Yes—how could you change over in the middle of a sentence, that sort of thing.

You have at the very edge of your active perception at the moment a hazy idea of a truer picture. Describe it, and we will go from there.

I can't describe it very well. I get a sense that the information is like a thread connecting the three of us and so any of us could begin and any of us continue while we are on that thread.

This is a beginning. We are about to tear down and reconstruct your idea of individuals and immortality, and the difficulty is that while you are between concepts, a failure of nerve, or of faith, will leave you with nowhere to stand, and you will retreat to some more concrete but less accurate position. But if you do so, that is probably the end of your exploring the subject for this lifetime.

Which is why the long preparation.

Which is why the long preparation, advancing concepts and complications and new appealing vistas and then half-withdrawing them. Playing you like a fish, keeping you on the line.

Yes, I felt Papa's presence just then. I get that I shouldn't concentrate so much on who is speaking, should I?

There isn't anything wrong with it, but it does tend to move the emphasis from the information to the speaker. However, the improved sense of "who" is speaking, and of the changing of the guard, so to speak, is also part of the process. You all tend to make of the afterlife a continuation of individuality in a distorted sense, misled by your wrong ideas of what individuality is while you are in a body. It isn't that it is an illusion, or a mistake; it's that what is, is mis-perceived, mis-interpreted, hence mis-reported and put into distorted concepts which naturally tends to distort future perceptions, perpetuating the cycle. That's one good reason why life has seasons of forgetfulness—to allow new understandings. It is why cultures and civilizations die, and also why they leave legacies. Life depends upon remembering and on forgetting.

~ 10 ~

Choices

Sunday, June 13, 2010

What shall we talk about today?

[EH] we can talk about my China trip, if you'd like. You might sketch the situation in a couple of sentences, for your readers.

In 1941 Martha Gellhorn persuaded him to accompany her on a reporting trip to China for Colliers. It turned out to be a grueling trip, and one with long-lasting repercussions, because Hemingway agreed to do intelligence work for the Treasury Department to see how well our money was or wasn't being spent in the Chinese war effort.

You can see the germs of many things in that China trip. And perhaps in your Upstairs sense of things you could say that Martha Gellhorn and Ernest Hemingway were to get together for a few years, spur each other to do certain things neither would have done in the absence of the other's influence, and then go off their own way. But there are other ways to look at it that shed more light not on the situation of two individuals so much as on two representatives of the human condition. I mean, she and I are well enough known that our experience can provide a context, for those interested, but this wouldn't justify any full-scale investigation into our biographies for those who weren't interested for other reasons.

All right, I see that. I am interested in it all, of course, but it has been only in the past couple of years that you have grown so close in my mind, suspiciously enough.

Yes, well, don't go in building in Hemingway-esque paranoia!

A joke, I recognize—but—you mean more than that.

Sure. When you start seeing the suspicious footprints all over your life's pattern, and you have no concept of guidance or an overall sense of purpose beyond whatever is physically obvious, you don't know *who* is influencing things in your life, but you start to see that *somebody's* doing it—and in the absence of any way of finding out who or why, it can set up thought patterns that lead to "They're out to get me. They're in the shadows, but I *can* sense them, and the people around me who say there's nobody there are either blind or they're part of it." And since there may be nothing on the physical level to pin down, and since at the same time there may be real forces at work that are similar in the way they show up in your life, you can lose your bearings pretty easily.

For instance, suppose you're like me as I was in the 1930s. I had a certain measure of fame as a writer. Then the Spanish Civil War comes on and I go over to report on it. Would I have done it in Marty's absence?

I mean, if I hadn't met her, and if she hadn't been urging me to put my shoulder to the wheel? Since I *did* go, and since that shaped the rest of my life, you find it hard to realize that I might not have gone, but, after all, I was writing of revolution and of things I knew that no one else had ever written about—Key West life—so if Marty hadn't walked into the bar, or if she hadn't had those magnificent legs, or if I'd had more sense as an individual *and* if I hadn't been being prodded by my own Upstairs component, to use your jargon, I might very well have stayed in Florida, rooting for the Spanish Republic, detesting the forces of reaction, but not getting particularly involved, telling myself I'd already gone off on one war to save democracy and it had cost me a knee and a lot of pain and fear and hadn't even made the world safe for anything.

Now, think about that. Really consider it. Because certain threads in my life led me to go to Spain, and because that and what followed that were so vivid, and so shaped my life and art, there is the temptation to think I never could have done anything any differently and still be Ernest Hemingway. But it isn't true. I might never have picked up certain threads if I hadn't met Marty, and my life would still look like it was the only way it could have gone.

Let me sketch it out.

I went to Spain and of course I got more involved *because* I went. Being involved, I expressed more of my political side, which involved setting aside some of my skepticism—some of my clarity of perception!—in the service of the cause, as always happens. Cost me my friendship with Dos Passos, because he kept individual ties paramount, and I let myself be blinded or anyway dulled by partisanship and the cynicism that always masks itself as clear-sighted realism. And, of course, like anybody who fought for the Republic or sympathized with them, this brought me to the attention of the FBI as a possible communist sympathizer, mainly because the stupid bastards couldn't be bothered to see that the left had all sorts of degrees all fighting each other. If anything I was an anarchist by temperament, and who do Communists hate worse than them? And who have more reason to fear and hate communists in power? And if I hadn't been on the FBI's list, certain activities wouldn't have come to my attention. And if I hadn't broken up with Pauline and taken up with Marty, maybe I still would have gone to live in Cuba for tax reasons and maybe I wouldn't, but the reasons would have been different and maybe I wouldn't have gotten sucked into what followed.

Now, you might say that *For Whom the Bell Tolls* was worth a certain amount of disruption in my life, and I won't say it wasn't. But who knows what I might have written instead, and who knows what I might have written beyond it, had I not gone to Spain. In some versions of my life I wrote the great revolution novel that *To Have and Have Not* should have been, and then wrote other things based on my life of course but not necessarily based on being a participant or a camp-follower in the war that followed.

Without the China trip, compounding exhaustion with involvement in government or semi-government duties as a spy; without The Crook Factory; without the sub-hunting activity for more than a year; without feeling obliged to report the war from the ground; without new concussions and combat-fatigue (for that's what it was) after Hurtgen Forest; without meeting Marty in London, and in fact perhaps without breaking up my life with Pauline in the first place, for it is still only a few years since Marty walked into the bar—can you see that my life would still have been my life? But it would have been a different version.

Marty changed the course of my life but of course she didn't move it to anywhere that wasn't a possibility for me, how could she? But she *did* change its focus. On the one hand we botched *To Have and Have Not* and got *For Whom the Bell Tolls*. We broke up my life with Pauline and Patrick and Gregory, and lost Key West and a very satisfactory satisfying life. I moved into an intensely political orbit for a while that perhaps wasn't really my true focus, and I moved into a sort of half-hearted Ernie Pyle existence.

Look, I knew better than to think that Britain and France were noble causes. Look what they'd done to Spain! They were run by the same bunch of government bastards that always run things. It doesn't change. And I didn't hate Germans even if I despised fascism—but Communism wasn't much of an improvement. The only thing is, when you've gotten into a war, the only thing is to win it. I told people this war was coming as far back as 1935 when nobody wanted to hear it—and I said then we ought to stay out of it. Well, you read in Carl Jung [in a book titled *C.G. Jung Speaking*] that he said the only thing for America to do was to stay out as long as possible because it was vital for the world that America not go down. How different is that from my own attitude?

My life should show you that what looks like an inevitable course isn't inevitable at all, it's just what you saw and what then looked inevitable after the fact. In fact, your life can go different ways depending on your decisions—depending on the threads you pick up and the ones you put down. There are only so many main branches to your life's possibilities, probably, but there are always more than you will be able to explore, because of course some choices make other choices impossible. You can't step twice into the same river. Try to envision Hemingway still in Key West, still married to Pauline, not going off to cover the wars, not getting diverted into leftist politics for a time, and you can perhaps see that, although you can't see what might have followed, *something* would have. Free will is not merely theoretical, and is not an illusion.

~ 11 ~

The Invisible Aspect of Writing

Monday, June 14, 2010

All right, Papa, now what?

Don't discount the value of so many conversations transcribed and sitting in the bank vault. You can see that people are responding to *Chasing Smallwood* as they learn of it, because it offers a helpful glimpse and example of just such matter-of-fact communication. You have the makings of many little books—easily digestible books—

I heard the analogy; just like your vast unfinished manuscripts.

Let's talk about that a little bit. This process is teaching you something about writing that you have always known in another context—which means, you've had the perception but have put a different interpretation on it.

What is writing but putting yourself into a very pleasant, very seductive in fact, altered state of mind? While you are living there, the work itself may be more an excuse to stay there than the main reason to do it. In other words, writing becomes its own reward. You know this. Henry

Thoreau left a couple of million words in his journal that went unpublished for 50 years after his death and probably he never expected it to be published. He kept it for himself.

Now—why?

Partly for the sake of preserving thoughts and memories. Partly for the sake of exercising his skill. Partly as a mine for future literary production. And mostly because for a writer, writing is how he gets into deepest contact with the other side.

That doesn't mean the writer *knows* this. It only means that he knows that writing is the savor in his life, and life is a tedium without it. Can't write all day and all night, of course, but then you can't make a meal of just salt, either, but you have to have it.

Now typically a writer has two things going: He wants to write for the sake of the process itself, and he wants to communicate. The first he can do as long as he can maintain contact with his wellsprings. The second has always depended on finding a way to be published, or to get access to the lecture circuit. In your day the economic barriers to getting your word out are much lower, but of course your competition for people's attention is correspondingly increased.

If you want to write a best-selling book, it means you have to beat some heavy odds. Either you're going to try for some lowest-common-denominator formula, or you're going to bring forth something of great originality that *strikes people*. The first doesn't interest you and would not be within your range of abilities; the second cannot be predicted, as it depends upon too many things beyond your ken or control.

Now you will notice in my career that I was never complacent with whatever sales level any given book received, and in fact was usually sure it *could* have and *should* have sold more, if it had had more enthusiastic support from its publisher. Regardless of the truth of this feeling, I was always frantic to get the word out, because I knew the value of what I was doing, knew the work I put into it, and I was full of envy and fear of other authors' success and I was paranoid about whether I was being sabotaged by lack of interest or effective promotion by those who were in my corner—Scribner's editorial and advertising departments, mainly.

I didn't know that I was being supported from the non-physical side. The closest I could have come to that concept is that I believed in my luck. (I also believed in my ability and in my habit of hard work.)

When you think your life and your life's success are all up to you, you can get pretty frantic. After all, you can never judge all the forces that are in play, you can't tell what may be working against you without your knowledge, you're likely to see conspiracies to kill your career among the critics because that's the way you connect the dots. It's a high-tension way to live, during the time you're not doing the actual writing, when you're in a different world.

But—then suppose you're not seeing the wolf at the door. Suppose you have a lot of experience in the bank and no need to shape it into something salable in a certain time. Then your situation is like Thoreau's, writing for himself, or yours. Or mine after I got back from Europe in 1945. I left—even disregarding the material I accumulated in Africa in the 1950s—a huge amount of material in unfinished form, when I lost my ability to access the creative mind. But that didn't mean what I had was unusable or discarded. When you think that *Islands in the Stream* and *The Garden of Eden* were both shaped out of it, relatively finished, and many small pieces like the discarded chapters on Roger that couldn't fit into *Islands* after I concentrated on Thomas Hudson—

Well, all the time that I was writing, I was doing two things, as you well know. I was working toward producing some finished product, but I was also—at the same time, and emotionally perhaps primarily—living in that altered state that any artist knows.

I always said I wrote with great difficulty. What I meant was that it wasn't easy for me to express myself exactly. First I had a general idea of what I wanted to convey. Then I had a better idea of it, and tried to say it. Then I picked apart that attempt and kept trying to say it better, and maybe this would go on all day and at the end of the day I'd have only a few paragraphs and I wasn't even satisfied with them, but would have to go after them again the next day. The writing was hard work. What *wasn't* hard work, what was joy in the same way fishing was joy, was the exercise of the skill and where that put me while I was doing it.

A connection that isn't obvious. You read Pirsig's book *Zen and the Art of Motorcycle Maintenance*. You know his point: The axis of the world is Quality, which you can't ever define but which you know when you see it. That whole book, whether or not he knew it, was about living in both worlds at the same time, which is what an artist is doing when he's being an artist—that is, when working at his art is holding him there. He doesn't have to know why, to have the experience. And there was never a true artist in any medium who didn't live that connection.

Of course, if you've spent the morning there, you're apt to be a little flat, a little directionless, when you descend to what people call the real world. And you're going to think you're just tired from working, because after all it's how you always feel when you quit work for the day. And the temptation to regain that feeling of intensity, of savor, without being able to work, is what leads so many to drink or drugs. Especially since not one artist in a hundred understands what is going on when he is in that special state. So, I'd come out of a morning's work and I'd count how many words I'd wrestled out of the void, and I'd go on with my day. And when I could recapture the feeling by fishing or hunting, that would keep me fresh, and would exercise the animal, as well. But I'd still be charging up for my next morning's excursion.

This will have to do it for now. I do recognize what's between the lines: what you lost when they destroyed your access to the other side.

Yes, but more. The shock treatments came because of my mental state. I know that now. I was in the end-game anyway. But yes, I'd lost everything. It didn't have a thing to do with being published, really. It had to do with being able to be in that state that had produced so much publishable work.

≈ 12 ≈

Three Revolutions

Thursday, June 17, 2010

What do we talk about today, Papa? I was thinking you were going to talk about what you did for our fiction.

I was fighting on a couple of fronts at once, and maybe each issue obscured the others.

I wanted to restore the written language, so that we could write as we speak. It had become so genteel, so euphemism-constricted, that it was being falsified. If you couldn't say shit when and where you would say it out loud—where it would be said in the circumstances—it soon led to certain kinds of circumstances not being described at all. My father never did understand why I had to describe what he regarded as situations unfit to be described in literature. He was proud of me, deeply loved me, I see that now, but the world he had grown up in and believed in as best he could didn't use these words in polite company and certainly didn't expect to read them.

And that was the second thing I was fighting to do—to restore honesty to our writing by writing about the way things really were, not the sanitized way they were pretended to be in the *Saturday Evening Post*, which was my day's equivalent of television, as you will remember from your own fifties' childhood, where it served the same purpose still.

So honesty in words, honesty in situations, and the third thing I was doing was a little harder to see, and I didn't actually see it this way until now, a long time later! What I *thought* I was doing, and *was* doing, was creating a more nervous, intense way of telling stories by leaving out as much as I could and telling only what I had to tell for you to get the story. That got rid of the flowery crap and the leisurely meandering around that were the weeds in the garden, as far as I was concerned. Just as Jim Joyce was playing with language to bring the mind to process it differently, though, so was I. I just never thought of it that way. I knew what I was doing was different, and I knew, what everybody knows, that my inspiration from it was cablese, the compressed allusive language invented for the transatlantic cable, to save cost. It's too bad you don't have samples of cablese; you'd find it interesting. Of course you wouldn't find it to be a revolution, as I did, because I spent my working life putting the revolution through!

But what I was also accomplishing, I see now, besides creating added intensity through compression, was requiring the reader to work in a different way if he was going to make sense of my stories—and my stories, realize, were much more of my life usually than the novels. When I was in the middle of writing a novel, obviously that's all I was thinking of, and it would go on for weeks—in the case of *For Whom the Bell Tolls*, for more than a year. But take my career month in and month out for more than 30 years, short stories were the constant. And what were they doing? They were teaching a generation of people to read between the lines, and therefore forcing them to create along with me, or misunderstand my stories. Not all of them, and the ones where you don't have to do it are the ones that make the anthologies, and that get taught. "Macomber," and "Kilimanjaro," and "In Another Country." It's the ones that don't really tell you that get so often misunderstood or only partly understood, like "Indian Camp."

I don't say I knew it while I was doing it, or even while I was living. But I see now that my third revolution wasn't merely style, or let's say was the *result* of the style. If what I'm writing, the way I'm writing, makes you live mentally in a place closer to the writer's world than any other form of writing, that's a revolution *and it's invisible*—even to me!—because it doesn't show any outward effect. I didn't even realize it!

You take C.S. Forester. I loved his stuff. But now do you see the difference between where he leaves you and where I could leave you, or anyway take you? His descriptions are so accurate, so vivid, his dialogue and actions so sure-footed, that he helps you to create a vivid picture in your mind. If you were to read him fast enough, it would form the pictures in your head as if you'd seen a movie. What he *doesn't* do, because he never tried to do it, is make *you* fill in the missing pieces. He doesn't deliberately leave out facts about whatever Hornblower is doing, to make you figure it out. He sure-footedly gives you everything you need to form the pictures and carry the story.

I, in leaving out everything I could, force you to work in the way the author worked. You have to live in the scene and realize what wasn't said. Now, you might not exactly know what was left out, but if you read it right you'll *feel* what was left out—its unspoken presence will have affected everything that was said. But that means you have to read it actively in a way you don't have to read [either] something written as chewing-gum, or something written as vivid description of a true rather than contrived problem; in other words, something that is "serious" writing, like Forester, rather than read-it-forget-it thrillers. And that active reading, though it leaves no traces, is still a different thing from any other kind of reading.

≈13≈

Habit Systems

Friday, June 18, 2010

What do you think, Papa? Looking through my eyes, can you see the mental processes that progressively distorted your life?

I didn't need your view to do that. When you die, you get past those limits on your vision. Getting multiple viewpoints is as easy after life as it was hard during life. The thing is, by that time, it's too late.

Too late to change your life as lived.

Too late to change your mind as shaped by how you'd lived. That's why the guys said to you that they regarded your minds as habit-systems. You took it down, but you didn't understand it. They meant that once you take away the physical surroundings—the body and its demands, sequential time and its demands, the limitations of point of view, all the features that make life in the physical unique—what's left amounts to a set of habits, a way of looking at things and reacting to them, a cluster of associations. And this is what your immortality consists of, for any particular lifetime. If you incarnate again, as I have, still that legacy remains, and functions, and preserves its individuality—it has crystallized, to use their earlier terminology. Much of what you recorded in your sessions years ago you accepted but didn't really understand, you see, and so now those things have laid a base from which you can move into deeper understandings.

It's a reiterative process, I believe they said recently. Not sure if they meant this or something else. Anybody reading this is going to wish I'd asked, so I'll ask, but you understand, I don't really care and in a way wouldn't want to know: You said you are back. Can you say anything about your present life, or (if that life is over already) your more recently past life.

Can I, yes. *Will* I, no. It's different from what we are doing in that unlike serious two-way information exchange, that would be like answering fan mail.

≈14≈

Hemingway's Father

Saturday, June 19, 2010

What would you like to talk about, Papa?

Your father.

My father?

Your father's effect on you, and to some extent your effect on him.

In light of your own relationship with your father, I take it.

My father—and my sons. Don't forget, it was the father's love for his sons that was the emotional tie to you in *Islands in the Stream*. That wasn't the only thing in it, and wasn't the only thing you took from it but it was the initial hook. There was a reason why you and I connected first along that theme. It wasn't the first time you read one of my books, but it was the first time we connected. I was just a name on a shelf before that. And *Islands* meant something to you long before you learned anything more than the barest outline of my life as reported.

All right.

You've seen, in working with people, that their parents often inflict the deepest wounds on them, and at the same time give them what they can develop into their greatest or most valuable gifts. Neglect can foster independence. Abuse can create toughness. Unreasonable demands can foster a sense of fair play that becomes paramount.

Now, that is just considering the unfortunate side of a father's or a mother's legacy to a child. The straight-forward gifts—teachings, examples, traits, even the hereditary talents that may be identified—they all get their recognition. It is the things we struggle with that we have to learn to see a more rounded way, in a different light. And of course, if you can't see your father and mother in that way, you can bet you'll never be able to see *yourself* in that rounded way. You'll be full of defensiveness and self-condemnation and shame and all the need to try to hide these or at least survive them. And, if that's true within you, it's going to be true outside of you, around you, as well. Your relationships with lovers, friends, even acquaintances sometimes, are all going to reflect these same characteristics, not only *as much* as if they were conscious, but *more so*, because you won't have any conscious control over them. You know all this, but perhaps not everybody who comes to it will.

So take my situation. I loved my father and he loved me as long as I was a boy. But just at the time I started to become a teenager, he changed, and of course at 12 years old I assumed it was something in me that caused him to back away. I didn't *think* of it this way, but I unconsciously felt that he didn't like what I was becoming. I know now what everybody knows, and of course my criticisms of him read ironically in light of the rest of my life, but you don't criticize somebody that harshly unless you love them. The opposite of love isn't hatred, it's indifference.

Just to clarify for others, I know that you're referring to your description of your father as a coward because he wouldn't stand up to his wife, in your opinion, and because he killed himself.

That's right, especially the second. I didn't understand that a man can come to the point where he can't stand things.

Just as Nick's father says in "Indian Camp."

My father became very harsh and very self-absorbed as his mental deterioration proceeded. Nobody knew all that much about such things in the 1920s, not among the level of society we were in. We knew there was something wrong, but nobody knew what to do. It'll give you a different view of my life if you realize that I spent my teenage years sort of tiptoeing around my father. Mental illness's cause not being recognized—though its effects sure were!—we held him responsible for his actions as if the man we had known was *choosing* to act that way. What was the alternative? To admit, even to realize, that it was all inside himself? And if it was too hard, too painful, to think of him *choosing* to be that way, the only thing left was, it had to be somebody else! And there was Grace Hall Hemingway, born to play the part.

But you didn't consciously realize what was going on within you.

Oh no. When parents are at war, children either choose sides or they say "a pox on both your houses" or they try to keep the peace somehow—by being extra good, by anticipating everybody's needs, by trying to *be* whatever the parents need as far as the child can tell.

I loved my father. It made it impossible for me to not hate and resent my mother. That's why I was never rational on the subject. No matter what the facts were, I could only see them in whatever way made her wrong.

≈15≈

The Myth

So, Papa, let me pose the question this way. I am more and more inclined to see your essence as one model of a complete man, intellectually, physically vigorous. Yet there is the negative evidence, your mental problems, for example. Your inability to get beyond certain fixed ideas—"my mother is a bitch; my father was a coward"—regardless of the facts. I can't quite phrase my question because I can't quite grasp it. I'm hoping you can take it and run with it. For all I know, you are suggesting it, in the first place.

No, not Ernest, not at this moment.

Welcome, Dr. Jung.

[CGJ] We have been presenting aspects of [Hemingway's] life in an attempt to use a model apparently well known to show how little anyone can be accurately judged, especially if judged without sympathy, or in other words condemned. His life had mythic stature: That stature inspired and disturbed people, depending on which piece of it resonated. His written work seemed autobiographical but was actually more fictional than was always recognized: Many critics, knowing that his fiction included reference to people or incidents in his life, assumed that he was writing in a sort of code, thinly disguising history in order to carry on a vendetta against those he disliked. What he was doing actually was somewhat different: He was borrowing freely from the people or situations in his life and using them as his palette, his choice of colors. There is a huge difference, and it is more than wish fulfillment or malicious revenge. You know from your own experiences writing fiction that you can borrow pieces from your life entirely out of context, entirely transformed, because they may serve to create an effect you're after. He did just that—but because of his compelling decisive persuasive style, and his publicized private life, and his own propensity to mythologize his autobiography, it became difficult for many critics to believe that he was working in a different dimension, not disguised malicious autobiography.

His tragic descent into his final illness.

"Tragic" is not a word well understood in your time. It doesn't mean "sad," nor "very sad." Rightly understood, it means, more, fated; beyond the individual's control; fixed by the gods. It does not mean merely "the result of accident, or of a series of bad choices." So yes, in its proper sense, Ernest's life was a tragedy, but the tragedy did not discredit the life, or prove that his ideals or strivings were bad models. They prove nothing. The boiler burst, under too much steam pressure.

So any tragedy would inhere in his having been constructed with too much steam power and insufficiently thick metal in the boiler?

Alternative tragedies would have been—no steam pressure at all; sides so thick that the vessel couldn't move for the weight of it; no fuel for the steam; no scope for a voyage. You understand? Your times' saying is that "you don't get out of life alive," a sardonic comment meant to imply that "you can't win," which is another popular saying. Your own joke on the three rules of life is similar. [The three rules of life. One, you can't win. Two, you can't break even. Three, you can't even quit the game.] The purpose of life is not "getting out of it alive" in the sense of the saying. It is a voyage, every life is. I shall step onto more charged ground. Yes. I know where you are going.

Well? So, if you know, you know also what it is like to be unable to adjust your emotional reactions to a different understanding of the facts—which is what you pointed out Ernest didn't and couldn't do.

And it hampers your mobility—mine, I mean in this case.

Your fluidity, your ability to flow with life appropriately. If being stuck, being frozen in place, were of service to you, I should have nothing to say against it. And, indeed, sometimes being stuck is the only alternative to coming apart completely, as in the case of the patient I had who later became a Nazi. I could do nothing for him, because his steam-chamber was dangerously over-stressed even at the slightest of pressures.

To be blunt: In martyrdom is fulfillment in certain cases. Given that we all die from life and the dying is no tragedy, why is the manner of the dying of eternal concern? The legacy and impact of John F. Kennedy and Abraham Lincoln and others was heightened and sealed by the sudden shocking manner of their deaths. Certain effects followed that would have been harder to attain otherwise, and if bad effects accompanied the good effects, still it remains true that you cannot ever tell—if you look closely enough, and far enough—which is which, good or bad. The evils in whatever path you choose are always obvious enough, so obvious that it may become difficult to imagine or sense the evils of the paths not taken, for evil is always manifested with good in a world of duality, and, again, which is which is often a matter of viewpoint alone. Good or bad often amounts to preference, and preference is rooted in one's values, and no one's values are absolutely correct or even unchanging. So if even martyrdom is not tragic in your contemporary sense of "extremely too bad" rather than in the classic sense of "inherent in the person's makeup," or "inherent in the situation," neither is a life wrecked by a burst boiler, accompanied ahead of time by steam escaping from joints forced open by the excess pressure.

Then if I understand you right, even the things we regret to see in his life, or our own, are to be accepted as part of the pattern; nothing can be done.

Not at all, not in any sense of hopeless resignation. They are to be accepted as the defects of his qualities, or your own—but that is not the end of the story, but the beginning. A deeper understanding sees that qualities have their defects, and it is by the close examination of the effects as they show themselves that you will perceive. No one's life may be summarized as an epic journey marred by wrong choices. Whatever choices were made, the life would have been "marred" by the defects of the qualities.

Suppose Ernest had been so made that he was a stickler for the truth, in the sense of never deviating from an accurate reporting of the external facts. He might have become an excellent reporter with no insight. He might have lived a blameless (or not blameless) life of absolutely no interest because of no importance to the culture. The defect of truthfulness might have been a lack of imagination, or rather a walling-off of imagination from his work. Imagination might have become confined to fantasy.

Ah, but he would have told the truth in all things instead of making up so many tall tales! Yes—but would the world be the better for the exchange?

You know that Thoreau said that a man should live in some fear of his own talents. You have remembered the gist, but have not understood it. It means, in short, that your life may lead you in ways you don't approve of and perhaps can't survive, even though by your makeup it is as it should be. So Hemingway.

I see. That's not so different from the verdict several of his best biographers have reached.

No, except that they, like you, may wish that he had made different choices. That isn't quite the same thing as realizing that every life is going to be the result of choices some of which will appear to be good, some bad. So. I yield the floor to my good friend the famous author.

I get that a humorous affectionate relationship has sprung up between you. Is this a result of this collaboration?

[EH] Any time you play on the same team you're likely to come closer. That's bonding, isn't it?

Have you come across each other actively since you had died?

That's closer to idle speculation than to real work. Let's stick to real work.

Okay. But I can't always tell ahead of time what's work and what's a diversion.

I know, and no reason you shouldn't ask anything you want to ask—but sometimes you're going to get a closed door. Nothing wrong with either end of that.

You have been talking of my life as it is understood and as I experienced it and as it might be understood by God, or by any all-knowing impartial arbiter. Three very different points of view! What's the point in it, do you suppose? Why are we bringing it up from different angles?

To show the futility of making judgments on people, for one thing, I imagine.

That, but more. If you are to bring out the real meaning of my life, you have to understand it not only as it was lived, but as it was *not* lived.

If I am to what? I didn't realize that's what we're doing here.

It's one part of it. I can serve as a pretty good, concrete example of several things we have to say.

Well, well. I've wondered.

Take my being Catholic, for instance. You can see *that* (and you can see *how*) it was a reality for me. It is widely overlooked, because inexplicable particularly to the scholarly viewpoint. So it is written off as a gesture, or as a hypocrisy relative to Pauline. But you can see how it isn't, and I can help you get a deeper sense of what it meant in my life—including all the complications that came when Spanish politics and then my own sense of sin divorced me from it—which amounted to divorcing me from the only *accessible* connection to the divine that I had. Who better to understand than another member of the club?

I'll explain the reference. [Ex-Catholics share a point of view that neither practicing Catholics nor those who have never been Catholic seem to understand. For some years, I have called ex-Catholics I have met Members Of The Club.]

So, there's work for you to do, and it will be fun, as it has been fun to date.

≈16≈

Different Exiles

Monday, June 21, 2010

Papa, let's talk some more about your life—or anything you want to talk about.

My life in Cuba. I was living in happy exile there. If you compare it to Paris, you can observe some instructive differences.

You lived in Paris for a few years after World War I while you were in your twenties and were working as a foreign correspondent for the Toronto Star, and teaching yourself to write fiction. You were in Cuba, let's see, after you lost Key West as a base, which means after you and Pauline split up, so I guess it means from the very late '30s until Castro's anti-American campaign, though not aimed at you, forced you out, in the last couple of years of your life.

That's true as background, but it doesn't give the flavor of the differences. In Paris I was surrounded by genius and near-genius and maybe-who-knows genius. Picasso, Miro, Joyce, Fitzgerald when he was there—so *many* authors when they were there—and I was part of it, but only part of it. I wasn't famous yet, but they could see that I had the talent and the drive, and so maybe would become famous. I was accepted, in other words. And I was a family man in the way only a young man with a young child is a family man. We were a unit and we thought of ourselves that way. And there were so many things to see, so many different things to do. Lincoln Steffens to talk politics and revolution to, the other correspondents from all over Europe and America, conferences to cover, skiing in Austria—all that. It was an active, varied, interesting life full of promise and I was working well among comrades even if they were rivals. And once I'd hooked up with Scribner's, I had my publisher, and I pretty much knew it all the way down. That time was all expansion and growth, a good time despite the troubles that always come at any time in our life.

Life in Cuba was very different, as life in your 40s and 50s is bound to be different from life in your 20s [anyway]. I had arrived, professionally and socially. I wasn't just one among many. Havana was not a literary center! So the pressure and the stimulus of personal competition among peers was gone. I wasn't a family man in the way I had been. My children were in the world and there wouldn't be any more. I was on my third and then my fourth marriage, and I was no longer assuming that once was for all. I had a vigorous inner life, but a bit less of an active outer life despite exceptions. Or, put it this way, what had been pretty much part of my routine in my 20s had become exceptions in my 40s and 50s.

And, biggest change of all, where do you go when you are on the top, but down? *For Whom the Bell Tolls* was a huge success. Going to match that, every time out of the box? Going to have to match it or be declared over the hill? It was a different kind of pressure, not an expansive one. And of course in the interim there were so many physical accidents, so much wear and tear.

And so much alcohol.

Yes, but maybe the effects that are so obvious to the observer of my life weren't as obvious to me on the inside, and maybe the alcohol compensated to some extent for other things in my life.

Needing to quit soon, but do you have something to wrap up about the differences between your life in Paris and your life in Havana?

Only in that there are different experiences of exile, and each one produces different effects. When you're running away from home to make your way in the world, that is one thing. When you have no home to return to, that's another. Nothing tragic about it, just life. But it's important to see what *is*, and sometimes people don't see—or maybe don't think about the importance of what is to be seen—how and why I lived my life *mentally* and *spiritually* at the heart of America, but physically only at the periphery. Like you, I was true to an earlier version that no longer existed, and maybe never did exist except in my mind, the way I had envisioned it.

≈ 17 ≈

F. Scott Fitzgerald

Thursday, June 24, 2010

Papa, let's talk about F. Scott Fitzgerald and me. Yesterday I was moved to buy five of his books, after having been unable to read the book of his short stories that I had borrowed. Other than "The Lost Decade," they seemed so shallow and even silly—just an impression from titles, and reading the first few pages of "A Diamond as Big as the Ritz" and "Bernice Bobs Her Hair"—that I returned the book and thought I was finished with. But then

I return with Tender is the Night, The Beautiful and Damned, This Side of Paradise, and Gatsby. I'm wondering: why.

There is a sense in which the public is always right, and you know it, so if somebody made that huge an impact on society, you may need to know why. If you are building a picture in your mind of the progress of the age—the way it moved forward, I mean, not the idea that every new thing is "progress" and is therefore something worthwhile—you're going to have to know something of its full proportions.

Maxwell Perkins' kids did a lot to shape the world that followed the war [World War I, of course], because they had been shaped by the world and continued to be shaped by it and shape it in turn. You don't know anything about Tom Wolfe or Marjorie Rawlings for that matter, or any of his authors but Fitzgerald and me, and even I am a recent acquisition, I think you could say. Well, you don't have time to absorb all the major influences of the time if you're going to accomplish anything else. How many years have you been reading about the Civil War and the history of your country, and how easily do you find yourself coming across new information that shows you that you only very incompletely understood what you thought you knew? And even to get what you've got, you had to pretty much ignore all but the highlights of what has happened in your time. You know? It's always a lot bigger than anybody can compre-hend, but you have to make the effort anyway. And if enough people make the effort, a common understanding does emerge on *this* side that can help you on *your* side.

So, go ahead about Fitzgerald.

I don't know that it has occurred to you, but you've been judging him by the people he wrote about, and figuring that they are trivial so he's trivial. But that's the same thing my parents did about me and my fiction. I wrote about lost, often despicable people, and they worried that this meant that either I was whoring for a popular following, or I was drawn to such people by some personal resonance, as you put it. But if you just read what I wrote, and the feelings it raises in you, you will know what I thought about them, because that's the feeling I intended to convey. So why should it be different with Scott? So give him a good try before you conclude that he's not worth your time.

I hear you. I hear you pointing out—and pretty gently, too!—that I've been condemning. All right, I'll grant him a full conditional pardon and try him as if I didn't know anything about him, which come to think of it, is approximately true. I know only The Fitzgerald Myth:

You'll find that people are usually better than their myth. I'd say "always" but you don't like "always." In any case, a myth is what grows around somebody; it isn't the man himself, or the woman.

You were plenty judgmental, in your day. Why?

Why? Ask yourself! When you are on your own, you have to do your own discerning, because you don't and can't accept authority's word for it. And it's a very fast slide from discernment to judgment—that is, to putting something or somebody in a box, and then comparing them to yourself, and condemning the differences.

So—what is Fitzgerald's importance?

Mostly let's save this until you actually read him, or even finish reading-reading *Gatsby*. But in a nutshell, he did just what he says in *The Crack-up* he did—he told people that he felt just the same way about things that they did, and they responded the way people always do when they suddenly feel *heard*, or when what they know is suddenly for the first time put out in a form like print or film that is beyond personal—they identified with *him*, and with his characters whether he approved of them or not, and with the life—you'd call it lifestyle—that they thought he was describing and recommending. You saw in *The Crack-up* that he said no author had been so thoroughly "frisked" as Ring Lardner but me. Well, his [Fitzgerald's] *style* and *mannerism* wasn't imitated as much as his *attitude*. People tried to write like Lardner or me, but they tried to live like Scott, or how they thought he lived, or how they could on their limited income. So he reflected the new ways of thinking and feeling, and then he reflected the ways of thinking and feeling that had been modified by his earlier writing, and it wasn't long before that road petered out. But—as I said—read him, then we'll talk.

~18~

Fitzgerald and His Talent

Friday, June 25, 2010

Okay, Papa. Let's talk. I finished Gatsby again early yesterday, and got into Tender is the Night—50 pages or so. It certainly starts off slowly. I'm having to restrain my impatience. If I had just picked it up for no reason, I'd have put it down nearly at once. After your prose, clicking and moving, it's hard to be patient with somebody describing the night sky hung like a bowl from a single star—

You might as well put in your appreciation for *Gatsby* that you wrote yesterday, though.

Okay. [Begin] *Gatsby* is still a terrific book. It seems to me, though, that Gatsby's life and success—if it may be called a success; anyway, his life that he built—reflect Fitzgerald's naïve romanticism quite as much as Gatsby's. It takes a romantic to dream up something like that. In a way, it's Hemingway in his immature period of trying to be published in the *Saturday Evening Post*, only complete with a devastatingly effective style. For the first time maybe I see Hemingway's meaning in saying that Fitzgerald had all that talent but hadn't done the observation necessary to portray something true. It's a terrific book, but it's a boy's story like *Treasure Island*, only transposed into material that wouldn't have been suitable to, or acceptable to, boys. It is a boy's idea of how the wicked world functions. Only—boys don't commonly assume that wickedness prospers—or even *could* prosper, and they don't factor in stupidity in human affairs. Time gives them these factors. [End]

Those of us who knew him could see that, always, of course. Speaking of impatience, I was always impatient that he hadn't taken the time to learn his trade—and one element of the writer's trade is to know and understand the human heart, not just his own. Where his plot and characters could be constructed out of himself, he did fine. *Gatsby*, "The Lost Decade." But when he had to report what he had not observed, or had to understand what he had seen but not understood, he was at a severe disadvantage. And it seemed to us that *he didn't need to be.*

It looked to you like a waste of talent.

Terrible waste of talent. It was one thing, you know, if you were born with no talent, or no opportunities. Then if you didn't get anyplace, didn't accomplish anything, whose fault was it? But to be given *everything*, so that with just a little application, a little discipline, a little consistent hard work *as a regular feature* of his life even if his wife was crazy, even if she was crazy jealous of his work and did her best to sabotage it, with all that natural talent he should have been able to be the greatest writer of his generation. Or—okay, so writers can't be ranked—let's say he *could* have been, and *should* have been, *would* definitely have been, a phenomenon, not just a phenom.

[For the non-baseball fans out there, a "phenom" is what the old-timers and the observers call the new kids who come up to the majors with a great prospective reputation; i.e., they're going to do great things. Often enough, a "phenom" is only a flash in the pan.]

So, Papa, do you still think that way?

Given what he was, the whole curve of his life could have been pretty well predicted from outside. What looks—inside time-space; on your side of the physical/non-physical line—like avoidable misfortune or waste or even open-handed stupidity may look different on this side, where what went into the makeup of that "individual" is more obvious, and where we are more aware of the interaction between person-group and social-group, as your guys are calling them.

Fitzgerald as a person was created as a metaphor for the 20s as an era, you're saying.

It might be closer to say, he was created out of the stuff of the postwar era, and his possibilities and those of the age were in close sync, which is why he met that amazing instant success. I said that the problem with Scott was that he had the idea of the rich as somehow special, and it wrecked him. Well, can you see that now? He used his resources to get enough money that he could spend like them, live like them—or how he imagined them to spend and live—and as a result he wound up imitating the stupid splashy nouveau riche and the vulgar arrivistes but that isn't the only thing he could have done. He could have used that money that came to him so easily to live a *longer* life, a *quieter* life, a more intense, *productive* life. And if he had picked up the strands within himself that were the artist in him and had laid down the strands that were "the envious poor boy who needs to be rich so he could win Zelda" he would still have been Scott; he would still have had a life, and a much saner one. It was his choice. And yet, of course the dice were loaded from the beginning. Still, he *could have* chosen differently regardless how the dice made him want to choose. He had Max, he would've had me and others, who could have been a steadying influence paying more attention to his work, valuing it more, with the partying and the "trying to be one of the boys" for when work was finished for the day.

But then there was alcohol.

You keep coming back to it, and you aren't quite right. Alcohol inflamed the situation and weakened his will and his confidence and it provided a cheap counterfeit version of the satisfaction that comes with living "there" while you're working, but if the rest of his life had been okay, he would have been okay and maybe he wouldn't have felt it necessary to drink so much. People drink to relieve pressure they can't live with and can't get rid of, as much as anything else.

Here it is seven o'clock, an hour and a quarter, and more or less on schedule I feel that it's time to quit for now. How did you work so many hours, Papa?

Partly I kept myself fit. All that exercise helped. Partly I inherited a strong constitution. Partly I disciplined myself with regular schedule and certain expectations of myself. All those things broaden your endurance, they build up your stamina.

IV

July 2010

Time

Thursday, July 1, 2010

Papa, being that tomorrow is the anniversary of your self-decided transition—and next year makes 50 years since then!—how about if you start?

There will be a time when 50 years as a space of time doesn't impress you as it does now. Consider how your reaction is different now from even 20 years ago, and then try to see yourself over here for 50 years.

And maybe that provides the topic of the day, for I am curious about the experience of time. You could always observe and report; you had that kind of mind. Let's try.

All right, let's try. That image that flashed through your mind a second ago was the key. It is *one* key, anyway, one way to approach it. Care to describe it?

Well, just for a second I had a sense of a moment being shot with intensity, I can't really describe it. It was as if your interest lighted it up.

That isn't bad. Now in everything I am going to say about time, remember that this is *one* aspect of our lives here. Unlike your conscious lives, we are not dominated by time. Like your unconscious lives, we roam unimpeded through it, landing now here, now there.

[Perhaps you can feel how that communication cross-faded to TGU.]

[TGU] You might profitably think of life on the non-physical side as dreaming alternating with lucid dreaming alternating with very focused experiences, all within a permanent out-of-body experience. Make the mental effort needed to imagine such a state of being, and a few things will become clear to you. Then, remembering that you *there* are more a community than a unit, remember that on this side our group-ness is more obvious to us than our separate-ness, and that will give you another aspect of our existence. Really, just remember that you there are we here, on different turf, just as we told you "way back when" in 1998 when you were writing *Muddy Tracks*, and this will give you a better sense of it than anything.

The chief reason why people are unable to get any good sense of the afterlife is that they *will* persist in imagining themselves as individual (which they are not, even in life) and separate (where there is no physical structure to produce the illusion and experience of separation) and conscious in the way you are in the presence of a passing moment (where there is no ever-passing moment). Think of us as your own unconscious mind—which is pretty close to the truth.

Don't fall back into the mental habit of thinking that things occur only in response to your activity or attention. It's all well and good to experience yourself as the center of life and the world, as in practice you do and everybody does, but it's as misleading in connection with this side as it would be on your side to think that everything proceeded from yourself.

≈ 2 ≈

Research

Papa, let's go back to your life. I noticed that, counting from your first appearance in May 2006, I have 64 sessions in which I talked to you entirely or primarily or partly—up to the end of June. So we have something to start from.

Then when you get that done, you could—you don't *have to* but you *could*—go back and re-read Baker, making note of the questions you want to ask, as you go along, and *stopping* till you've asked that question, then going on. You can accumulate a couple of associated questions if you wish, but don't get a whole pile of them in the name of efficiency, because by then you will have read on beyond what you're asking about. Don't worry that one or two questions won't be enough to fill sessions! It isn't like that's been a problem so far.

No, it hasn't. Baker I presume is smiling somewhere to hear you recommending that somebody read his book.

You know my objections to biography, and they still hold. But corrected from an inner view, they're very valuable. And yes, I recognize that it is just as well that I didn't try to write my own memoirs. Settling scores that way is nothing but pettiness, a talking behind somebody's back.

≈ 3 ≈

Reflections on Fitzgerald

Speaking of talking behind somebody's back, let's talk about Francis Scott Key Fitzgerald.

Well, you know, I was under a terrific obligation to Scott from the very beginning. It doesn't matter how much you know you're going to succeed, you need somebody who has succeeded to tell you so, or, if you don't need it, it certainly helps. And he didn't just tell me, he went way out of his way to help me. All of which you know. I might never have gotten to Scribner and Max if not for Scott. Plus, he was a very appealing personality until that juvenile part of him surfaced, and even that was charming for a while. It was great having him for a pal.

From the beginning, Scott was a little intimidated by me, and I worked to be sure that he was. I am being brutally honest, here. I wanted to have the edge. I hadn't had any college, I hadn't really been in the Army, even to the extent he was. I hadn't yet had a success, and certainly hadn't had the instant success he had had with his first novel. So I played the cards I had. I had been wounded in action, however much of an "industrial accident" it was; I knew boxing, I had a bunch of things I'd learned about the world; I was a competent functioning journalist. I was becoming better self-educated day by day. In short, I was more of a complete man than he was, and Scott was easily impressed by the accomplishments of others. So I used what I had. I didn't want to be the tail on anyone's kite.

But you didn't mind others being the tail to your kite.

Well, that was their choice, wasn't it?

You didn't leave them much other choice, though. They could become a tail, or go their separate ways, like Morley Callaghan, or could contend with you in an endless war of maneuver.

Nothing particular about that. Thoreau said, "No man is ever party to a secure and settled friendship." It's a continual war of position, he said.

You rifled that out of my own store of quotations.

So?

Hemingway the plagiarist, imagine!

Not plagiarist; thief, in this case.

We are both smiling; I don't know if people will realize it. So, you and Scott?

The little you have read should give you what you need. You can describe him by what you've intuited.

What I can't imagine is why This Side of Paradise was even accepted for publication, let alone became a bestseller.

That's because you don't realize the difference in audience between the early 1920s and your time nearly 90 years later. Even in 1960, less than 50 years after its publication, it was a period piece.

I can't imagine it being published post-Hemingway.

Don't you believe it. It is still read and enjoyed by people at its level, and there are plenty of them. But what has changed is—well, so many things.

Your own publishing revolutions not least among them.

Well, that's true but not the whole story. We didn't set you reading Fitzgerald in order to criticize him or his work or his readers, particularly, but for the light it would shed on my work, and I don't mean merely my literary work. I was living a more complete, rounded life, that can only be appreciated by melding the Baker approach, and my works themselves, and the foundations of the Myth, and the huge inaccessible mental world I constructed and continually modified by so much reading and thinking and reacting and conversations with people.

The stuff that was largely inaccessible to Martha Gellhorn.

Invisible in plain sight, that's right, because she was focused only on one piece—the written result—and not on the whole. She is said to be a good reporter, but in my experience she missed most of what she saw unless it matched her categories. She never did understand that mingling with the disreputable elements of the world is the only way to understand what's really going on.

Anyway, Scott sensed all that [Hemingway's greater wholeness], and he was so impressionable, and his external position in the world compared to his own sense of himself left him so insecure, he sort of latched on to me in a real friendship that over the years turned sour because fundamentally we weren't at all the same kind of people. But I owed him! And I did like him! Yet I was so impatient with him, and I got more so as time went on. I knew or thought I knew that all he had to do was choose to not be a certain way—to grow up, in short—but he never could do it. And it didn't help that Zelda and I got so we couldn't stand each other.

When I was struggling through *Tender is the Night* I came up short when suddenly I realized that the rock that sank him may not have been drink or the waste of all that talent but the strain of remaining loyal to that terribly mentally ill person he was married to. For just a couple of pages in the middle of the book he gave a glimpse of it—then he more or less papered it over, perhaps out of a sense of loyalty to her.

I think that's right, although you'll notice that Dick Diver begins with a strong sense of purpose, and Scott never had that. Writing to become a rich best-selling author is not the same thing as writing because you can't not write, and continually trying to be better then you have been, trying to write better than you have done. So in that sense, Scott whoring for the *Saturday Evening Post* was not a betrayal of his talent, it was just Scott continuing to be Scott, where for me it would have been fatal. It didn't actually involve him betraying his ideal, you see; he wanted to write because that was the only way he could think of to become rich enough to marry Zelda, and unfortunately for him, he succeeded. But if he could've done it by selling bonds, he would have done that.

Your parents and Fitzgerald? For that's what I hear you prompting me to ask.

My books were all intensely moral and they portrayed my morality by depicting immoral people. They used the language such people use, and put them into the situations such people get into—and when I say "such people" you must realize (but I'll spell it out) I mean, everybody! But my parents—my mother especially—objected because they couldn't get past the story itself to the meaning of the story. Scott's work, on the other hand, though not particularly moral, they found much less objectionable. Just a matter of packaging and perception.

Not confined to them, either. I think a lot of people don't see through your stories to their intense sense of morality, of right and wrong conduct, or useful and useless people (though that isn't quite the right way to phrase it) and purposeful or undirected behavior.

I was a Boy Scout, in short.

Well, you were! You were still the boy shaped by Theodore Roosevelt, hide it beneath cynicism though you might.

True enough.

Is there a wrap-up point here, or have we been just rambling?

I think you'll find this has helped you get a better sense of me and my life, even if by a carom shot off of Fitzgerald.

≈ 4 ≈

Hemingway's Sons

Saturday, July 3, 2010

Papa, I forgot, in yesterday's session, that it was your anniversary, even though I knew full well it was July 2.

So what? No reason to build a shrine around it.

It's just that I like to associate things. Anyway, what should we talk about?

Gaps? [In the record of Hemingway's life, I knew.]

All right. Let's see. How about talking about you and your sons.

Difficult subject. They suffered, you know. They weren't first except occasionally when I was teaching them something. I couldn't very well include them in my working life, could I? You know as well as I do, writing is done *alone*. And that means that *thinking* and *feeling* and associating ideas and emotions is done alone. If you spend a lot of your life doing that, your family and friends get what's left. That's normal. But if besides that your inner self isn't very easily communicable, by the same law of your nature that makes you a writer, people who have a right to know your inner self may feel deliberately shut out.

But isn't that the universal human condition, to be more or less shut out of each other's inner lives?

Go back to your own boyhood and remember. Did you feel a part of your father's inner world?

No, not really. I thought it was because I wasn't interested in what interested him: racing, horses, farming, whatever else, really. Gambling and enjoying his friends. I sort of took up my mother's impatience and general disapproval, so I didn't ever really get inside the hedges.

Well, condemnation isolates, right?

Sure did. And with you?

I had only their earliest years, and that changes things. I have very fond memories of Mr. Bumby [first-born John], as you and the world know. The other two came when I was older and more burdened, and of course they weren't first. And the presence of nurses and people to take care of them makes life a lot easier for the parents, but it isn't very good for the child. They tend to get shut out of their parents' outer lives, as well as their inner. But I wasn't thinking as much about them as I maybe should have been.

≈ 5 ≈

Individuals as Communities

Monday, July 5, 2010

Yesterday I re-read Adios Hemingway, a novel by Leonardo Padura Fuentes, a Cuban writer. Just a detective novel by a Hemingway aficionado, but one who, reading about the life that you lived, has serious reservations. In fact, he is repelled by The Hemingway Myth, the pointless killing of animals, the meannesses, the out-of-control behavior, even while he recognizes the generosity, the warm-heartedness, the serious craftsman.

You would find it a sobering thing, to see the opinions others hold of you. Even the exaggerated good would be a reproach; the bad opinions would sting as much because they were out of true proportion as because they were true.

You say "the exaggerated good."

Well, if people see only the good sides of you, isn't that a reproach, showing you what you might have been, if you'd had a better handle on your other selves? And if they see only the bad sides—or let's say the unpleasant sides, put it that way—it is still a reproach, showing you how often you fell down, how many things you did that you wish you hadn't. And if they had a truly balanced view of you, do you suppose you'd agree with the balance?

I've always known you were a highly moral man.

I was a *perfectionist* man. Like Jake [Barnes, in *The Sun Also Rises*], I wished I was a better Catholic. But, remember, we've been trying to get you into the habit of seeing yourselves and each other as the communities you are rather than the units you think you are. So if you look at my life you might profitably look at it again as an example of seeing from this new point of view. That is the point of your extensive reading of and now about Hemingway, remember—a public life that can be re-examined with insight gleaned from the inside. So think of "me"—the essence of the person—as the ringleader of so many individual elements. Think of "me" as the guy who got stuck paying the bill for whatever the guys inside broke. Of course, I also got the credit for what they accomplished.

I feel where you're going, but let's spell out some what and why.

Hemingway the *borracho*, for instance. Do you know—can you imagine—the trouble that brooding drunk cost the rest of me? Even the happy drinker brought problems as well as relaxation and exaltation. And what about the ones who married women, seeking something that others didn't want and couldn't stand? How about the violent clashes within me of so many elements that sometimes couldn't stand one another? And above all, what of the resulting fly-off-the-handle temper, and worse the mean pursuit and getting-even and the right-at-any-cost element? I ask you, imagine yourself as ringmaster of so many strong contending elements—and the nervous strain that holding them altogether took, and produced. If you can see me as holding together what our mutual friends

TGU are calling a person-group, a lot of complexities and perplexities in my life *and in your lives* will be cleared up for you.

I've said it before, but once again, you can't really say this in life and be heard; it sounds like special pleading, asking for mercy, or even for what people call "understanding" which often amounts to forgiveness without repentance. Nevertheless even if it can't be easily said, it remains true: I, you, we, everyone—we are not individuals in the way your society assumes that we are, and therefore we don't function in the way we are assumed to function, and therefore most of our lives go unexplained and, as Thoreau said, they *have to* go unexplained, because even the explanations would have to be explained.

Theft again.

Can I help it if you leave stuff around to be stolen?

Smiles on both sides. Okay, and so—?

Well, if you look at my life and you try to see it as reasonably consistent, you get these puzzling anomalies, don't you? How can one person be so controlled and so uncontrolled? So generous and so suspicious and even grasping, so great a friend and so treacherous a friend, so gracious and so snarlingly offensive, so this and so that endlessly? And you say he has "moods" or "streaks" or sides to him that this or that brings out. But these explanations don't explain! They sort of explain *away*. Think of yourself. Who—trying to see you from outside and having a pretty good experience of you—could do more to understand you than to construct a more or less fictional individual who could have done and said what you have done and said, more or less consistently, more or less staying in character? And even that construction is going to show puzzling sides to it. The reason why isn't far to seek. It's because such a construction is a cover story, a papering-over of reality with an image that looks like what could be expected—at the price of not resembling what it really is!

Yes. This is ground we've covered before.

I think you'll find that it isn't enough to say a thing once. You repeat it, and the person hearing it is in "a different space" as you say; in actuality a somewhat different group of themselves is reading it than read it previously. You may have to say it ten times before enough of the person-self's constituent parts have heard the message.

That's an interesting concept.

Just consult your own experience. You read something; it makes an impact. You read it again and it makes a different impact, as if the words were different. It isn't the words, it's the "you" that's different! And if it's a different enough mixture, the words may seem almost brand-new, and you're thunderstruck that you never thought to understand them that way when you read them before. Well, *you*, in that sense, *didn't* read them before. Other parts of you did.

Yes. And what's the specific practical application you're putting this to? For I can feel there is something.

To transform your lives, it is necessary for certain new ways of see-ing (hence, of being) to percolate all the way down. They don't do this right off; it takes repetition in different contexts. So when, a while ago, we spelled out the way of seeing yourselves as a person-groups function-ing within social-groups, we were loosening the hold on you that the socially accepted—assumed—fiction of the individual has on you. Once see yourself differently, and everything can change. But to see yourself differently is not usually the work of one flash of insight, but of the slow working of that insight into this and that corner of your existence.

≈6≈

An Out-of-body Experience

Tuesday, July 13, 2010

Papa, let's talk about your wounding, the out-of-body (or near-death) experience, the aftermath including light, letters, and Agnes, and fear.

All right. Your first unasked question is—how much of the story as understood is accurate. You've read that I carried a man to safety, and you've read that it would have been impossible, and you've read that I started to, then was hit again and fell and was carried in. You have become wary of anything I said anytime, because of my tendency to spin yarns about my life and exploits. In fact it was this very tendency and your dismay about it that helped hook us up a few years ago. So I'll try to stick to the trail of the truth.

I was where I didn't have to be, but was [there] legitimately. That is, I was in the line at Fossalta voluntarily but I wasn't exactly sky-larking. I was doing my job; it's just that I was closer than I needed to be. Anybody who wants to know, knows that in the middle of the night, out of the darkness, a mortar blast from the Austrian side hit where I was. It killed the guy next to me, killed the guy on the other side of me, and wounded me and another. It shredded my legs with shrapnel—mostly my right leg. Fortunately the junk they were filling their shells with was mostly little stuff—at least, that's what hit me—so even though I got more than 200 pieces in me, most of them were pretty small. You can see they'd have to be, or they'd have taken my legs off, or the right one, anyway.

Still, the body isn't built to handle that kind of punishment. I got buried in thrown dirt like the others, but that doesn't mean a couple feet of it, it means a thick spray like you might get sprayed with water by a boat passing you close by. Only it was dirt and mud and stone, not water.

I didn't notice, because I was on my way out. The shock of the impact, of all that inexplicable pain out of nowhere, of the sheer blood-pressure tide internally, blew me right out of my body. I never romanced that aspect of it, notice. Even in the pages I wrote after my African disaster in the 1950s, when I speculated about the soul, I said what had happened but I didn't embellish. That should tell you something.

It tells me you didn't think anybody would believe it.

It tells you more. It also didn't have any place in a boy's dream of glory. Nobody wrote of near-death experiences the way they really happened. It was all hair's-breadth escapes, or valiant death-bed speeches, or silent farewells. *Nobody* wrote about boys getting their souls blown out of their bodies and then getting a second chance at life. So it wasn't anything I romanticized. Every boy had read about wounds, though they were always clean glamorous wounds, not that kind of maiming that a serious wound really is, so boys romanticized that too. Death, wounding—especially with a romantic limp—were all part of daydreams, the way impossible loves and broken hearts were. Near-dying wasn't.

I remembered it. One minute I was in the trench with the others, talking and keeping our heads down, and the next my soul was flying away from my body—and that needs to be said right. It wasn't that my soul was flying away from *me*. I, the soul, was flying away from the shredded body I had been living in. I was going out—in the same way Carl [Jung] experienced it in his experience in 1944, a long quarter century later—and then, just like him so many years later, I was coming back. I wasn't aware of any reason for it. It wasn't like somebody was working on me and brought me back, and I don't remember any consultations my soul had with anybody. It's just, one minute I'm in the trench, and then I'm flying out of my wounded body, and then I'm hesitating, at the end of my long tether, then I get reeled back in and I'm covered with dirt and pushing myself up out of it, and my legs are on *fire* with those red-hot needles all through them, and I see I need to get myself taken care of. There's nobody else around but the one wounded man, and Boy Scout that I am—not literally, it's just an expression—I figure I'll be a hero, so I pick him up and try for the back trenches. My legs are on fire, like I said, but they work, and I am too busy to calculate whether I could walk let alone carry somebody. Well, I didn't carry him very far, and I don't know if I could have anyway, but I got hit with a machine gun bullet in my knee—making a mess of it—and in my foot that I didn't notice. I was down and I would have died there whenever I bled out, if the stretcher-bearers hadn't gotten to us.

You know—you have read—that my tunic was covered with the other man's blood, and they thought it was mine, and if it had been, I'd have been a hopeless case. But I convinced them, in a foreign language, just after I'd been shredded and then hit again, that I wasn't to be left for dead. Try that sometime, for drama, at 18 years old.

Then I had them take my pants off, because I had to know. Wounded-hero stories, and valor in action and all that romantic shit we had been fed all my young life was one thing. Being afraid my legs were ruined and I was going to lose one was a different thing. July 8, 1918 was when I learned what all those lying stories about the glamour of war were worth. But they told me it wasn't as bad as I was afraid of, and they patted me and told me I was going to be okay, and it was better to be in a hospital than in the trenches anyway, and they took me out of the lines, and that was my experience with battle. A hell of an efficient way to learn about

warfare: Go to the front and get wounded right away and still be conva-
lescent when the war ended.

⁓8⁓

Aftermath

*And thereby you got the opportunity to spend months absorbing soldiers'
tales and seeing their attitudes, and storing up knowing, like Jack London
in the bars in the Yukon, filling up with stories or the materials for stories to
bring back to the world.*

Oh yes, and I see the point. I could easily have gone over, spent half
a year doing my job, never getting hurt, and gone home unsatisfied that
I'd ever really gotten to the war. What kind of material for stories would
I have had? Who would have wanted to read stories about ambulance-
driving? Or I could have served for months and gotten hurt near the
end, too late to hear so many stories and absorb so much atmosphere. Or
I could have gotten killed and stayed killed, I guess, and somebody else
would have had to change the way people wrote and read and thought. It
was a good plan, if you want to look at it that way. But I'm afraid I wasn't
quite looking at it like that in July, 1918.

*I'll quote the letter you wrote to your father in 1918 that Baker cites on
page 52.*

["It does give you an awfully satisfactory feeling to be wounded . . .
. Dying is a very simple thing. I've looked at death and really I know. If I
should have died, it would have been . . . quite the easiest thing I ever did .
. . . And how much better to die in all the happy period of undisillusioned
youth, to go out in a blaze of light, than to have your body worn out and
old and illusions shattered."]

*How much of that was true and how much of it was what you thought
you ought to be feeling?*

In a way, I didn't know then. I was still all illusions; you don't get
illusions knocked out of you all at once no matter how hard the knock.
There's always more. It was true enough as far as I knew then.

Meaning, it's what you thought you thought?

More like, it's what I believed, but it didn't say a lot of things I had been learning fast but wasn't ready to say or even admit. It would be years before we turned against the war when we saw what had really gone into it, and what had really come out of it. So you can't expect me to be admitting that I was wondering, even in the middle of the night, if it had been so smart to get into the war when I didn't need to, or go to the trenches and get wounded when I didn't need to do that either. My father hadn't wanted me to go, he knowing the difference between his father's true stories of heroic battles in the Civil War and the chances of having my young life snuffed out unnecessarily—for there were plenty of boys ready and eager to find a way to get into the war. So I couldn't very well say, "the illusions I absorbed weren't true, or anyway were dangerous, and you were smarter about it than I was." And anyway, it wasn't all that clear, inside me, for now that it was over, I was proud. I'd been wounded because I'd been at the front, and by my own choice. I had tried to save a life, and it was witnessed, and I got a medal for it. I'd stood up like a man, in other words. If I hadn't charged enemy positions and saved battles that were being lost and done all sorts of boys-dream stunts, well, my real wounding was worth a lot of imagined stories about how it was going to be. And, I wasn't a boy the way I had been just a few months before.

I have read that for months you had to have a light burning at night or you could not sleep. I have felt I understood, but I'd like you to speak to it.

Your conscious mind is one thing, but as Robert Graves said, it is your solar mind, your daytime mind. At night you're ruled by a different part of you. That's when the moon comes out. Now, these are analogies, but that doesn't make them untrue. I had Jake say, it's awfully easy to be hard-boiled in the daytime, but the night is a different thing. My other mind—or maybe you could think of it as my body's reaction—something knew I had been there in the dark and death came out of the darkness without warning. Yes, we knew we were being shelled, of course, but until you've been hit once, your only experience of shelling is that it's a lot of noise and commotion that often injures and kills other people. It's what I said about bullfighters—the key is how they are after they've once been gored and know they aren't invincible and incapable of being badly hurt or killed. It's only then that you see what they're made of really.

But, the point here is that death and pain and possible mutilation came out of the darkness, and that's what my body knew, and for the rest of my life, but especially for the first couple of years, darkness meant danger and suffering, and who can sleep with the body manning the outposts against imminent attack? So yes, it was a good long time I slept with the lights on, and if I wasn't proud of it, I wasn't ashamed of it either—and actually I was a little proud of it, in a way; it showed that my medals and my wound-stripe and my service itself hadn't come free. But it certainly put an end to thinking that war was glorious.

A good thing to know, even at the price.

There's not much point in volunteering to be wounded in an industrial accident. War can be necessary sometimes and people can do things that make you proud to be part of the same species as them—but in a while you realize that the things that struck you as glorious don't have a lot to do with striking damaging blows, but of enduring, and using skill, and daring. In other words, you're proud of a man for what he could rise to, not to what he could sink to. You see plenty of both

≈ 9 ≈

Wounds

Thursday, July 15, 2010

Papa? Shall we continue with the questions I have accumulated? What about Agnes? How did you feel, all the way down, when you got that Dear John letter? Obviously you were angry and hurt—but was that all? You weren't 20 yet. Was there also some relief mixed in?

[Agnes and Hemingway fell in love when he was her patient. He went home to America in January 1919, thinking that he and she would be married as soon as he could support them, but within months she wrote him, breaking off the engagement, redefining their love affair as kid stuff.]

This is the way biographers and historians go astray, by thinking that their subject may have—then it becomes *must have*—shared their own reactions to things. If you married too young and lived to regret it, it's easy to think that anyone would who did the same, and therefore that anyone who wanted to, and expected to, marry young must have been at least a little relieved at being let off by circumstances. But, you know, being married suits some people in a way that it doesn't suit others.

Then, tell it as you experienced it.

It was pretty much the way I showed it in *A Farewell to Arms* except that I wasn't nearly that experienced—I wasn't experienced at all, in fact—in love any more than in war. I had been badly hurt, which means, badly scared. If there's anything that leaves you more alone than being badly hurt as a young boy, it's being hurt among foreigners, right away, before you've had time to shake your faith in your physical immortality. You've been blown up, out of the blue. You died or started to die, and you came back covered in dirt, knowing you've been hurt but not yet knowing how bad it is, because the pain hasn't started. You've done the best you could to live up to your ideas of how heroes acted, and then you've gotten a couple of machine-gun slugs in you and the heroic-rescue-while-wounded-himself is over too, and you have to be carried in. And then, still being brave and the pain not yet having started to come flooding in, because the nerves haven't recovered yet, you have to tell these people who don't speak English any better than you speak Italian that you are not dead, it isn't your blood, and when you get them to understand that, you have to see your legs, because you know you've been badly hurt and you can't walk now after that machine-gun slug got you, and you don't know if this means that you are going to lose that leg. (I put a little of this into Harry Morgan, "I got a lot of use for that arm," 20 years later, though I don't think anybody made the connection.) So you look at it, and of course it's a mess of blood and the kneecap isn't the way it ought to be but it looks like the bones aren't obviously broken, and maybe it'll be all right, but you don't know what the surgeons are going to be able to do or not do, and you're holding on to your ideas of how a man acts, and you've never been nearly as scared as you are, you trying hard not to show it.

And then the pain starts coming in, a fast tide that keeps mounting and mounting and never ebbs but keeps on building and it gets to be all you can do to hold on. You don't want to cry and beg somebody to make it stop, because the heroes you've read about get hurt and it never says they cried or were terrified of consequences: They took it with a smile or if they couldn't smile they took it with a stiff upper lip, not like you inside. And if you're still a teenage kid, maybe it takes you a while—weeks, I mean, not minutes—to realize that maybe the stories don't tell the truth, either because editors don't pay for the truth or because the writers don't know. And maybe you don't realize right away that it isn't how a man *feels* that counts in such a situation, but how he *acts*. So maybe you disappoint yourself, and you spend the rest of your life coming to grips with the fact that you weren't able to feel the way the real heroes feel when they get hurt. And if you start thinking maybe you aren't what you wanted to be, then you have to *try* harder to be it. You fake it until you make it, like your partner used to say. And this puts you on shaky ground, but it gives you some kind of ground, anyway, to stand on, because otherwise you aren't a wounded hero, you're a scared kid a long way from home who wants his mother, or anyway what a mother should be, what he imagines other people have as all-accepting all-admiring mothers, and where is the place to stand if that's what you are and if that's how people see you are?

And then when they've patched you up and you are through with the worst of it, the pain and the terror and the shame that you'll never admit, at first because you believe those hero stories that you didn't live up to and then because you're embarrassed to have been green enough to believe them in the first place, then you are in this heaven, all these women taking care of you, and you're in a clean, more or less empty hospital, because you're one of its earliest patients, before it's really geared up to go. And by then you're not in the same kind of merciless overwhelming pain, but a sort of intense fluctuating ache that isn't any worse than a headache compared to a fractured skull, say. And you are back in control of yourself, because you've got the pain licked, and they aren't going to take off your leg, and you aren't going to be a cripple even if you did get a slug in the knee. And it looks to other people like you're sort of a hero, because although real soldiers know the difference, other people can't tell, and then it turns out that if you're careful and you learn how to imitate, then the real soldiers can't tell either. So you can at least put on a brave front and you can cautiously put out a few hints, and so you can hold your head up after all. And of course when the Italians use your industrial accident as an excuse to give you a medal, that's good cover too, even if you don't actually see the metal in the flesh.

[Stating that the pain doesn't begin right away contradicts an earlier statement that it did. I don't know which is right. When, editing this, I asked about the contradiction I got that both were true: Pain as overwhelming reality hasn't started, in the sense that mind and body haven't actually begun to process the new sensations, yet it is there waiting. A better way to put it might be that the part of the person-group that is fully experiencing the pain, immediately, it not the part that is in charge of the consciousness at that moment, and so the full awareness is delayed. I don't see that this necessarily reconciles the contradiction, but it is what I got.]

And you are surrounded by women, and some of them are pretty human, and they get grouchy and they see through heroics, however well done, and others aren't interested in you as any particular person rather than as a handsome kid in general, and then there is one who is.

Now, I never talked about this, because by the time I could talk about it, too much water had gone downstream, and I wasn't that kid anymore, and I had walled her out of my emotional life, and so I couldn't really remember what we had been to each other. To put it in terms of person-groups, the parts of me that had fallen in love with Agnes went away, and I never heard from them again. And, to put it in terms of robots, I never was able to trust women in the same way, couldn't trust my feelings in the same way (for I'd been fooled, I told myself after the fact, and therefore it was a failure of observation and interpretation), *had to* be the dominant one so I'd never again get hurt like that, and I was always prepared for them to go. Anybody can see, looking at the way my life played out, that when I needed to separate from Hadley, or Pauline, or Mary, I needed to force *them* to be the ones to make it happen, because that's the only way I was prepared for it by my experiences with Agnes. In other words, from the time I got her letter, I had a robot that made sure that in any circumstances that could be seen as being the same thing all over again, that would be the only way I *could* see it. And whatever I did to make it happen, I couldn't see, because it wasn't the same part of me doing it.

Yes, I do understand. It was a different kind of wounding, and nobody ever treated you for it because nobody ever really understood what it had done to you. Your generation was tougher than mine, and that wasn't always a good thing.

No, it wasn't. But either way has its advantages and disadvantages.

So you and Agnes fell in love and it was right, in the way your war experience wasn't right.

That's it exactly. The hero stories didn't match my experience, but the love stories *did*. I could reach out and encompass her and be encompassed by her, and it was a very pure, very satisfying love that promised to just keep getting better. It didn't matter that she was eight years older than me—and remember, that meant she was very nearly *twice* my age! We were careful not to think about it that way, of course (and I lied to her about how old I was) but I was just 19 and she was 27.

You don't mean twice your age, you mean the difference between you was almost half your age.

That's right. It was a lot, and it meant that when I was 30, she was going to be nearly 40, and I was way too young to see that as possibly a problem, because for one thing I needed somebody to mother me, and for another thing, boys aren't as likely to see things that clearly as girls are, at least not if he's in love, and I was. All I figured was that every year we were together, the difference in age would matter less. But Agnes saw it, and couldn't help seeing it, and finally she was able to see things differently, after she and I were apart long enough.

But you know, you don't ever forget your first love. If it doesn't work out, you either put the whole thing aside as a misinterpretation, or you read it as a betrayal, or you live as if you'd never felt those things, said those things, gave yourself in that complete beautiful unselfish way.

You'll notice that Frederick Henry isn't set out that way. He, unlike me, has had other women. He started out just looking for sex and was surprised when he realized he loved her. He was more experienced than she was, and you might say the experience with her re-educated him, so that he became innocent for the first time. Just as he was experienced as an ambulance driver, and as a long-term veteran, so he was experienced as a lover and as a taster of women. He wasn't me at all. He was me as I like to think I might have been, but he was different enough that I could write of him.

And the marriage and the childbirth and the death weren't the same either, of course.

You'd say they were what my life might have been. I had to kill off Catherine, because I had had to kill off Agnes within me, and so I had to kill that part of that innocent open-hearted boy. And the life we might have had, and the children we might have brought into the world, they went too. What the war hadn't killed, her letter did. In fact, if it hadn't been for the war, we never would have had our romance. And if I hadn't been a starry-eyed kid to begin with, I wouldn't have been within 3,000 miles of the Italian front. If I hadn't still been a starry-eyed kid, I wouldn't have been where I was in harm's way—although I easily might have been later, of course. And if I hadn't been the starry-eyed kid whose world had just been shaken by a hard jolt of reality, maybe I wouldn't have seen her as my ideal other half, my better half as people used to say.

Ernest, this tells me so much about your life!

Yes. You've come a way since all those disillusioned questions three years ago.

It's embarrassing, a little, except they were sincere and troubled, not accusatory or judgmental. (I hope.)

You learned a good while ago, there is no real room for tact when you're communicating mind to mind, and none for lies and evasions, either.

No. When I noted this question about Agnes, page 52 of Baker, I had no idea I'd get so rich an answer. I see now why last time I was moved to skip around my list to three other questions. Thanks for the guidance—you and anyone else involved. You were a hell of a man.

Community

Saturday, July 17, 2010

Papa, you will have seen "Witness" with me, I suppose—or anyway can see what I know about my having seen it. (Which is it?) I wonder if you share my feelings about what it says of our loss of community.

[After other things, here deleted, Hemingway seemed to segue to TGU:]

John Book may be regarded as a representative of modern, western, scientific, materialistic, separated man. Highly separate from his surroundings, very inner-directed, dividing the world between Self and Everything Else. This is a very chilly existence. In the Amish world as portrayed, he experiences another way to be—less modern, less Western in a sense, less scientific in a sense (we'll have to explain this later), less materialistic, less separated. Now bear in mind, isn't an absolute division. It isn't as if he were one pole and they were the opposite pole. They are merely at different places along the polarity. Either-or belongs to John Book's mental world, not yours!

We used the word "scientific" because that came mostly from you and it wasn't absolutely wrong, but with another mind we might have been led to a different comparison. Since we have consented to use it, let us define the one aspect that applies here: the examination of a thing as if it were not connected to the person-group examining it. Book is very much divorced from his surroundings, and the Amish are very much less so. That's all we consent to mean by using that word in this comparison. As we said, not absolute opposite polarities, but different points on a scale.

For John Book to fit into the community and experience its appealing features, he would have to function differently, not merely in abstaining from violence but in truncating his world. This was well brought out even in such innocent scenes as he and she dancing to his car radio's music. You *can't* be both one thing and its seeming opposite. You can be drawn to both, you can balance both for a while, you can to a limited degree alternate from one to another, but ultimately you can't live in two worlds with contradictory ways of seeing things. The strain will tell. She had no exposure to the outside world but him—yet that was almost too much. He had no exposure to their world but her and the life of the community as he observed it as a sort of temporarily tolerated outsider—and it was almost too much.

Sunday, July 18, 2010

Okay. Papa, I don't know if it is worthwhile for us to continue the discussion I thought we might have about community, but I'm available if you wish to do so.

I made my community as I went along. I had no choice, because I didn't fit into the one I left when I left home in 1917 to go to Kansas City. The rest of my life was one of continually assembling and losing floating communities of people with each new change in me—for as you know I was no unchanging commodity. Some years I might not be the same person six months running.

"Hemingway was always willing to give a helping hand to someone on the next rung up," somebody said, and what they meant was that I was always climbing and using people and forgetting the ones I had no further use for. But that is a misreading. What they didn't understand is that I was continually redefining myself by what I did and what I read and what I wrote and what life brought me to. If you look at my life in terms of person-groups as we've been encouraging you to, you could see me as pretty continually altering the pattern, bringing new pieces into play and letting other pieces go dormant or lie fallow. Each changed person-group thus naturally attracts and is attracted by different other threads. Some individuals continually matched these active threads, and many couldn't. Therefore some people like Dorman-Smith were friends for life, and others were friends only for a while, while one certain combination manifested within me, dropping away as other combinations manifested in turn.

If you will look at yourself, and at your friends and family, you will see that some traits are relatively unchanging and others are dynamic, subject to radical revision of form or function according to changes in environment. Similarly, of those you know, some change little over a lifetime and others change once or twice and others change a bewildering number of times, often as a result of no obvious cause.

If your internal community—your active person-group—changes rapidly, you will find that your *effective* environment changes equally rapidly regardless of appearances. That is, if the environment continues to consist of the same people, some will fade in importance to you and some will increase. Thus, the importance to you of this or that individual will change, and the internal composition of any given individual may change along with yours.

I was a magnetic field, exerting a strong pull among my friends and acquaintances, pulling forth from within them parts of their person-groups they maybe never saw otherwise. Naturally this sometimes made them feel like or look like hangers-on, and naturally they would often resent it even as they continued to be fascinated.

You're describing a cause of charisma, it sounds like.

Charisma follows wholeness—and wholeness can never be merely Downstairs connections. It always involves one's Upstairs connections, shining through.

And when one loses that connection, for whatever reason—

Then the charisma goes out the window, and you're living on your reputation, as long as it lasts you.

Thus, Hemingway in the 1950s.

Thus, Hemingway after the plane crashes in Africa. Thus Hemingway with his access dimmed, his enthusiasm wanted, with his friends mostly gone, with his body failing and his confidence: and he with five more bulls to kill.

A portrait of desperation. If the planes hadn't crashed?

No plane crashes meant fewer injuries, but they couldn't bring back Charlie Scribner and Maxwell Perkins, and they couldn't bring back the ten years I lost to politics and warfare, and they couldn't bring back the worlds I had lost (as had everybody else, of course) as the pre-World War I world had been lost to the 20s, and that to the Depression era, and that to the second world war and that to an increasingly alien post-war world that was increasingly insane, with nothing to hope for except not to outlive the world that was being destroyed around us. No plane crashes couldn't reshape dozens of bad decisions and all the losses that come from time and temper and the results of insecurity.

Have we gotten off the topic of community?

No. But you are coming close to seeing why you were given a title for the study of me as "Hemingway: A Man Alone." I was alone as I made my way, I was alone even as I was surrounded by friends, I was alone in any environment I successively created, I was alone in my work, in my thought, in my reading—in everything but my play, which ought to shed some light on my play, and even there, as I found out, in the end you are alone. But as Harry Morgan found out, "a man alone doesn't have any fucking chance."

So the alternative was—?

Not every situation has an alternative, at least not necessarily a good one. What was I to do? Being what I was, I had no community I fitted into. When I hit my stride in the 20s in Paris I had one, for a short while, but it was destroyed around me by an influx of tourists and by the natural attrition of the working life of artists. In Key West I found a different sort of community that I enjoyed until The Hemingway Myth interfered too much and then divorce with Pauline made staying there impossible. And after that I had *querencia* in Cuba, and I couldn't even play that one out because politics made it impossible. [In bullfighting, *querencia* referrers to the bull choosing a place where he will fight to the last.]

So your community was a long-distance community stitched together by letters.

As yours is stitched by phone calls and Internet. But this is a very different thing from what your grandmother experienced.

Yes it is. My father's mother lived from 1889 to 1974, almost entirely in the same town, in the same house, surrounded by the same neighboring families, part of a real, physical community that held the same values and more or less saw things the same way. She was a farmer's wife among a farm-

ing community, and she didn't have any wish to be anything different. She died before her society moved irretrievably away. Or maybe she would have been able to adjust, I don't know.

The contrast between her life and yours should tell you something about the contrast between the human community as it was and as it is, and as it is becoming. The comparison isn't as simple as any passing mood might make it seem. It isn't a straight downhill or uphill progression, and of course some societies are moving in one direction while others are moving in the other. But what you *can* say is that we are breaking into new ground. This particular movement is being driven by machinery—at least that's the "how" of it, as you would say. The "why" of it is that it is time, and if it weren't driven one way it would be driven another way, but in the same direction. [That is, if it weren't driven by one thing, it would be driven in the same direction by another thing.]

I imagine that this is clearer to me than it would be to our readers. So I'll throw in a word, here. I have had the sense that humans are becoming something more complicated, more connected Upstairs while still walking around living our lives Downstairs. This is a big change, if true. It isn't that simple, probably—few things are—but the outline is probably true enough. Hence these conversations, perhaps.

Hence these conversations, and that's why you were fashioned, or fashioned yourself, or helped fashion yourself with input; we don't care how you think of it. You were equally drawn to history and to psychic potential. This enabled you to see the *perspective* of the change and see the *potential* of the change. You know what it means and what it promises. Hence, you become a translator.

And so—?

And so the question of what you call virtual community in your lives; the impermanence taken for granted; the clearer and clearer sense of lives being *pushed*, being *directed*; the urge toward realization *now* of the potential that otherwise might be considered a potential for Someday. And so one use of my life's story, for I as a man alone did show some aspects of things that will be clearer all these decades later, and in a context that centers not on my writing but on what my writing reflected. Think of it as a recycling project. Turning Papa back into a man; turning the success-machine back into meaning. Turning one life into an example that may help reorient many lives. And this is as good a time to end this as any. On to another topic next time, as may suggest itself.

≈ 11 ≈

Hemingway and His Father

Monday, July 19, 2010

All right, let's talk about your relationship to your father. This is in my mind since reading in Reynolds last night.

From my perspective now, the subject looks a lot different.

Probably true for everybody.

I loved my father, and I criticized him so severely—sound familiar at all? And I stuck up for him in my own mind, and wanted to protect him and wanted to get him to change, and felt betrayed that he wouldn't change, and felt personally attacked not just by him but by his fatherhood when he seconded my mother's judgments. It is all tangled up, and it will take a bit to untangle.

My father, you have read, was a great companion for a little boy. He and his son—I was the only son at that point—went fishing and did the things that a father and son could enjoy together in those days if the father loved the outdoors, and the outdoors were available, and the father could take the time, as mine could. Why do you suppose I became an expert trout fisherman before I even went to the war? Because it was a love I picked up from dad, and continued after he and I were living in different worlds.

You have read how he started moving away from the family when I was about 12. To put it plainly, his life became less and less bearable to him, and of course the family was a large part of his life. At the time I didn't understand even what our society knew about what is called mental illness, and anyway in Oak Park mental illness wasn't allowed to exist, it would lower the tone. So, he was "nervous," and it came out in fits of what you might call modulated screaming. You can scream without ever raising your voice. You can reject everything and everybody around you by seeing them as not measuring up to some code you drew up. And you could get to the point that God himself couldn't follow your rules to your satisfaction. In fact, you had to get to that point, because what you needed, and didn't know you needed, was for nothing to measure up; it explained your feelings of rage and loneliness.

He didn't get there in any one leap. He fought it, and sometimes gained ground and sometimes lost ground, but it was always there, the struggle. And because he was struggling with it night and day, it was exhausting; had to be, but it was invisible to us except when it showed as temper or unreasonable expectation.

When he lost his joy in the world itself may have been when he lost the battle, because that meant he had nothing to help him refill the wells. But it may be that losing the joy of nature was the *effect* and not the cause. I don't know.

We live surrounded by our own mental lives, and we don't primarily see what's going on around us even with those we are closest to. It's natural. Who could give somebody else 24-hours-a-day attention, and even if they did, who could know them from inside? So, most of what goes on around us touches us at the periphery, not at the center. Our family's struggles surprise us, even if we're in the middle of them.

My father must have loved my mother. At the same time, he had to live with her, and a person who does have strong feelings and desires and expectations can be exhausting to live with, if yours aren't as strong. And if yours *are* as strong, you're liable to get into a long tug-of-war, affection fighting alongside egotism, and somebody is going to win and somebody is going to lose, and there isn't likely to be a rematch.

When you win that tug-of-war, you're happy you won, but maybe you think less of the one who lost. And of course it may not be all that clear even to the ones involved. For one thing, it may play out over years. For another, circumstances may blur the result. But over time it becomes clear enough.

And if you've lost, you may despise yourself for being weaker-willed, and may resent the other for that continuous unspoken *pressure* all the time. But maybe you still love her, or him, depending, and that complicates the resentments and the self-criticism. And maybe you aren't all that self-aware, so this analysis would have surprised you. Maybe you're taking it all out on everybody around you in bitchiness, and neither you nor they know why.

If you look at it that way, the story of my father's life after a certain point in his marriage is the story of his living with a continuous unbearable pressure that could find occasional release to some degree, but ultimately just kept getting worse. As the pressure got worse, it acted the way continual pain will, it wore him down. As it wore him down, it pulled down his mental ability, so that he had a harder and harder time seeing things straight. Therefore over time he blamed more and more external things, and had a greater and greater need to blame them.

Look, don't think I don't know that I'm painting something of a self-portrait here, except for the cause, which is different in my case. But I'm talking about my father, and what I saw and didn't understand as a child and didn't interpret correctly as a young man and *couldn't* understand as an older man, for by then the pattern had gotten hold of me.

What I saw was a man browbeaten by his wife who nonetheless inexplicably and unforgivably took her side against us—me and my sisters and then Leicester too. That is what I *saw*, and what I *knew*, and when he killed himself in 1928 when I was not yet 30, I could only read it as: She killed him. And, along with that: She'll kill me too if I don't get the whip hand. You understand, I'm not now saying that how I understood it then was right; I'm saying, that's how I saw it. There's a difference.

I'm not entirely wrong in that, either, it's just that it wasn't as simple as I saw it. The pressure of living with her and her ancestors and her standards and her certainties and her strong will *did* wear him down. The fact that he loved her nonetheless did provide confusing crosscurrents. His mental illness probably *did* stem from that situation. In a different situation perhaps he would have lived a happier life. In fact, I'm sure of it. But it wasn't a situation with a villain, it was a tragedy of good intentions and two people who really couldn't live together happily because they couldn't harmonize. Surrender isn't harmonizing.

Tragedy is right.

My *emotional* indictment of my mother is accurate enough. But the *facts* are mostly wrong or distorted or out of context—and now I can see why, of course. Just like my father, I was seizing on what seemed like logical factual reasons to support what was an emotional certainty and, like him, and for the same reason, I couldn't admit what I was doing because I couldn't *see* what I was doing. An obsession becomes an obsession because many strands of emotional logic keep calling you to something that can't be satisfied. So you lay out all the reasons why you feel a certain way, to put it to rest. But it doesn't! [i.e., laying them out doesn't put it to rest.] You feel just as strongly, maybe even more strongly. So you lay out all the facts again, trying to make the urgency go away. But it won't, and if somebody reasons with you or contradicts you, it's like you're being prodded with a stick. (And why would they want to do that to you? They must have it in for you, for some reason.) And if they go along with you, you know they're pretending to agree to something they don't really believe, so you despise them and distrust them, both, a little, even while in another part of your mind you're gratified that they see it as you do. If there is a way out of this kind of a box, I never found it.

Lincoln practiced benevolence, I think. He never purposely planted a thorn in another man's bosom, he said once.

But then maybe it turns inwards. I don't know. Once you develop that way of seeing the world, it's hard to get out of.

≈ 12 ≈

Mr. Lincoln's Way

But you know, I don't think he did see it that way. Well, maybe we can ask him. And maybe for all I know he has been knocking on the door. Mr. Lincoln? [I had made Mr. Lincoln's acquaintance four years earlier.]

[AL] If we go brooding over the little slights and wrongs that we feel we have suffered, we're likely to magnify their effects—and to what purpose? Maybe we imagined a slight where none was intended, or maybe the wrong was truly intended but wasn't mainly aimed at us but was a collateral effect of someone's selfish desire to have something at your expense. What of it? I never found it worthwhile to pay a lot of attention to the things my enemies did to me or said about me. It made a much more pleasing picture to remember all the kindnesses I had received, from so many people. And after all, it takes no more effort to determine to be cheerful than to allow ourselves to be miserable. I often said, most people are about as happy as they set their minds to be. I had troubles enough, and deep sorrows. Is there anyone on earth who doesn't have them, or hasn't had them, or can guarantee to himself that he won't have them? But should your troubles overwhelm your cheerfulness, you are just that much farther behind. It seems to me sheer folly to conspire with your enemies to overwhelm yourself.

It seems to me that both of you had to deal with what we call mental illness. (I know the guys don't believe in the existence of mental illness but I haven't been able to get what they see in its place.) I don't have any way of knowing which of you had more to deal with. I'd be interested in your assessment.

[EH] I can hear you clearly enough: Too much liquor made my problems worse. But—did it? The concussions didn't help.

[AL] I believe that I inherited my melancholy from my father. Nothing in my life's circumstances was noticeably different from those around me. If I was poor and many of them were not, when is the earth ever free of rich and poor? And that is the only form of deprivation I can see in what was a singularly happy life. The melancholy was not the natural effect of circumstance, but something I was born with, like my wit and my love of fun. Maybe they're the same thing, melancholy and love of fun to overcome it. Certainly they drove together in my life.

I seem to hear you say, it wasn't circumstance but inherited predisposition that drove you to melancholy, and to the necessity of overcoming melancholy. Whereas, Ernest, I seem to hear you saying, if I was melancholy, there were reasons enough for it.

[EH] Two different ways of looking at things. I get it. But my father still had to live with my mother. He still had to live with the feelings that raised in him. It wasn't just that he was prone to melancholy, or mental illness, or "nervousness." He had been pushed by his life.

Don't you believe it.

Welcome, Dr. Jung.

[CGJ] You can always find good reasons for anything that happens, reasons that excuse you from responsibility. It was circumstance! It was fate! It was something external. This is true only from a point of view that thinks that what happens to us happens *to* us, instead of *with* us. In fact, though, our lives are much more mysterious than that, more patterned, more interconnected not only with space and time but with what we used to call the eternal and spiritual.

Dr. Hemingway came into the world with a certain broad range of possibilities, and honed and refined (and therefore narrowed) them as he went along. This is how we live. His *internal* choices helped determine what his *external* challenges would be. It isn't merely a matter of his internal choices determining how he would cope with external events. No, although it goes against common sense, nonetheless I saw it continually in half a century of practice, what he made himself determined what would happen to him.

You must not make that true description of the process of life into something simple-minded. He did not *consciously* decide what would come to him. Nonetheless what we choose determines what can or cannot come to us. There is a time delay in physical reality, and there is a perception of separation both by space and by time. Nonetheless, it is so. Had Dr. Hemingway consciously adopted Lincoln's determined cheerfulness, and his benevolence and his determination not to blame his troubles on others, he might have been able to bear the troubles of his own life as well as Lincoln bore his. It would have been good work, and would have lightened his own load. However, remember that we cannot judge truly. No one knows another's life as the person himself does, and no one knows his own life as his total self does. Judgment is tentative and for the sake of understanding. Within these limits it may be helpful. Beyond them it is limiting and destructive.

My God, what a fortunate life I lead! Hemingway, Lincoln, and Jung!

And any others you vibrate with. Life is much richer than people commonly suppose.

Well, it's 7 a.m., which means that somehow I've been doing this for an hour and three quarters, minus a few minutes to make coffee. A great joy, my friends. Ernest, maybe we can come back to your parents and you tomorrow.

If not tomorrow, there's always some other day.

Thanks to you all.

≈ 13 ≈

Sex

(12:40 p.m.) Ernest, I have some time if this is a good time to pursue the question of your parents.

The "wrong time" wouldn't ever be on our end. You don't get a busy signal or an answering machine except from your end.

All right. So, about that marriage.

It isn't the marriage per se that we're interested in, but the effects on the children of the marriage, of the continuing discord and the results of that discord on my parents. It is true that I blamed it all on my mother, and it is true enough that between her and Agnes I developed a deep distrust of women, and an expectation that women brought trouble. At the same time, I needed what women carry with them—and I don't mean sex. I still needed nurturing, and the worse I got, the more I needed it. And the more I needed it and didn't get it, the worse I got. And the more I looked in the wrong place, in the wrong way, the more lost and desperate I became, and then at some point I gave up, decided sex and all that was just a cheat, and that what I really wanted and needed didn't exist, or didn't exist for long, or didn't exist if you looked behind the illusion.

Shall I act as interpreter, in case what is clear to me is not clear to others?

Feel free. It's your job; after all, *you* are the one in the physical.

For the moment. All right, I am hearing you say that you needed mothering and didn't get it, or didn't get enough of it. So it was a natural progression to seek it in a combination of sexual activity and emotional nurturance from older women. But the more you confused sex with nurturance, the less satisfactory the result.

True enough. Why don't you sketch out your centaur theory?

To put it briefly, we function in two ways. Physically we are male or female individuals, with our mental, emotional, physical particularities. (I don't use the word peculiarities here because it will suggest abnormality, which is not my intent.) But on another level we might be looked at as representatives in the flesh of the masculine or feminine gods or goddesses. That is, we carry that divine energy and it is carried sort of regardless of our personalities. A woman who feels herself valued (or, less commonly, undervalued) because of her sexual attractiveness may feel unseen, because her humanness is getting lost amid her divine aspect. It's a way of seeing that could be easily mocked, but I think there is something to it.

Well, if I'm attracted to four women to the point of marrying them, and lots of others to the point of sharing sexual relations with them, it ought to be clear that I was seeking something, and it is easy enough to say, "sure, you were looking for sex!" But if I was seeking it, and finding it, why would I need to seek it farther? That answer is too simple. Not that *I* necessarily saw that it was too simple! Just, now I see it is.

What is sex, anyway? Physical pleasure, but if you have sex with someone you don't care for, the aftertaste is plenty bitter. And if you have sex with someone you *do* care for, but it doesn't give you that something you need but can't define, it leaves you unsatisfied, and perhaps inclined to search elsewhere. And if, occasionally, you do get something of what you need, sex doesn't have to have anything to do with it one way or another—Gertrude Stein, for example.

And I'm hearing to ask you about homosexual or lesbian crosscurrents in this context. Maybe it's the mention of Gertrude Stein.

That's something else I didn't understand. I saw it all around, of course, and I fought against the hypocrisy that didn't let us write about it. But it is only now that I see it without what you would call the political overtones—the thing itself, in other words, not the thing as a political movement or a social fad. Everybody says Hemingway was so vehement about queers, he must have had his doubts about himself, and spent his energy over-compensating. It doesn't seem to occur to them that in this like other things I reported what I saw, and did it not from some neutral place but from a very definite moral stance. In fact, let's say a few words about that.

To *describe* a thing is not necessarily to *approve of* it. Anybody really looking at my work—my stories particularly, because it's more compressed—*must* see that I am writing from a particular point of view. You may have to dig for it—I wasn't painting billboards!—but it is clearly there. Did any of the professors ever find a place where I showed that I *approved of* or *encouraged* homosexuality? Do they think I approved of the senseless cruelty or war that I also reported? I wish they'd open their minds and use their heads and lay off the psychoanalysis. My attitude toward homosexuals and lesbians was often tolerant as long as they weren't behaving in a political sort of way, weren't rubbing people's noses in it for the sake of feeling superior. Now you know—or would have known if you'd been in Paris in the 20s—that sometimes they do. Why shouldn't I attack them for doing it in the same way I attacked Mike or Brent [characters in *The Sun Also Rises*] for being worthless sponges? I wrote about what I saw, and although in my day we didn't have the phrase "politically correct" we had a lot of people who tried to enforce it. They didn't enforce it on me, provided I could find an outlet that would pay me. [Meaning, provided he could find a magazine that would touch the topic. I add this just in case it isn't clear to everybody.]

We've hardly touched on the topics we could pursue, and it has been less than an hour, but I'm going to have to fold my tent for the moment. Thanks.

≈14≈

Three Aims

Tuesday, July 20, 2010

I'm not quite sure of how to proceed. Ernest?

Remember, in all this we are proceeding along more than one track. There is the correction of The Hemingway Myth for the sake of providing a model of completeness that the world misunderstood—not for the sake of doing me justice, although there is that, so much as for the sake of providing the model. The model is *needed!* And to correct the myth, it is necessary to understand; therefore it can't be a whitewash job, and it can't be superficial. But it isn't a matter of research for new facts—mostly it is a matter of interpreting what is known. That's one strand.

A second is to provide a model of possibilities, showing how communication proceeds and showing what can be done, and how easily. This could be a great encouragement to people. And just as correcting the myth can't be a whitewash if it is to do any good, so explaining the process can't overlook the difficulties and pitfalls, which involves your giving the process a certain amount of thought so as to be useful.

Then, most important of the three but depending on the other two, this will provide people with a new model of the physical/non-physical interaction, hence the true function of 3-D existence, and by implication we will show that the non-physical exists—that is, that the afterlife is not only not a fantasy but is a necessary part of life, without which life wouldn't have meaning or make any sense. And it will do so in a way that shows that religious belief was tapping into the same reality.

≈ 15 ≈

Seeking Wildness

Okay, what about you "shooting up the town" that summer of 1919 when you and your friends were up at the lake region in Michigan. The way you would tell the story later in life, you and your friends "shot up the town" for fun. In reality, apparently you all started to shoot out streetlights as you drove through the town in the middle of the night, and after five or six of them, realized that this might not be such a great idea, and got out of town, lying your way out of it when a timid cop questioned the car full of rough-looking kids that you were. Reading about that in Reynolds, it struck me that later in life it was important for you to think of yourself as having been tough and a little bit wild. It implies that the real life you had experienced was too tame for you, and you wanted to redefine it as wilder, tougher, more reckless, closer to the edge. Accurate? And if so, what's the underlying meaning of it?

Accurate and perceptive, and this is what you bring to this, linked to my mind, for most people couldn't see beyond the bragging. Yes, that's exactly it. Within myself, I thought my life was tame, and I always wanted it to be wilder, more dangerous, and since it wasn't, I was pushed in two directions, or I mean it expressed in two ways. One, I re-invented. I *was* a writer of fiction, after all—which means an imaginative re-fashioner of ideas to create an illusion that would reflect truth more clearly when done right, and would at any rate create and reflect a different world whether true or not. Two, I moved to engage in activities that would tap me into that wilder, freer, more vital existence—warfare, hunting, deep-sea fishing, competition of any kind.

Both directions met limits, and both imposed penalties. You can't invent and invent and invent about your life without at some point risking that you will lose touch with what really happened, the material you're inventing out of. If you do, you get captured in a feedback loop, you'd call it. You lie, or you invent, or you tell tall tales—they're the same thing, sometimes, or near enough—and then you start to believe those stories because you don't do the rigorous self-examination that would be needed to get back to the bedrock fact, and increasingly you don't do it not merely because the story is a better story but because you can scarcely bear the truth. If you develop a bias toward seeing your life a certain way, and the emotional need strong enough, after a while it will require more strength of mind and active consciousness to move out of the accustomed mental routine channels than you can give it. Something extraordinary can do it—someone you love, holding you to the truth, or some *thing* you love doing the same thing—a higher loyalty in some way or other, overriding your self-preservation, in a way.

You can see how this started to play out, in ways innocuous and not so innocuous, as I began to lose the physical energy needed to keep my consciousness honed. Even before shock treatments, I wasn't exactly losing my memory, I was losing access to the channels that would've given me access to them, because the accustomed channels had been so much deepened by years of use. So, truly, in effect I no longer remembered or could remember my life as it was, but as I had preferred to reinvent it after the fact. And of course losing access to the real memory is deadly serious to a writer, and to a person. Once you lose touch with the original, you have only the invented, and the invented has a bias that will self-reinforce as you go along. So that by the 50th repetition, all your emotional conclusions (call them that; I don't know how else to put it) are exaggerated, systematically warped.

And if you've spent your life brooding over wrongs, or worrying about being stabbed in the back by malice or neglect, or haunted by feelings of guilt and sin that you tried to keep repressed, they're all going to be exaggerated into false guidelines about how life works and how far you can trust people and what hidden dangers are lurking on every side, and when you aren't actively or even frantically denying them, these feelings are going to overwhelm you, and maybe you wind up in paranoia, unable to weigh fears or suspicions because the life-experience that would have provided you with a corrective has been overlaid by an increasingly falsified narrative that only increases those story-lines.

Like that film I saw about the guy who lost the ability to form short-term memories. He wound up relying on his own moment-to-moment notes, and when he deliberately falsified one, he later acted on it as truth.

Yes. It is a good description of the process, and helps you understand what I just said.

Just as reinterpreting memories can get you into a wilderness of false evidence, so trying to live an ever-wilder life has its disadvantages, especially if your guides to conduct are unreliable. It can get you wounded without warning or glory or meaning before you're 19. It can get you into politics in ways that don't serve you or what you believe in. It can get you somewhat off your path, so you wind up in your fifties hunting with a spear because you're searching for a more primitive part of yourself.

≈17≈

Grounding Abstractions

Friday, July 23, 2010

All right. So—"Papa"—do you have anything you'd like to say about your time with the Kansas City Star during World War I before you went overseas, or with the Montréal Star after you return?

Your more careful reading has showed you my life less from hindsight and more from how it looked to me going forward—or anyway it is showing you how *I* looked, going forward.

Yes indeed. I have a picture of you, it occurs to me, much like my cousin Charlie—so much enthusiasm and drive and intensity; so magnetic a personality.

Did the abstract not get concrete, right all at once, just then?

It did! It really did. I had read of how you were, and I had an idea of it, but suddenly connecting it to something I'd seen popped it out for me.

What you just experienced is a sudden grounding of an abstraction. But I don't like either of those two words very much. "Grounding" seems like "bringing something down to earth" and is accurate in one sense but is not accurate if it is taken to mean "deflating the overblown" or "making concrete something that was vacuous." And "abstraction"—well, I never trusted abstractions, even though we deal in them continually. Let's say, instead, that you just connected a component so that the juice flowed through it. That's what grounding means, in this case. And it wasn't an abstraction, that idea of me that you had had, but a visualization, even an idealization.

When you connect a visualization or ideal image to a functioning current, it becomes a part of the flow—part of the electrical circuit—and is able to contribute on a moment-to-moment basis, rather than sitting separate and unconnected except when specifically addressed. When you suggested to your friend Michael that he address various "past lives" he knew of, he experienced a sudden coming-alive of those parts within him. What had been masks on a wall became living intelligences interacting with him. That was the same process.

Yes, I can see that. And all my boyhood reading, of Lincoln, say—

You were much too young and too inexperienced to truly understand what you were reading except as generalized background about a slice of American history from 1809—or from his boyhood, really, or young manhood—to 1865. Even the background wasn't in any connected circuit. The Civil War was as much a disconnected series of set-piece incidents as anything else. It was not the *process*, the *connection* that you gradually learned it to be. It couldn't easily be otherwise—you have to learn the alphabet before you can spell; grammar before you can write.

So this was giving you the basics, and at a very young age. There would be time enough to retrace and retrace your steps, adding understanding as your life provided you with experience.

Hmm. In this as in so many things, I've had to do it backwards from the way other people do things, I see.

There is undoubtedly a Complaints desk somewhere.

I'm smiling too. But it's striking. It's like, there is a flow, a circuit, and there are components. And sometimes we build (or receive) another component and other times we plug another component into the circuit.

It's just a non-inflated way of restating what you've heard often enough before: Your job in life is to keep connecting the dots so that all parts of yourself productively interact. Work on this analogy; develop it a little. It has promise.

Seems to. I will. All right. You and newspapering.

Don't forget, you have another advantage that somehow has not occurred to you: Your very first job out of college was as a newspaper reporter.

Which gives me a faint echo of your early life. I hadn't thought of it, it's true.

Also an echo of your cousin Charlie's life. Your journalist cousin Charlie that you found so attractive.

Is this why you nudged me—if it was you, as I am beginning to suspect, though until now I'd assumed it was my own idea—to give Angelo's editor [in my novel Babe in the Woods] Charlie's name and part of his personality?

Whether you thought of it or were nudged—how would you be able to tell, and what difference would it make? You're always being nudged by a million things in life, mostly without your knowing. That's just how life is. Don't worry about it.

Well, for the sake of the studio audience, so to speak—

I had a cousin named Charlie Reilly. He was seven years older than me, and I admired him and found him enormously attractive as an individual. He was outgoing, knowledgeable about the world, self-confident, enormously cheerful and attractive to people. He died in an accident at age 39.

But you see that having a glimpse into his life, and yourself having had two experiences of journalism, you have an introduction to my life that is both an intuitive and a logical connection. The one gives you a picture, the second gives you flow.

There is a tremendous lot of information packed into that insight. It's going to take some time to unpack it.

Do it with writing rather than trying to do it in your head. You can't *fix* it, like an artist fixing a charcoal sketch, without setting it out somehow. If you don't do that, it just swirls around in your head. Analogy, remember.

So—you on the two papers—

Suddenly you can see that it wasn't Ernest Hemingway acting as a young man, but young Ernie, feeling his way into life, the way your cousin did. Both ways of seeing it are true enough, actually, but biographers are prone to reading a man's life backwards.

Reynolds doesn't.

Well, he's always drawing connections forward, and that is valuable, but only if the reader remembers that the subject of the biography didn't know all that. The *subject* of a biography doesn't know the barest elements of his story. How could he? Who he marries, what kids he has, how he lives, where and when he dies—nobody knows that ahead of time, but the biographer knows before he begins to write, and if he isn't careful he'll write a portrait instead of talking to the person.

But that's all they think possible.

Well, that's what they *think*, but that isn't really what happens or even how they experience it. It's just that when they come to set it all down, it comes out within the format that says, "he lived, but he's dead now," instead of "he lived and here's how it was for him," and certainly not "here's what he thinks now, looking backward."

They couldn't very well do that and keep their respectability.

Not yet, no. But if they *knew* more than they *admitted*, and incorporated it in some way—as Carl Jung often had to do—they could make a more alive portrait. Sandberg did it. So did Reynolds, in fact. But it doesn't always come through—like most things in life it depends on the person, come to think of it. The reader determines what is in the book he reads.

We've done our usual 70 minutes, but I'd still like to hear about you and the newspapers.

Plenty of time for that. Today's session wasn't a diversion.

No! And it's funny that I have to keep remembering, I could contact this or that person.

You have to complete the circuit before it will become an automatic process for you. Until then, you'll need reminding on a case-by-case basis.

Hmmm. One more example of how we function all disconnected.

That's one way to look at it. Another is to say, it's an example of how you can *learn to* function connected, and what's in it for you.

≈17≈

The Young Reporter

Saturday, July 24, 2010

Maybe too early to be doing this, but I seem to be awake. So, Ernest, anything you'd care to say about life on the newspapers?

It was a fast education, something I could learn to do, writing rules I could absorb immediately. A once in a lifetime opportunity for a kid, and if I'd stayed with the K.C. *Star* instead of going off to war, maybe I'd have kept my job when all the vets came home, and maybe I'd have been afraid to lose it, and maybe that would have been the end of my career as writer.

Hard to imagine, now—but I know what it can be like, being afraid to lose a job even when you don't want it.

Let my life show you what it is like to believe too strongly in certain illusions. We got into World War I for economic reasons, more than anything else, but we went in with nearly everybody thinking it was for reasons of honor and right, and *in a way* that wasn't so far wrong. But our participation was based on so many lies that any underpinning of truth was ultimately discredited and disbelieved in. So people who got wounded, or whose friends or family members got killed, had reason to believe it had all been for nothing.

I get the sense that you really don't want to talk about the newspaper year. Why is that?

Maybe there's nothing to say that will contribute to the purpose of redirecting The Hemingway Myth, and maybe it isn't important for any reason. Not everything you will ask will meet response.

It's just that I have this image of you now, since yesterday's comparison with my cousin Charlie, and I can see you (metaphorically), I can vividly feel your presence, all eagerness and aliveness, anxious to ride to the next fire or patrol with the cops or get in on the next bit of gossip. It's like your job isn't a job at all, but a great amusement park, and a ticket to the show, and your entry into the grown-up world and your escape from the safe and boring and cloistered world you had grown up in.

See? You don't need me at all. What can I add to that? That's it exactly.

Well, the Montréal Weekly Star, then, where you'd haunted your way onto the staff as a stringer at space rates.

Not exactly a stringer. More like a freelance feature writer, but tied to the one organization. It was the post-war [sic], it was my only chance and I was lucky to have it and I knew it. It was still a license to snoop into people's lives, and a way to practice my trade of writing and observing, and even though I was a decorated veteran, it was still an entry into the grown-up world. I was still younger than you when you got out of college.

⁓18⁓

Pitfalls for Biographers

Monday, July 26, 2010

I am blank this morning, so I hope somebody is primed to go. Who's up? How about you, Papa?

Sure. Your queued-up questions refer to my relations with my parents.

Yes because (a) I don't think your biographers quite have it and (b) I wonder about how much you have reconsidered, after the fact. I guess we have talked about your having lost the father you had had, and your being unable to accept the man he had become, but what about you and your mother, really. Or, no, what about the layer upon layer of different reactions to them within you? For I sense that you were more than one person to them, and you perplexed yourself, perhaps, as you experienced the crosscurrents.

I suppose you'll wind up bringing me to the defense of biographers, if this goes on long enough! I can see the limits of what they can do, and I can see that it is worth doing, if they had more resources. It isn't enough to have the external evidence, because that can become a matter of picking and choosing what will support a simple—perhaps simplistic—view of a complicated subject. And it isn't enough to have the evidence and have some ideas about psychology and then practice what you call psychiatry without a license. And neither is it enough to accumulate many points of view—external evidence, all of it—and sort of average it out. And this is more or less what they have to work with, along with intuition and insight and prejudice.

Oh, I hear you. What they need besides several excellent biographies, and memoirs centering on other people that mention you, is direct contact to meld the external and internal evidence.

They do. They don't realize it, but that's exactly what they need *and can have*, but in the present state of things, even if they use the direct-contact approach, they dare not admit it. It would be fatal to their respectability. It would be as disgraceful as informing their work by using theology, or by astrology, or by any other discipline or art that is outside the range of narrowly defined "intellectual" pursuits.

My biographers are in a quandary, always, because they know they can't count on me to serve up facts instead of tall tale, or grudge, or self-serving myth, or faulty memory, or just lies. Partly this is because so much of my past was painful for me to admit, partly because I was making up a story that *I* found plausible to explain otherwise inexplicable actions and reactions of mine. Partly, too, there was resentment of people prying into my own business, the inner springs of my emotional life. And of course, having started off reinventing myself in order to move from being a near-sighted kid from a well-to-do town into a sophisticated man of the world, how could I go back and rewrite the story as it had really been— particularly since so much of the story as it had been *was not accessible to me*? The boy who had been was not the young man who succeeded him, and was that much farther away from the man—or men, rather—who came after that.

This is closely tied in to your continual growth, isn't it? You kept swapping out bits of your person-group, and they didn't connect all that well.

Now, as long as you can avoid the temptation to look at this as a psychological malady, I think we can explain it using the new concepts you've been given.

I rather think I can explain it already. Your person-group was only loosely linked, with your will, or your central drive, or the underlying part of your over-all being that was directing your life as a whole, the only part of you that provide continuity.

You could put it that way. My life was *growth*, and it was the movement from where I started, *away*. I mean, it wasn't exactly aimed toward a final goal. It isn't like I was born intending to have to blow my head off. But it *embodied* the myth of the boy who made himself into something different, using will and steady purpose and endurance. But *what* he made himself into was less a part of the fabric than the inborn need to change, to grow, to move.

I hear Martin Eden, though I'm not sure that's a good comparison.

Jack London was very much aware of the external obstacles that held people down. Perhaps he wasn't all that aware of why he wrote that story that way, because of course the part of him that was setting it down—taking dictation, in a way—didn't know he was going to kill himself, didn't know that money can be a trap if there is too much of it, just as much as if there isn't enough. You might talk to him sometime. You'll find him to be quite a different kind of voice than you've met so far.

Well, maybe later. I'm interested in Papa Hemingway, at the moment.

I haven't lost sight of your question. The point is this. If you have a person-group that has external goals that aren't necessarily the ones that are obvious to the conscious personality, many of his actions are as puzzling to him as to anybody else. You've experienced it. Maybe everybody has. People up to now have been mostly aware of the disparity in perception when they get into trouble, and so this fact of life has been associated with pathology, what they call mental illness. But that would be like saying that if you're breathing, chances are, you're subject to this or that, because without fail, everybody we treat for this or that also exhibits a habit of breathing! You see? It's a *human* condition that is mostly unnoticed unless it is seen in connection with a problem. This is true partly because there is no theory that would explain it as normal (because the prevailing theory is taken for granted, hence is unseen) and because in a pathological condition it is usually there in an exaggerated form.

So when the boy that I was came home from the war, obviously he was chafing at being back in another man's house with another man's rules and expectations that sought to return him to his childhood state. That's how the boy experienced it—and certainly Reynolds got that aspect of things. There isn't any need to jump to your present-day one-size-fits-all theories about post-traumatic-stress syndrome, either. Sometimes being honorably wounded is a tremendous validation.

What Reynolds sort of got, sort of missed, is the mechanism of rebirth. He like most biographers imposes a unity on my life that wasn't there, and sometimes misses the unity that *was* there. But it's complicated to describe, because it's a thin line, and it is nearly quibbling, and yet it is important.

Well, we have a little time still.

The unity that *was* there is the unity that can be seen in a horoscope. It is the overall drive and composition of the life, but it is well beyond the conscious personality's grasp. Just as you may be born with an innate talent and never suspect you have it until something reveals it to you, so most parts of the total bundle that you are remain mostly unknown and even unmanifested. Some biographers grasp at this but usually they come off sounding mystical and theoretical. Besides, so much of a man's life seems to contradict the idea of a central driving force. It can just as easily be read as a series of chance occurrences "and if it hadn't been for the fact that Sherwood Anderson was still there, and that they met," there wouldn't have been any Ernest Hemingway as literary phenomenon. It isn't so, but if the biographer or the reader of biographies isn't aware of the existence of the driving force as a real phenomenon, not as a metaphor, that may be the only "common sense" interpretation of the life that they can come to. In that case, Hemingway's life was shot with luck and it was only by a series of miraculous coincidences that we got what we got. In the absence of the right concept, you see, the evidence can seem to point to an inevitable conclusion that in fact is merely the result of unconscious assumption.

The unity that *isn't* there but is assumed is the unity that would result from the same person directing the show first to last. Doesn't happen. It probably *can't* happen. In most people the changes are slow and seem like a progression rather than a changing of the guard. In a few people, it looks like they never change. In people like me, the composition of the active members of the group changed sometimes moment to moment, or anyway, in a short time in rapid sequence. When you come to write this up, part of your task can be to unpack this and show how it manifested.

≈19≈

Undercurrents

All right, Papa, nearly 4 a.m. Your parents and you?

It isn't that I'm shying away from the subject but that like all the guys upstairs as your mind constellates them, I circle around and provide context so that you get a better idea of how any given thing is placed in its context. It's important that you see how things interrelate. It's much less important that you see any given thing in isolation—as if "in isolation" could exist.

So, to understand me—as an example of life, you will remember, not as a sort of embalming or even of reconstruction—realize that I, as you or as anyone else, contained a series of mechanisms, or robots as you are calling them, that tended to act on their own when triggered, and acted sometimes with and more often without the knowledge and modulation of other parts of the person-group that was me.

Have you never erupted in rage, or found yourself *compelled* to act in some manner, in response to some stimulus, quite independent of the will of what you would normally call "you"? You know you have. We've touched on this before. That which I would do, I do not. That I would not do, I do. It's a very old problem.

When I came home from the war, I was not the person who had left home for Kansas City after high school. How could I be? Yet it was very convenient to live at home, and thus not pay rent, and be surrounded by support, during my year of convalescence. How else could I have stretched out my insurance payments? And that was all that I had. Beyond that finite series of payments, I had no job, no career, no real direction. Even if I could have asked my father to pay my way through college, how could I reduce myself to a somewhat older college boy when I had lived among veterans? It is true, I wasn't exactly a veteran, not technically, but I had gone in harm's way and had gotten wounded, and I had had the willingness if not the eyesight. That would have to be close enough. A few months in the hospital, absorbing the life and atmosphere of real veterans, was enough to separate me forever from the life of college boys.

And even if I could have had my job back at the *Star*, in the face of so many de-mobbed journalists, I couldn't have done it, hobbling around with a cane. Is that any way to chase ambulances? And anyway I wanted to be a writer. I had my insurance payments to buy me the things I needed, and I had a house to live in; let me use my time writing.

But it meant fitting in where I didn't fit.

I don't say my parents were unreasonable. Maybe they lacked imagination, to see that the changes in me were not necessarily bad, but were just different. But they couldn't stretch so far.

My father tried so *hard* to live by a few rules, and he took those rules to be absolutes, in the teeth of the evidence all around him that they *weren't* absolutes. What was he going to do with me? And still more, what was he going to do with his daughters, who defied his rules openly instead of surreptitiously as I did?

As I look at it now, I can see that he took it—as he did everything else—as evidence of his personal failure. His children were going to hell figuratively, and maybe literally, and he couldn't do anything about it.

Oh, we had some blowups, my parents and me, for they were together in that. My father was more religious, my mother more *noblesse oblige*, but neither one of them had any doubt about their standards, and I wasn't living up to them. And I alternated between trying to get along and trying to get them to give me space, as your generation says.

Only—and this is the real point here, not particulars of my biography except as illustration—it wasn't *me* reacting to that situation, so much as it was what you are calling robots. It isn't as if there was a consistent individual giving direction. *At most* there was a consciousness observing the interplay of external and internal.

I know you understand what I'm saying. Can you translate it?

I do know what you're saying. Let's put it this way. When certain triggers were pulled, a robot within you went into motion. Different triggers evoked different robots. But you as a 20-year-old didn't have any insight into this, nor much control over any of it, nor much memory of what you never observed because you weren't there at that moment, the robot-du-jour being there instead. So you would retain a memory of the situation before and the situation after, and some part of the actual explosion or conflict, but not the psychological links that would have made sense of it.

Yes. And so I'd put on some patches afterwards to explain it to myself and to others. And naturally since I knew I didn't *intend* any of it, it must be either the justifiable result of intolerable pressures from them or their misunderstanding me, or something like that. And such patches over time acquired their own consistency regardless of what any outside observer would have said had happened.

Nor was I the villain of the piece. My sisters certainly didn't think so. My parents were expressing their own robots too, naturally. So any what you call victims-and-villains scenario would miss the point. It was conflict, not warfare, and nobody in the conflict was "wrong" in their own eyes or even objectively except in this or that particular instance.

There's always conflict open or suppressed between a grown son and his father, and it's worse if they have to live together in the father's house. And the conflict between mother and son can be worse. The father at least wants to see the son independent. The mother maybe doesn't. The son wants independence—but he also wants that security of the nest, especially if he can get it for nothing.

Nothing particularly special about that situation at the Hemingway's in 1919. It was exaggerated because the war had given me a huge amount of freedom sooner than I would have had it otherwise, and had filled my mind with experiences of other ways of seeing the world and enjoying the world, and Oak Park looked awfully provincial to me.

But perhaps the important point is how easy it is for the biographer to assume a consistency of *motive*, a consistency of *participant*, a consistency of a *situation*, whereas in fact everybody's robots changed their motives from moment to moment (potentially) and this in effect meant that different people were standing in for each of the people involved, which meant that what looked like an easy-to-summarize situation was at best an average of what really happened.

If I was told to leave the cottage until I could stop swearing and loafing and taking advantage, that's true, it happened. But happy times also happened, times when my parents and I not only managed to get along but had renewed glimpses of what we appreciated in one another. The Ernest who wrote a loving note to accompany the gift of a lily was as real and as much part of my total person-group as the Ernest who fought wildly to show them that the world was larger than their ideas, that *he* was larger than their idea of him.

Beware believing biographers! And yet, absorb their point of view of that life (for that's what their work amounts to) and use it to pry beneath the surface for the varying aspects that are so easily glossed over or made consistent in the telling.

If you were to ask my parents to describe my life and actions and attitude after I returned home in 1919, they'd probably say I didn't want to do any real work; didn't want to contribute my fair share of the household expenses or upkeep; didn't want to follow the rules I had been raised to follow; had been coarsened in language habits and morals; in general, I had gone seriously downhill. For this is what they could see. What they couldn't see was the writer struggling to be born; the war veteran struggling to remain a man and not be forced back to being a dependent boy; the traveler who was oppressed by new/old narrower limits. Most of all they couldn't see that scared boy over-compensating with over-confidence. I made sure they didn't see *that*! I hadn't really gotten into an army. I hadn't really been a hero. Maybe I wouldn't be able to really be a writer. Maybe I wouldn't really be able to get out of Oak Park. That was a terrific load of worry to carry. It was a hard way to start life—and for the moment I couldn't do much about it.

And what I couldn't see is that nothing between my parents was as simple as it looked, because they too were not simple, nor was either one a singular person, but person-groups often expressing through automatic reactions, or robots. Maybe no child sees his parents accurately either as individuals or as a couple. I certainly didn't. And, as I said, after the fact I nailed up a few posters expressing the situation as I wanted to remember it, and left it at that. So for the longest time, my father was a coward and my mother was a bully and that explained my childhood and background. That *emotional* history became the only history I could hear, and so the facts were rearranged, reinterpreted, forgotten, distorted, invented, according to the *emotional* need.

Did you ever see it clearly?

Moments of clarity would be terribly upsetting to my mental stability, for they would mean that I had nowhere to stand. So, I couldn't afford them.

And you put robots into place to screen you from anything that would provide that knowledge.

It's almost more that my robots installed robots. It wasn't conscious on my part. I couldn't have afforded that it *become* conscious.

How did it happen, Ernest?

You mean, I think, *why* did it happen. I suppose you could say, because I never examined my life—my inner life—the way I examined life around me. That might possibly have made me more aware, and might possibly have helped me to get control of some of my automatic mechanisms that did so much to complicate my life. But that's almost asking me to be a different person.

Yes, I can see that. I'm sorry you paid such a high price, though I can imagine your life being equally creative and far less turbulent.

Maybe. The thing is, though, everything interconnects. Start tinkering with the mechanism and you don't know what happens down the line.

True enough. Okay; I guess we don't need to talk more about you and your parents in 1919 and 1920 unless you want to sometime.

You've gotten the main point of it. If people get the idea of how complicated their lives are because of how complicated *they* are, that will do.

≈20≈

Making Things Real

Thursday, July 29, 2010

Good morning, Ernest. On page 81, Baker quotes one of your Nick Adams stories, in which Nick is getting married. "He wondered if it would be this way if he were going to be hanged. Probably. He never could realize anything until it happened." That last sentence captured me, for some rea-

son, and I couldn't help wondering what it meant. He could never realize anything until it happened. What did you mean?

Nothing particularly important. I could *imagine* things in lots of ways, but I couldn't really make them real to myself, couldn't grasp a new fact ahead of time. Sort of how you felt as the year 1999 turned into 2000 and you found yourself in a new century forever and couldn't quite grasp it. You felt like you should feel differently, somehow, and instead you were just you, where you were, and although the century had changed there was nothing to tell it to you but an abstract idea.

So why does this seem an important thing to grasp, I wonder. I'm having to wonder aloud, as it were—because the fact that it seems so does not explain itself.

Tease out the implications and perhaps it will come clear. That's usually how you make sense of a thing that isn't clear. It has to do with *me*, you know that. And there is something implicit in it, something hidden, but not so much deliberately concealed as hidden as much from me as from you—for although I was a careful workman, I didn't always know why a given sentence fit, or was important, or why it *had* to be there to deliver the effect I wanted to convey. My job was to *recognize*, quite as much as to *fashion*.

I would have thought you would know this one.

And maybe it will mean more to you if you work it out than if you are given it.

Well, I can see that. The only thing I know, starting in, is that this line told me something about you, I just didn't and don't know what it is. You couldn't realize a thing until it happened. Yet—I keep counter-pointing— you invented stories out of who you were and what you had seen and what had happened to you. So it isn't like you didn't have any imagination! Well, I'm groping, here. Realize a thing. Make it real to yourself? Adjust (something) to new circumstances? It's a weird feeling, because I know that in a sense there is nothing special here; the sentence means what it obviously means, and that's the end of it. And yet—

Well, ever since I connected that picture of the open, eager, learning young boy, continually in motion, constantly wanting more, continuously reinventing himself and his possibilities, with my cousin Charlie, I've had you. Having seen Bub, I've seen you at the same age, even though you were half a generation older than my father. And I know that if I don't fix this image before I read again into your later years when you were a different person, or when different members of your person-group had come into play, I will lose maybe forever a chance at a special insight. And this "never realized before it happened" has a clue for me. What is it?

Maybe just note it and go on, for you have gotten it front and center now, and perhaps that's all you needed to do in order to provide the conditions for an insight to emerge.

Well, I hope so.

So let me go to the next question. On page 97, Baker says that in September, 1925, when The Star ordered you to go to Constantinople to cover the war between Greece and Turkey, Hadley said you shouldn't, and wouldn't speak to you for three days when you insisted on going. Hadley is usually portrayed as very submissive, very willing to do as you wished. A quarrel and a three-day cold spell doesn't sound like submission. I already got that you entered the marriage determined not to be dominated, but what was the inner story here?

You see here just another example of how compression works against real understanding when it comes to biography. Biographers come up with a certain understanding of your life as if what's true sometimes is true all the time. She was afraid.

Afraid you'd get killed, or hurt?

Look what happened to me last time I'd gone sticking my nose in somebody else's quarrels. Of course there is no comparison between driving ambulances or visiting trenches, and reporting on the war from a safe distance. But who knew but that I'd used up my luck three years before? And if I got incapacitated, or killed, or permanently maimed, where would *she* be? It didn't sound to her like the cruise she'd signed up for. I was going to be a *writer*, a serious writer, not an ambulance chaser, heading out to any war I could find. It was irresponsible! I was leaving her alone. There were any number of daily news reporters—not feature writers—who could do the job, so it isn't like I was really needed. And suppose I got hurt? Or suppose I didn't get hurt, was I going to develop a taste for running off to see the wars? Is this what she had to look forward to? That was the general idea.

It still amazes me, to send out a question, having no idea of the answer, and then receive something that seems so obvious that it is hard to believe I didn't know it ahead of time. Of course that's what the quarrel would be about.

It wasn't only that, either. This was the first time she tried to put her foot down, and if she hadn't, maybe I wouldn't have gone—though I probably would have anyway. But that made it certain.

You couldn't afford to have her be older and providing money and then determining what you would do.

Exactly. It was life and death, in a way. I wasn't going to be one of these guys who wound up like pet poodles. And anyway, I was still only 23. I had *life* flowing through me. I was always raring to go. I knew I wasn't going to get hurt, and I knew that Hadley couldn't judge the situation. I knew that her fears were just fears, they weren't any more rational than if she'd been afraid that I'd get run over in the streets of Paris. I mean, it does happen, but you can't let yourself be afraid of going down the street just to be safe. And you can't let your wife decide which fears you're going to listen to and which ones not, or what's too dangerous and what isn't. Women want security and men want danger, and they have to find a way to live with the difference, and the way isn't surrender.

But you got malaria on the trip, and in fact had a pretty miserable time of it, it sounds like. Punishing yourself regardless?

I wouldn't have seen it that way.

No, you wouldn't have, then. But now?

Just as you can't use tact when you're talking mind to mind, so you can't avoid inconvenient realizations when the other person shows you connections you've never made. Yes, I guess so. I got my way but I saw her point more than I let on or could afford to let on even to myself—because I wasn't going to let Hadley become Grace Hemingway to my Dr. Clarence Hemingway! And of course I knew that I was living on her money and was relying on her in many ways big and small, emotionally not least. But I *had to be* my own man. It wouldn't have been good for either of us if I had let myself relive or replay my father's life. So there I was, living in a way I theoretically scorned and saying so about others—loudly—and not quite letting myself see the situation, which is easy enough to do if you set your mental sentinels to deflect uneasy thoughts as fast as they arise. And of course it came out in my getting sick. I couldn't have seen it then because I didn't think the world worked that way, and anyway I couldn't admit the preconditions. But yes, I went off on my own—promptly got my typewriter broken by a drunken cabbie, a typewriter I needed, that had been a gift from Hadley, that I had to get fixed on the other end of the trip—and got malaria and lice, and so punished myself for disobeying mother, all without having to realize any of it.

So the Freudian aspect of it—punishing yourself for disobeying mother, or mother's stand-in, your wife—does seem true to you?

Oh yes. Just because a lot of nonsense is quoted about psychiatry doesn't mean there isn't a lot of truth to it. Hell, I knew it right at the beginning of my adult life. I *did* read Kraft-Ebbing, you know—and with Hadley.

I knew that, but as much as I know about you, it is still recurrently a surprise to realize how much you did know, how, as Callaghan said, you read everything, and how you learned what you wanted to learn thoroughly and well, to the degree that you wanted to learn it.

So tell me, what is the significance of the quarrel?

The significance of *your concentrating on* the quarrel is that you understand Hadley and our marriage better. Just because some aspect of a thing was never written about doesn't mean it didn't exist or wasn't important.

Well, it's 4:30 and even though this is only about 10 pages, I think we should stop.

Take one more look at the sentence you wanted clarity about.

I don't see any particular connection between "can't realize" and your quarrel with Hadley. Unless it means, like me come to think of it, you lived so much in the present that other times weren't real to you.

Well, not that they weren't real, but they were real in a different way.

Yes! I see it, whether or not I can say it. Your imagination and your memory are both Focus 27, as we would say in Monroe-speak, and your moment-to-moment sensory life was C1. [I think of focus 27 as the imaginal equivalent of everyday life. C1—consciousness one—is Monroe's term for ordinary consciousness.] Was that the important distinction?

You tell me.

Of course it was. And they were very complementary. It explains the lack of continuity in your life, your frequent re-examinations of things, your high-pressure existence.

Well, it does *in potential*. You'd have a job to do, to spell it out. But that's the insight you were looking for. And if it makes you feel any better, I didn't know either.

Huh. Well, I'm going to go back to bed for a while—it's 4:45, now— and think about this. It seems pretty important.

≈ 21 ≈

Living in Two Worlds

It explains a lot. Hemingway lived in both worlds routinely. Again, a model of wholeness. The C1 sensory everyday world he enjoyed as anyone does. The imaginal world, F27, he accessed all the time—reading, writing, remembering, visualizing. I don't say that he knew what he was doing and why he was doing it—but he did it. It requires an explanation of the two worlds. I thought I'd have to sit down and provide it, but it occurs to me, of course I can just ask for it. So—

[TGU] Think of the physical world moving through space in its usual predictable way. There is a non-physical equivalent of the physical world that moves right along with it—"flying formation with it" as you have sometimes put it. This is at once the "space" your non-physical components reside in and the "place" your memories are stored, and your visions and imaginations are test-driven. It is a part of physical and non-physical both; it is unique in that. This is because it may be considered to be tethered to the physical on one end and to the non-physical on the other. The word "end" in this context is a metaphor, of course. Thus, approached from the physical, the realm of Focus 27 appears non-physical because of the many ways it differs from physical life. But approached from the strictly non-physical, it appears somewhat physical because so much of its underlying conditions and permutations are integrally tied to the physical, what we call Earth.

Someone living a life intensely physical and intensely imaginal is going to live stretched between the two, one might say, or at best alternating between them. It is relatively rare to find someone evenly balanced between the two, in love with the physical and non-physical alike. Much more common to see a preference for one or the other, and often enough a *perception* of only one, usually the physical. (Someone perceiving only the non-physical is usually confined in some way, as irresponsible for taking care of his or her body.)

≈22≈.

Revival

Friday, July 30, 2010

I share another thing with Hemingway, perhaps because a boyhood of asthma keeping me up at night accustomed me to spending my time reading, actively ignoring the physical world. I live in that imaginal world routinely. It is no different thing for me to spend much of the day reading, which I have come to think of as spending time mostly in the imaginal world. Unlike Hemingway I have never been intensely physical as well. My sensory pleasures are few and relatively unimportant. But he seems to have been balanced instinctively, not so much one foot in each world as—well, anyway, Ernest, what do you think?

You're getting to it. The biographer who says "Hemingway pretended to be a big outdoors man but owned 7500 books" misses the point. There wasn't any *pretended* about it, and there wasn't any *but*, either. What good would a writer be who never read? What would he have to write about if he didn't live? It's a proverb, you know, that young would-be writers should stand up and live before they sit down to write. And what did I object to, my whole career, but writers—critics especially—who hadn't *done* anything before writing? I don't mean they had to be soldiers or sportsmen or any particular thing; just, they should have had something besides reading to bring to the task.

I certainly can see that! I always wanted to write—taught myself the basic elements of clear composition—had perhaps from other life connections an innate ability and an interest in using the ability—but for the longest time I had nothing to write about, because I hadn't so much lived as merely been dragged around by my body while I read.

Why do you suppose that so many young writers cannibalize their family and friends and neighborhoods to provide characters, and their interests (or, often enough, the "latest thing") to provide storyline? It's because they want to exercise the skill but don't have the subject matter. Now, this is not a seminar on writing, nor on Hemingway. It is about life and the nature of life. All of this, when you put it together, will serve to provide people another way to see what it is they're about. To do that, it must show those who are ready for it what *life* is about. We've decided you can perhaps preach the gospel, without preaching.

You can't just leave it there. Say more?

Is it not clear enough that one of your anchors is the matter-of-fact acceptance of the fact that the physical world is underpinned by the non-physical, and that physical life is a specific part of unending life, and that a given individual is integrally (if you will pardon a small play on words) a part of a whole? How common do you suppose those knowings are in your time and place? The ones who know the first and the second and the third of these three truths are relatively rare, and those who know any two or any one of them are likely to perceive themselves as being in opposition to those who know the others. Hence people are churched or unchurched, but not both; metaphysical or common-sense-ical or religious but not all three.

The religious won't listen to you, and neither will the materialistic-minded. So you find yourself speaking to the metaphysicals, as you call them, continually pointing out that their view of religion is a cartoon view. *It makes you sound religious to them*, just as your views, as expressed to your daughter's Christian minister brother-in-law, sounded non-Christian and therefore ungrounded, to him. It is the point of view of the interlocutor that colors the message they hear.

Well, I have seen that this keeps edging toward that rather unpopular message.

What do you care about popular? You tailored your life to let you go your own way regardless of popularity. The difference between popular and unpopular is the same as the difference between being an émigré and a refugee, as the old joke has it—timing.

I don't feel anything like adequate for the task of setting this all out, so it's going to be up to you to lead me along. By the way, what happened to Ernest, here?

Come to think of it as a big band playing jazz. The tune carries forward partly by first one and then another soloist taking the mike, then returning to the background.

Not a bad analogy, I guess. And of course by now I am used to the underlying reality of it. So tell me, how can I best help my friends to break through their intense dislike of, distrust of, often hatred of, religious expression? Many of them can't bear to even use the word "religious," holding to the word "spiritual" as the only acceptable connection to that reality.

You can't. Or, let's put it this way, anything you or anyone can do to help somebody else is to hold up a subject in a different light, for them to accept or reject as they are able. Each individual is really a person-group with some who can hear, and some who cannot; some who will welcome your input as a valuable alliance, and others who will reject it as interference or as potentially malign. *You* don't have any way to know that, and even if you did or do, you can't be tailoring your exposition to meet any one person's prejudice—particularly as no one regards his own prejudices as anything but truth!

What you *can* do is to exemplify an attitude of open-hearted acceptance of other ways of experiencing the world (including the non-sensory or non-physical worlds), because only in fluidity rather than in rejection and judgment is health to be found, and growth.

Yes, I heard the use of "exemplify" rather than, say, "exhort" or even "suggest."

Always easier to advocate than to exemplify, but not nearly as effective.

Well, I'll keep working on it! It doesn't come any easier to me than it does to anybody else.

No way for you to know that.

No, all right.

≈ 23 ≈

Pain

Saturday, July 31, 2010

I'm very tired, very sleepy, this morning. Papa—you and physical pain. It seems to me you must have gotten awfully used to it, in your lifetime. For such an intensely physical man you certainly had an amazing string of injuries. I haven't ever happened to see your horoscope, but it must have some terrific squares in it. And, say, that brings forward another question that I haven't quite had in the front of my mind, but that has been formulating. So, take your choice of questions: (1) something about the role of pain in your life and (2) your attitude toward (or against, rather!) mystical or occult fascinations such as, I gather, both your mother and later Hadley were drawn to.

No need to choose. We can deal with one, then the other, and if not today, later, depending on where the material leads us. What do you want to know about pain and me?

How did it affect your life?

You've seen that no biographer fails to mention the string of strange accidents I experienced. Some people like Gertrude Stein chose to pretend to believe that I was "fragile" but that was just her choosing the jibe she figured would annoy me most. More commonly, people assumed I was clumsy and actually unskillful at things I pretended to know very well, for once people discovered that I romanced about one or another aspect of my life, they assumed that I must be a complete phony and a liar, and so nothing I claimed could be true. (I wonder how I persuaded the men at the docks to pretend to weigh me in with all those fish?) And others engaged in your "psychiatry without a license" and tried to find deep currents of self-destructiveness in me that led to some of those things, like the skylight that fell on me in Paris.

Yes, those are the three sorts of reactions I've noticed, plus another that just assumes you were unlucky.

That's the one I would have subscribed to myself. I didn't have a lot of patience with mystical explanations of common sense things.

I'm going to challenge you on that. I think it would be way more accurate to say that one member of the Hemingway person-group didn't have any patience with what it dismissed as hocus-pocus. But another member of the group was highly superstitious—and I mean what look like trivial superstitions, not just trivial expressions of deeper understandings—and a third closely related member of your person-group was very closely tied to Catholic ritual and mystic participation. And for that matter I think your life was shot through (if you'll pardon the expression) with an attitude that mingled the physical and non-physical in practice but not in theory. It's just that these members of your person-group weren't all that well acquainted.

That's an interesting perspective, and pretty much true. There is a whole essay here on how we live more or less unaware of how we live. I'll leave it for you to write, as your mind is a lot more theoretical than mine, but I see the effects of the situation, now you bring my attention to it. And it merges your two questions nicely.

We're always being stage-managed, I figure. I certainly am. Most of my bright ideas come out of the blue and oh-so-coincidentally seem to lead to some place I have been being led to already! And the guys—including you, I suppose—sit there innocently saying "Well gee whiz, look at that. Who would have thought we'd wind up here?" I've come to expect it. To rely on it, in fact. So—your reaction?

As I say, it seems obvious to me now. And although you might think that as soon as we're dead we get all the insight into ourselves, that's only true in a way. In another way, we become *conscious* of something only when something lights it up, as you have just done. That's another essay for you. Make a note.

Let's go back to pain.

All right, pain. It's part of life, right? We learn that early enough. Especially if you're going to get your enjoyment in the open—hunting, fishing, even farming—anything physical—you're going to lay yourself open to the possibility of getting hurt. And I intensely loved the world, and being in the world, so I was out in it as much as possible. I know it's unfashionable in your world you live in, but in my world we had a code, and the code said real men were tough and could take it. In practice, women had to be tough and take it too, but there was a difference in kind. Men were expected to be strong and if need be violent. Women's strength was expected to be in endurance and in extension, come to think of it, rather than in violence. In other words, men expanded the boundaries, women held the world together. Your time may not like the division, although I can't quite see why not, but anyway it corresponded to our lives. It met our circumstances.

Anyway, men could take it—and that meant being able to deal with pain. It also meant being able to deal with fear and do what had to be done, regardless, and why anybody would make fun of *that* value just doesn't make sense to me, and never did. Is there some value in being *un-able* to cope with pain or fear?

None that I can think of. Maybe in my time we see it as less gender-related.

That's just because you don't understand what you think we thought. We were still fairly close to the pioneer era, you know. We weren't that far removed from frontier existence, and frontier values tended to persist beyond frontier conditions. What frontiersmen ever expected his women to be frail or oh-so-refined or incapable of facing realities like childbirth or children dying or primitive nursing of wounds or fevers? You think frontier women were *soft*? Not in *that* way! And they weren't expected to be and it wouldn't have been any advantage to anyone that they should be. You're confusing the expectation that they would be more spiritual, more connecting, more nurturing and expressive and openly loving (though nobody would have put it that way) with the idea that they were supposed to be less capable, less able to cope.

It's all well and good to smile at the stiff upper lip attitude to pain, but in practice that's a very practical approach if not carried too far. You didn't see us popping pills and haunting the emergency room (not that we even had them) and treating ourselves for a thousand imaginary ailments. We *assumed* health, and *assumed* that pain and sickness were a part of life, and we didn't come apart when we experienced them. It wasn't heroics until carried to too-great lengths.

So if you are all the time fishing, you have to expect that sooner or later something might happen and you get a hook in your finger, or you hurt yourself pulling in a huge fish, or something. It's just part of the situation, and when you experience it, you deal with it.

But you had some downright strange accidents.

And a lot of unnoticed everyday incidents, like everybody else.

Oh, sure—but the effect on you?

Well, that *is* the effect, in a way. I expected that accidents happen, and I wasn't devastated when they did. I was proud of my ability to cope, and I knew I could function under pain and I was reasonably proud of that too—but of the two, I was a lot prouder of the first, because any-body but a weakling could deal with pain when it came along, but not everybody could deal with emergencies.

I feel like we've scarcely touched the topics, but I'm worn out already. I see it's my usual 70 minutes and—how many?—10 pages. More tomorrow, maybe?

I am not going anywhere. Where would I go?

Fishing in the Gulf Stream?

It wouldn't interfere with anything. We aren't the subjects of time here in the way we are there.

V

August—December 2010

*Illness and Injury • Watching Star Trek • But You Must Work • Writing
After the War • Being in Training • Consequences • Mind to Mind
Contact • Outlandish Stories • Legitimate Suffering and Mental Illness
• Person-groups • Judgment and Self-Criticism • Sensory Evidence • A
Man Among Men • Hemingway's Wavelength • The Garden of Eden •
Roger and Thomas • "What was I supposed to do?"*

Illness and Injury

Sunday, August 1, 2010

*Not feeling so hot. Not the best background for communication, per-
haps. I was up at six, decided to go back to bed, and here I am half an hour
later. Just to preserve continuity? For I don't feel like much. And yet, I wind
up feeling better as I work, so why not? How about it, Ernest? Is that how it
was for you?*

It's true, work provides continuity. At the most elementary level, just
the need to get up and go pushes you to do that rather than to declare
yourself out of action. But of course illness comes with a reason, and so
you overlook or ignore it at your own risk. If I thought I was coming

down with something, I took to my bed and stayed there until I figured the coast was clear.

But you were afraid of drowning in mucus, I gather.

Well, probably I never would have seen the difference consciously—at least, I don't remember being aware of it—but I put illness and injury into very distinct categories. An injury was one thing. You tried to avoid them, and you cleaned up after them, but they didn't pose a continual threat. Illness was harder to prevent, and could be harder to deal with, because your body was working against you, or that's what it felt like. It deprived you of a place to stand, where if you'd gotten injured, the uninjured rest of you could work together to recoup.

Interesting

You keep watching those Star Trek videos and you'll be saying "fascinating" all the time.

[A friend had given me videotapes of the complete original Star Trek TV programs from the 1960s and I was watching them—which meant that Hemingway, in effect, was watching them through me.] No doubt. While we're on the subject, what do you think of them?

≈ 2 ≈

Watching Star Trek

They were television, and I never cared much for television, though I must say it is better without commercials interrupting it all the time. But it's still TV in TV's constricting format. An introductory sequence to get your interest, then three or four longer more or less same-sized segments each ending with a dramatic situation designed to prevent you from turning to another channel during the commercials, then a coda like the introduction, not only to wrap up the situation's loose ends but to leave the watcher feeling good so you'll want to watch again next time. It's hard not to be distracted by the constraints of the format. Scott [Fitzgerald] could have written for television. He would have been pretty good at it.

And you?

I could have provided the basis for specials, and Hotchner could have done the adaptations, just as we did do. I couldn't have worked to order like that. Besides, they wouldn't have wanted anything real that I could have given them, and anything they would have wanted, I wouldn't have been able to give them except by whoring. Faulkner could have written for TV too. Anybody who could write for the movies could write for TV. I couldn't. Too much like grinding out sausages, especially if the sausage has to *look* good regardless of *tasting* good.

So what about the Star Trek universe?

You're coming to them backwards, so I am too. You know the movies, so I know what you know. You never watched the TV show, so it's all seen in retrospect by you, hence by me. (It would be a different experience, my watching it through someone else's mind.) So, like you, I see these young skeletally thin actors through the lens of the older, bulkier actors they would become. So we know something they don't know. We also know of the success after failure of the whole Star Trek concept; we know the interaction and growth of the characters and the increased complexity of the storylines and messages and yet we are seeing them when they didn't know it themselves. *But their non-physical selves did!* You see?

That's how we live our lives.

There's a continual interaction between physical, living each moment of time, and non-physical, aware of the overall pattern in ways the individual in the moment can never have the data to share—yet the non-physical will help to physical to greater awareness if that's part of the pattern. It is in this sense that you can talk about "planning" your lives. Everything people have said about the non-physical patterning of your lives is true from a certain direction—and that direction must come with an awareness of the effects of a different continuing experience of time and the effects of time.

I see it. So—the characters and plots?

Perhaps you can see that the very compromises that made it commercial also compromised the message and made it that much less able to do what it tried to do. *Enforcing* peace is like spreading non-violence by winning fistfights or laser-gun battles. It's like the flaw in the premise you saw in "The Day the Earth Stood Still": The galaxy wants peace so much that it reserves for itself the right to annihilate men, women, children, animals, plants—the whole planet—if they decide that man's violence is going to spread to the rest of the reality. But they don't enforce quarantine, or use any intermediate form of policing (which in itself would recognize that peace, like war, is contained within at least potential violence)—they just threaten to kill everybody.

But if a film or if television shows had attempted to dig deeper into the paradox *without* finding scapegoats such as madmen or villains, the result would have been looked on as theoretical or unrealistic or even as polemical. It is very hard for an artist to get beyond the bounds of the commonly accepted and experienced reality. It's 20 times as hard— maybe 1,000 times as hard—to get beyond those bounds in teamwork— and what are script-writing teams but attempts to do together what is best done individually, except that the medium makes it impossible.

I see some pretty heavy-handed messages tailored in the early days of the Vietnam War.

Early days in retrospect. But 1968 was after all in the third year of massive involvement. It didn't seem "early days" to you, did it?

No, that's true. I was forgetting.

Only in "the future" could certain disturbing messages be even hinted at; and they had to come wrapped in the form of conflict that was accepted as being dramatic. I'd say it was a contribution of Star Trek to substitute intellectual confrontation for violence sometimes, and that wedge—mostly inserted via the logical character of Spock—was as subversive as anything else they attempted. No point in analyzing the characters, although I gather I'm going to be seeing quite a lot of them.

About 79 or 80 episodes all told, I think. They certainly produce a different mental "feel" than reading your work.

Thank you.

I'm smiling too. But seriously, there is a difference and I don't think it is only film versus book.

It isn't only that, but you are out of time.

~ 3 ~

But You Must Work

Open for business, Papa?

Not now—I'm busy re-running those Star Trek episodes.

That one got a chuckle, not quite a laugh out loud. I can see you couldn't watch Shatner if you kept kosher. Or maybe his director thought he needed to be that way to be "dramatic."

Or maybe they never put the thought into their performances that you are assuming they did. Like Bogart and his leading lady in Casablanca, they figured it was just a job, not art.

Now why would I—let alone you—be unable to bring in her name? Ingrid Bergman? It isn't like it isn't something entirely familiar to me. How many times have I seen Casablanca, after all, twenty? Yet there was this blank and I just covered it with "his leading lady" and kept moving, so the gears wouldn't clog up. But—can you give me a clue? The same thing happened years ago with Joseph Smallwood being unable to remember Missionary Ridge or Hood instead of Bragg, and I couldn't figure out why—but in this case not only could you not have forgotten her name, but neither could I—yet when I reached for it, that name was not there.

It's out of my league. Add it to your list of questions—which you have been neglecting to keep.

All right, I wrote it down.

Write down enough of them, and you'll be able to sort them into categories, and the sorting will bring out enough relationships to half answer them. You've acquired many more than you suspect, in the course of the past few years.

Now, a word about your writing.

I know what's coming.

Feel like you're about to be Dutch Uncle'd?

Feeling like I deserve to be, maybe.

No, it isn't quite that we regret that you aren't working better and longer. What you *have* systematized is working well. At how many points in your life would you have been able and willing to get up in the darkness and write away into daylight, communicating? And by immediately reading it into your computer, you have preserved the record in typed form, thus accomplishing step two right away and not adding another pile of backed-up work to the pile. Sending it to your friends has acted to prod you gently to accomplish so much the more. But now that you have provided headers for all the sessions, you need to start working on the next part without waiting for this process to end, unless you *want* this process to end—and we know you don't.

No, I sure don't. So—a certain amount of time daily doing a different kind of work?

It's only an analogy, but—think of how you told your group yesterday how to go about receiving messages. First have a question, then receive it (go into receptive mode), then report some of it (moving into the more active mode of writing it down), then return for more, asking more questions if need be. Writing all this isn't that much different. And in fact this provides a kickoff place for a brief lecture, as much to your readers (and potential collaborators) as to you yourself. That process—reception, reporting, analysis—is a natural rhythm. Repeated, referencing previous understandings (and incomprehensions, too) in the formulation of new questions, it will assist you to penetrate continually deeper into whatever subject matter you may choose (or may be led into). *But you must work.* Or rather, you must work if you wish to progress.

Some people use journals for one reason and others for others—and many use them now for this and now for that reason. They are very handy but of course there is nothing sacred about the means of communication. Others may prefer the computer, or notes, or sketches. We do suggest that you employ *some* medium to leave a trail, not for the sake of an historical record but so that you will have anchors for yourselves—for consider your situation.

You live continually moving—carried along the eternal present, so that today's conditions are not yesterday's, nor tomorrow's, nor one minute's the next's. Continuity is thus in the non-physical hands of your higher self, your unconscious as you call it. Have you ever thought about that? How much continuity can a present-moment consciousness provide? That's why people make lists and use appointments calendars, after all.

Your thoughts, your emotions, and often your daily routines, fluctuate unobserved, you identifying with each in turn. Nothing wrong with it—that is the nature of life in the physical. But it means that it's easy for you to lose track. Hansel and Gretel tried breadcrumbs. They learned that it's better to use something not subject to being carried away, like stones, the very symbol of permanence and imperishability. If you wish to preserve a trail for yourselves, we suggest something less perishable than access to memory. The memory itself can never die, but if you lose access to it, how much good can it do you? So, some record of your work is worthwhile. Even if the record is kept in habit, that is very valuable. What is sitting-zen but a reminder of purpose, by the very act of once again sitting? End of lecture. If you want to make this process a continuing series instead of a burst of information/interaction followed by digestion followed by another burst, you need to be spending some time organizing past material as you go. Otherwise you will keep doing research forever and never write the report.

≈ 4 ≈

Writing After the War

Tuesday, August 3, 2010

Okay. So—let's see. Ernest, are you still re-running Star Trek episodes?

I think I've gotten about as much out of them as was put into them. It's no big problem to tear myself away.

How was it that you could find markets for your stories in magazines that depended on advertising? [In other words, how did he escape the need to write stories with happy endings.]

You didn't see any of them appearing in the *Saturday Evening Post*, did you? They [his stories] had a different audience, one that would sit still for ambiguity, or indirection, or sardonic content. And of course after I'd made a name with *The Sun Also Rises*, my market was any magazine that thought my name would help sell.

[Publisher Arnold] Gingrich and Esquire.

By the time that came along, I was in my 30s, and I was established. But we helped each other. I was a good name for his masthead and his was a good audience for my future writings. And he paid very well, and got his money's worth.

How did it happen that you ceased to write for magazines after the war?

As much as anything, no financial need. And I had my eyes on such a larger project—my land sea and air book—that I didn't want to have interrupted by *trying* to write short stories, and none particularly occurred to me.

Too much isolation, too?

Well, that requires some telling. I wasn't isolated in the sense of not having people around, and many of them were intelligent, stimulating people. But people seen in a party context is not the same thing as people seen in the context of living with them, of doing something together, easy or hard, short or long.

Eating and drinking has a sameness, I take it.

Oh, I hear your refrain about too much alcohol. I'll go this far—once you get dependent on a thing, obviously you lose some freedom of maneuver, you have to be sure it's around, and maybe it's the same as your coffee all the time. But it's still a social lubricant. It's still a ritual like breaking bread together. It has its place in life.

But we were talking about isolation.

A writer's life is lonely—or, alone, anyway—because nobody can go to those places in the mind in company. And your reports when you come back are just a pale reflection of what you saw, what you lived, what you are. Now, if the rest of your life balances that time, that's well and good. Or if you unbalance while you're working on a long project but then you take time later to rebalance, to get back in touch with external life, that's good, and that's what I always did before the war.

But it was harder afterwards. Easier just to host parties at the *finca* than to move about—and after a while of living like that, people coming to you, you not going to them, you get used to it, and you get more and more vaguely uneasy breaking out of that comfortable routine. Even if it is an *un*comfortable routine, it becomes more comfortable than going out. It is a form of agoraphobia, I suppose. You wind up like you were when you were a kid, with the outside world seeming very strange, vaguely threatening, very unfamiliar. That's one reason I carried all that luggage. Not the only reason, but one reason—I tried to bring my world with me. I became incapable of going anywhere with a change of clothes and a toothbrush. And if we weren't going to a known place like the lodge in Idaho, it was harder. And of course in any life, you lose people—you take casualties, as I always put it—and some of them can't be replaced. Max, Charlie Scribner. It distanced me even farther from the outside connection to my inner world of writing.

If you had been healthier, if you hadn't had a concussion and its after-math in 1944 and if you hadn't had the airplane crashes ten years later, could you have kept writing by concentrating on the world that you had known, that no longer existed?

That would have depended on what resources came to mind. Writing about any true thing is health-giving. But writing just for the sake of writing as an exercise wasn't enough. I suppose I could have written a memoir—besides

A Movable Feast, I mean—but what good would it have done? It mainly would have demonstrated what an unreliable memory I had.

≈ 5 ≈

Being in Training

Friday, August 6, 2010

Well, it's 6:15 now. I suppose there have to be days like this, when nothing comes and my mind is stuffed with cotton.

You don't suppose diet and exercise could have anything to do with it, do you?

It's called being in training, and you have to take it seriously if you want to have enough wind to go several rounds. You saw how I lived. It wasn't only physical exuberance that led me to include hard exercise in my life *as part of my routine*. It was necessary, as necessary as living in a way that provided new input. It's one more aspect of wholeness, and this is something that I scorned the literary crowd for. They lived too much in their heads. Now, nobody lived as much in his head as I did, but I lived intensely in my body, too, and it balanced. Suppose I'd tried to write about bullfighting from a flabby, under-exercised body? How vital would my prose have been? How sharp would my perceptions have been? How fast and accurate would my mind have been, finally? You've got to keep the machine tuned. But of course you don't keep it tuned just for the sake of keeping it tuned, but to use it.

≈ 6 ≈

Consequences

Saturday, August 7, 2010

A couple of questions have come to mind. First, Papa, a question of "what if?" It seems to me that if you hadn't gotten involved with Pauline Pfeiffer, your life would have taken a radically different course. Without Pauline, no

rich Uncle Gus. No Uncle Gus, a much more constricted standard of living.
No Key West house, no safari in Africa, hence no Green Hills, and maybe no
particular affinity to Cuba because no discovery of Gulf Stream fishing, etc.
Ultimately perhaps no discovery by Martha Gellhorn, no trip to Asia, etc.
a lot of consequences. Is that how you see it too, and, if so, what alternative
life do we see?

It's enough to make you believe in consequences, isn't it?

It's enough to make me think it was a pretty costly engagement that had
significant plusses and minuses for you.

I know you don't understand about or approve of the [1933-34]
safari, but that was the fulfillment of a dream I'd had since I read about
Col. [Theodore] Roosevelt's safaris. You know full well I'd wanted to be
an explorer. And I wouldn't have given up the Stream, once I'd been out
in it, for anything.

So, the downside?

Oh, it was pretty much what you know it was. Some of my strands
were well content to loaf along, living the life of the very comfortable
rich. And others weren't, so they made me work hard for the money,
and they pushed me to exert myself physically and mentally to earn the
luxuries. Uncle Gus tipped the scales, and gradually I moved in the direction Agnes always feared I would, right when I wasn't yet 20 years old.
Why do you think I criticized Scott Fitzgerald so much for not working
enough? And, his example helped keep me from becoming just like that.

Not that I would have anyway. I was first and foremost a *craftsman*. I
needed to work and I knew I needed to work, not for the money or the
fame so much as for the thing itself. We've talked about it. Living in that
place, the place you couldn't get to easily otherwise and not without ill
effects.

I know where you are, but readers may not. The place is that mental
space where you invented from. The ill effects are hangovers and blurriness if
you got there from drink instead.

≈ 7 ≈

Mind to Mind Contact

You had a very good quotation by Sheean. You might use it.

[The quotation, from *The Hemingway Women* by Bernice Kert, page 48: "Years later Vincent Sheean remarked, having spent time with him when the two were war correspondents, then Ernest created outlandish stories as unthinkingly as other people breathed. Most of the time his listeners could not separate his reality from his fantasy."]

I knew this was an important clue, that didn't mean quite what people assume it means.

Yes. Some people take that to be an admission that I was an inveterate liar, or was out of contact with reality. How do *you* take it?

Aren't we more concerned here with how you see it, having known it from the inside?

The point is that *you* are on the inside when you contact another person. We know what you know—why should you expect it to be different, the other way round?

But in fact I don't know, except in little bits and pieces.

That's a pretty big "except," don't you think? Once you've gone from "there can't be any communication between minds" to "yes there can," it's a long way you've gone. After that it's a matter of practicing and learning the knack of it. But if you expect too much, the fact that you don't get what no one could get, could discourage you. Let's put it into concrete terms. If you make a friend who is well informed about something and is perfectly willing to share his knowledge with you—how much of it is he going to be able to transfer to you at any one time? He can willingly answer questions, and if his range of knowledge is enough that one thing leads to another, maybe you could go a long way on a little. But he can't just transfer it all, like Mr. Spock doing a mind meld. What he can do most efficiently is tell you what he has reason to tell you; that, and answer your questions. Sound familiar?

Now, when you emotionally or maybe we ought to say empathetically *connect* with somebody, you get flashes of insight; you don't get laid-out expositions of facts. If you have the background to see the connections of those flashes of insight, all right, it's as if you were given a lot of knowledge. But you weren't. You were given a lightning-flash that lit up the terrain that was already familiar to you. If what it lights up *wasn't* familiar to you, what you get is much less, maybe only a dazzling brightness lighting up one specific thing you happened to be looking at.

You can't expect to know everything a disembodied mind knows, any more than you can that of an embodied mind, because it doesn't work that way. Your physical brain gets in the way because it can only process so much at a time, and it is continually busy making the adjustments that bring it to the next moment of time. You can't put the Encyclopedia Britannica on the head of a pin, and if you could, you might have a hell of a time reading it. Without the limitations of the physical body/brain, operating in time-space, yes, what I know, you know. But that isn't what's going on here. How could it be?

This puts a different light on the whole process. Thanks. It gives me something to chew on, and I'll do the chewing.

≈ 8 ≈

Outlandish Stories

Now, to return: You know what I know, to the extent you can bring it within your physical limits. So what about my outlandish stories?

What it tells me is that you continually lived between two worlds, or more probably you lived in both worlds at the same time, all the time. And it blurred the boundaries for you, didn't it? After I got familiar with the mental state that Bob Monroe called Focus 27, where we create instantly and continuously, a non-physical state that tracks physical reality, I recognized that children live as much in Focus 27 as they do in ordinary consciousness. The boy sitting in a cardboard box that's really a spaceship, or a sailboat, or a stagecoach, knows it's a cardboard box, but he also knows it's a stagecoach or whatever. The two realities don't separate until teen-age, or maybe the age of reason. And some people's imagination is stronger, or maybe they never lose the key to the kingdom.

You have it. And I never lost it, which is what I meant when I said all writers are liars. I never did realize that most writers were not like me *mentally.* I knew they weren't usually as physical; I knew they didn't usually work as hard or read as much or want so intensely. But it's only now that I see that it wasn't laziness on their part necessarily or willingness to sell out, as you would say. *They didn't have the key.* They didn't create by letting themselves go, in the way I did. And when Scott wrote to order for the *Saturday Evening Post*, giving them what they wanted, I can see now that it wasn't a betrayal of anything for him to do that, because it was entirely different for him. *He* had to work to *get the picture. I* had to work *to express what I saw.* That was all the difference between the way we created, but it was everything.

Not sure that will be clear enough for everybody.

I always said he had all that talent and should have been the greatest writer we had. But what he had was the ability to write easily and smoothly and compellingly all in one flow, that I never had. What he *didn't* have was ideas, and pictures, and a tremendous reliable internal connection that would have fed him stories as fast as he could have written them out, like Mozart having the skill and having the access and producing like a fountain. So he wound up writing trash, exercising a profitable skill, but not using it to *say* anything. *Gatsby* was his moment. He snagged a connection and it lasted long enough for him to create a rounded finished piece—and wouldn't you know it, his public was disappointed, because what they expected and wanted was his usual horseshit. But I never saw it till now, that it wasn't laziness on his part, or lack of work, or even Zelda. He didn't have the access. He was given a great talent, and nothing to say and no way to acquire anything to say.

Whereas you—

I plucked stories from the air, like Mozart hearing fully developed tunes. But unlike Mozart, I had to sweat blood to *craft* the result. I might have just told tall tales, you know, if I hadn't been a craftsman. I might have found a niche and filled it, and if it wasn't for my broad center of competitiveness—it's pretty wide to be called just a streak—maybe I would have. But I wanted to be great, and I wanted to do right what I saw all around me being done wrong, so I couldn't settle. And I never did.

You certainly didn't. You changed the language and the way we use language and the way we see things.

And if it hadn't been for Gus Pfeiffer's money I wouldn't have gotten trapped in The Hemingway Myth that obscured all that.

Maybe you'd have won the Nobel Prize a decade earlier, or more.

Don't you believe it. That kind of prize comes for only two reasons, neither one good. Either they give it to you for some political reason of their own, making a point, or they give it because they have to, because you've outlived and outworked all the non-entities they already gave it to, and they just *can't* not give it to you. Although even then, it's political, and if you don't give them an excuse to give it to you maybe they won't anyway, it's so embarrassing to them that they didn't do it earlier. If I hadn't written *The Old Man and the Sea* and given them the excuse that this time I'd written about an uplifting subject and an admirable man—as if Spain and Robert Jordan weren't enough—they never would have figured out how to climb off that limb that was making their prize ridiculous.

But it's getting to your limits.

75 minutes so far. Not a problem yet. I don't think we're finished with the imaginal world and common-sense consciousness.

Well, go on.

Your stories about your own past, that kept changing and getting better. It wasn't any different, was it?

I wasn't ever as calculating as my biographers seem to think. I'd tell a story and it was a story. If I liked it, why shouldn't I tell it? And Sheean saw, you see. He saw that the storytelling came naturally to me. It wasn't a *skill*, it was a background. In fact, the thing I had to watch against was

Yeats' artist's temptation: creation without toil. Telling the story was as easy as anything. Writing it was hard, and exacting, and it was work. All during the war, I *told* my stories, I didn't *write* them. It was lucky I was able to get back to working at all, afterwards.

≈ 9 ≈

Legitimate Suffering and Mental Illness

Sunday, August 8, 2010

Just spent most of an hour posting [on my website] a couple of conversations from May. We'll see if I drained the batteries or did something efficient. It was interesting to read the pieces from May 24 and 25. I had forgotten that it was from Carl Jung that I first got the concept that Hemingway represented a complete man, that his great attractiveness to people stemmed from his wholeness. Obviously that didn't prevent him from experiencing and ultimately succumbing to serious personality problems, but it does change the picture. All right, so here we go. Dr. Jung, I have been using a quotation of yours as a part of my signature in e-mails for some time, but only yesterday—at your prompting?—did it occur to me that I didn't quite understand it. It rings true intuitively but it could do with some explanation. "The foundation of all mental illness is the unwillingness to experience legitimate suffering." What is "legitimate suffering," and for that matter what is mental illness, and how are they thus so intimately connected?

[CGJ] You have asked the question even though you are anxious. This is good. Always, when you meet an obstacle, push through it, beyond it, or it will surface again in a more difficult form. Challenges never get easier except sometimes as a result of prior failure leading to reduction of capacity—in which case they still are harder relative to the capacity one brings to them.

To understand the sentence, one needs to understand the definitions. Mental illness. Legitimate suffering. For that matter, unwillingness.

You have been told [by TGU, in the past] that there is no such thing, as such, as mental illness, but we will stick to common parlance. For our purposes, we may define it as the inability to

*Wow! I see it, all at once! In connection to Hemingway! Sorry to inter-
rupt, but it was so striking, to go from not understanding to understanding.
Please, proceed.*

Define mental illness as the inability to experience reality in an
undistorted form. Define legitimate suffering as—for instance—bearing
the knowledge of what one is, or what one has done. And define unwillingness as a conscious choice, become unconscious because repressed, to
see in distorted fashion.

That is so simple, so obvious once said.

You will find that our readers find it less obvious, until we put into
words the understanding that leapt mind to mind between us. However,
it is true that some will be able to join in that intuitive communication,
and thus will get it as you got it.

So, to plod. (I *was* Swiss, you know. We Swiss are great plodders.)

Ideally a mind experiencing a life does so with inputs open and
understanding functioning without distortion, and in this way smoothly
assimilates what occurs externally so as to experience it internally and
thus come to greater consciousness of its own nature and limitations and
possibilities. (By the way, those three words are restatements, one of the
other. To know one's nature is to know the others, and to know them is
to know what one is fundamentally.)

This is the ideal. Of course it is rarely if ever approximated.

To the degree that one refuses to see one's shadow side, one distorts
one's experience of reality. "It wasn't me. It was circumstance. I was an
innocent victim. He provoked me. Anyone would have reacted in the
same way."

Such distortion, if continued long enough and consistently enough,
obviously results in the person becoming ever less able to respond appropriately to circumstances, because circumstances *as reported* to the conscious mind are reported in the distorted form required by the refusal to
acknowledge and accept one's own actions, motivations—ultimately, a
part of one's own character.

*Yes, it jumped out at me when you began—Ernest Hemingway was not
sufficiently aware of his shadow side, and therefore couldn't acknowledge or*

often remember certain types of actions, and such actions—those that led him to break with friends, for example, or that led him to be unable to restrain his competitiveness—repeatedly had ill effects on his life. Yes, Ernest?

[EH] I don't think Carl was quite finished.

[CGJ] No. Our friend is particularly enthusiastic today.

Let's blame it on the coffee. I would never do something like interrupt. It wasn't my fault! They made me do it! Anybody would have!

[CGJ] All right, we are smiling, but a little bit goes a long way. If you meant it, that would be a good example of the mechanism.

To continue the thread I was following, though it may be obvious, one can reach a point from which there can be no return, because incoming reality *as perceived* bears so little resemblance to incoming reality *in and of its own nature.*

Thus, Ernest had to blame certain situations on others because it would have become unbearably painful to admit to himself his own responsibility. That is the common way to understand the situation. However, in the way we are sketching out, we would rephrase it this way. Ernest's person-group comprised such extremely disparate elements as to be held together largely by the fictions he told himself about who he was and what he was. He shaped himself to an ideal, and the price of that was disenfranchising parts of himself that didn't measure up to the ideal.

He could not acknowledge them, and therefore he lost the ability to integrate them, and therefore they functioned suppressed until they exploded, then were suppressed again. A part of his conscious personality knew that the explosions occurred, but experienced them as autonomous—a primitive would have described them as evil spirits that had entered and taken him over—and therefore had extreme difficulty taking responsibility for what seemed to him not really his own doing.

Another part of his conscious personality remained unaware—as best it could!—that the explosion had taken place at all.

But this in turn caused further problems, for in the aftermath of an explosion one sees an altered situation, that has to be accounted for somehow. If ex-hypothesis one denies that an explosion took place at all, or denies at least that the explosion had anything to do with one's own action or being—well, *somebody* has to be at fault! Find them!

Oh, I see the mechanisms, all right. And I suppose that few people who read this will fail to see it from personal experience.

You can see, then, that if this process is allowed to get too advanced, a person may wind up inside so elaborate a labyrinth as to be unable to return to clarity without trusted outside help. And the farther one has proceeded inside the labyrinth, the less able one will be to trust outside help of any kind. Carried sufficiently far, the only way out is via death and release, which thankfully is available to all.

But. If a person is willing to see the person-group as it exists—the disreputable characters as well as the saints; the bums as well as the hard workers; the drones and the dullards as well as the inspired creators— then there is hope, and health. For if one can hold an ideal while remembering that while in human form with human limitations we cannot *attain* (but can only approximate, or tend toward) ideals, then one still has a touchstone for conduct and aspiration, but one need not deliberately ignore the unavoidable shortcomings, nor be crushed by guilt nor overcome by hopelessness.

And it hurts to see what we really are rather than what we would rather be. Is that it?

Not everyone is mentally ill. Not everyone holds an ideal unattainably high, and suffers from the failure to attain the unattainable.

Ernest?

[EH] This should render my life more comprehensible. On the one hand you're being told that I was an example of wholeness. On the other hand you're seeing how unable I was to deal with certain themes that ran through my life, and you see how my life spun out of control. You tend to put too much blame on the alcohol. The cause is as Carl said—I couldn't see myself or my life straight, and so I got farther and farther off course.

[CGJ] That isn't quite right. You found it too painful to see the past as it had been, so you shrank from it and walled yourself off from incidental reminders as best you could. But your life—look at it now!—was not, objectively, something to shrink from realizing. And if you had seen yourself more accurately you would have seen those around you more accurately. It would have relieved the anxiety, the paranoia, the depression, it would have turned down the valve on the rage and the manic highs.

But it was all tied in with your idealization of yourself that was the means of creating yourself and holding yourself to your impossibly high standards of craftsmanship *that you did largely achieve.*

I can certainly see it. By holding yourself to a high enough standard, you can make it guaranteed that you are never going to do good enough or be good enough to satisfy yourself. Hence the bragging, hence the anxious competitiveness.

[CGJ] And hence the need and the use to you of the Catholic Church, Ernest. Your critics don't seem to understand the psychological importance to you of confession as a way of shedding guilt. But the structure of the Church "in our time" didn't match with the rest of our world, so it wasn't enough, and this without entering in to the question of the Church's politics in Spain and elsewhere.

So, to wrap this up? For we have been going more than an hour.

I sum it up as I continually summed up situations. Do not judge another's life. Judgment—condemnation—never liberates, it only oppresses, isolates, and condemns judge and judged alike. You never have the data. Ernest's life cannot be understood as if it were a simple man's, nor a man comprising a harmonious low-pressure collection of threads.

[EH] Yet my life must not be seen as a series of bad decisions or of unfortunate external circumstances, either. It was as I was, and if I had realized that consciously as I realized it unconsciously, I'd have had an easier time of it.

I thank you both. I think many people besides myself will find this helpful. But don't think I don't see manipulation when I experience it—at least once in a while!

We smile as well.

≈10≈

Person-groups

A delicate question, Papa. One whose answer may prove difficult. Reading Baker, page 222. This is in 1931:

On a visit to the MacLeishes at Uphill Farm in Conway Massachusetts, Ernest was standing before the fireplace when the MacLeishes' daughter Mimi came in to greet him. Something in his manner frightened her and she ran off to her bedroom. Ada found her crying and saying over and over that this was not the Hemingway she knew. Ernest spent nearly an hour talking to the child upstairs, and afterwards compared her to the child Ellie in "Disorder and Early Sorrow," the story of Thomas Mann's that he liked best after Buddenbrooks.

There is no further mention of the incident. What was that all about? I don't know the Thomas Mann story, so I don't know what you were referring to. But something in that description makes me think that the girl accurately saw you as being different. Did she?

You understand, nobody at the time had any context for seeing her actions as warranted. Neither would you, if not for the person-group concept.

Yes—that's where I went with it.

People say, "he's changed," but they almost always think of it as a change like an evolution, a flowering and a decaying. They don't so often think of it as like changing partners in a square dance. Do you remember what Fitzgerald said? [Writing to their mutual friend Morley Callaghan of Hemingway, Fitzgerald said he thought that Hemingway needed a new woman for each big book.] That was pretty perceptive of him, and it worked out in practice. Marty for *For Whom the Bell Tolls* and Mary for *The Old Man and the Sea.* But that wasn't as perceptive as it might have been if Scott had known about person-groups. Do you see it?

Oh yes.

They say *in vino veritas*, but wine has nothing on children. She saw that she wasn't dealing with the same person she had known—yet, same body, same voice, and taken for granted by the others. It frightened her badly. Here's how to explain it, in case it isn't obvious.

There was a group called Ernest Hemingway. Some of the group were dominant and some were in the background. Some were private and some gregarious. Some were scholarly, some extremely physical, some curious, some didactic. You understand, traits just like anybody, only I'm explaining it not as traits but as separate personalities I was holding together by my life. Every major change in my life was accompanied by a major reshuffling of players, some before the fact, others after the fact. It is obvious, surely. She was badly frightened because there had been a major shift and yet I wasn't totally strange either. It would be as if your brother appeared to you one day—in the body, I mean, not as an apparition—and was the same old brother you'd always known and at the same time was significantly someone else. As if he was possessed, say, or as if he had been in an accident or had had life-altering surgery *and no one but you noticed*. Of course it scared her badly, more because nobody seemed to realize it then because of the strangeness itself. But none of us knew.

I wonder what inspired Carlos Baker to include the incident.

Ask him. *I* don't know.

No, I'm not going to ask him. But it was striking, and the Fitzgerald quote you had me append made it even more so.

Surely it stands to reason that nobody is the same makeup in the same proportion under any and all circumstances.

It is now, sure. I mean, I see it differently in light of the person-group concept.

It says a lot about the importance of good companions, good habits, good intentions, doesn't it? But none of them can guarantee a thing. If life comes along and changes your circumstances, you will adjust your internal alignment to match, or, if your internal makeup changes, you will find your circumstances changing soon enough.

It's almost as if parts of us take a breather while their substitutes get into the ring.

More like new troops being sent in to reinforce or replace old ones. But not very much like either. It's just [the] internal and [the] external matching, as they always do.

All right. Speaking of that, I want to talk about one of your robots. It seems to me that you could never bear to be in the wrong in your own eyes. So, when Pauline came, you eventually wound up blaming the situation on the Murphys as the rich, and on dos Passos as their pilot-fish! That was very unfair, Ernest.

No judgments, though, right?

All right, that's right. (Why can't I get off this word "right" that's inserting itself everywhere today?) So talk about it, then.

Sketch your theory about robots. How to get rid of them, I mean; how to get free of bad habits.

I wouldn't have thought of them as bad habits, but I suppose that's one way to see them. Robots—automatic servants we have programmed some time in the past to always react to a given stimulus with a given response—function beyond our conscious control. They work out of our unconscious. Therefore we usually aren't even aware that they exist, let alone that they are functioning at any given time. We can change their programming only by contacting them out of the feeling (which means out of the specific consciousness) from which they were created, and applying analysis to the cause/effect or stimulus/response within which they operate. However, given those two conditions, feeling and analysis, we can change them easily, for they are our own creations and are there to do our bidding.
But now I've lost the connection to dos Passos and the Murphys, etc.

Put the two incidents and Scott's theory together and see if you don't have a more convenient, more powerful, explanation of my life.

I (like you, like anybody) was not an individual in the way our society saw it—yours or mine. Instead, I was the common denominator for a group of what might be called semi-individuals, or something—as everybody else is too. When the lineup of effectively operating sub-individuals changed, what people could experience changed. "Hemingway became the prisoner of his own myth," or "he fashioned a mask and then couldn't take it off," or "as he grew older, certain tendencies grew greater and he changed."

As my lineup changed, though, certain parts—those I held to most fiercely—did *not* change. I was a writer, a great writer, a craftsman with integrity. This was not going to change if the rest of my life crumbled around me. At the same time, changed circumstances internal and external brought new forces, new sub-individuals, into new relationship with that great craftsman aspect of me, and so as Scott said, new book, new woman, except that reverses the order of things.

Now, to be crude, are we talking about a different person to have sex with? Is it a matter of whose sex organs come together? Hardly. It's a matter of woman as enchantress, as vision—as anima projection, I can hear that Carl and you would call it. *That* is powerful, and another time ask Carl to talk about it, maybe. In any case, a new woman to be enchanted by called forth new parts of my inner being, and they related to—or let's say they were observed by, and portrayed by—that central core of me that did *not* change in and out, but remained always at the helm, that determined great craftsman. That's why I had unshaken integrity there always, you see. I couldn't afford to lose that. I'd have lost myself, and been totally adrift.

That does shed light on some things. But even though the result is a bit lighter than usual, I think we need to stop for now. It has been our usual 70 minutes.

≈11≈

Judgment and Self-Criticism

Friday, August 13, 2010

I sure hope you guys have something cued up—or queued up, either one—because I'm working with a head full of cotton.

[TGU] But, you're *working*. That's all to the good.

Yeah, but too much reading yesterday, and all the other bad habits I have.

So? Do your own criticizing, if it interests you. We aren't interested in criticizing, even if it seems that way to you sometimes. You know from your own experience, hardly gained, that criticism never helps unless it is asked for and actually wanted. Otherwise it is nagging, more or less, even if the content is accurate. People can't hear until they can hear.

Yes, I know that first-hand. It's hard to hear criticism especially if it is being added to self-criticism for the same things.

People are very hard on themselves, and even an ounce of criticism from someone else, especially if meant unkindly, may be too much to bear.

This relates to Hemingway too, doesn't it?

Yes, of course. Remember, we are using the man and his life as examples of how something widely known may become more understandable when seen through the keys a different view of life provides.

So this enters right into the question I had in my queue about the violent alternations of good-Ernest and bad-Ernest.

No, not all that directly. But it will tie in eventually.

Proceed, then.

The consciousness that is responsible for the group of elements that we are calling the person-group, we may as well call the ego. Don't jump to the word "egotism," however. The ego as we will use it is merely one's sense that the consciousness of the present moment *is* the self. This, of course, it is not and could never be, unless one wished to concede a different ego for every moment of time. (The true self can only be outside of time-space, naturally; there is no place to stand, inside a continually shifting time-consciousness. Jesus said, don't build your house on sand, you will recall.) But the ego *is* the sense of one's self at any given moment. It is the lens through which one perceives the world and the time.

That ego—that very restricted consciousness—has very little idea of how many disparate strands comprise it. It doesn't usually recognize itself as a lens for a person-group. Instead it invents itself, imagines itself, [as] *one* thing, with a consistency of makeup and purpose that is at very wide variance from what actually is.

If it perceives "bad" traits within itself; if it remembers "bad" things it has done or thought of doing; if it feels the presence within itself of elements espousing or embodying values it discards or indeed despises— one common reaction is to feel ashamed and guilty that these elements exist. You should know!

If one's ideals are high enough, if the pretense to be more or better than one is is strong enough and badly enough needed, you see the ego enter into massive denial. That denial, as we have said before, may lead to rewriting of memory in order to reduce the pain to bearable levels. And it will certainly be likely to respond to an external reminder as to an attack—for that reminder will cause pain, and will evoke the fight-or-flight response. Puzzling, then, isn't it, that people respond so badly to criticism?

Very funny. But certainly what you are saying rings true.

Notice how unnecessary it is, considered abstractly, that criticism bring pain or that self-knowledge bring criticism.

You want to say a little more about that?

Remember the story of the man who asked another man's servant how the other man was, and the servant said he was well, except he kept looking at his own faults "and cannot come to an end of them."

I do vaguely. "What a worthy servant," was the man's reply. But I can't remember who recounted it and where I read it. Anyway, I get your point— the higher the ideals, the finer the sieve through which we examine our conduct.

We would prefer the analogy the Egyptians used—the scales. One's soul needed to be lighter than a feather to pass on; otherwise, back to the mill, that is, Earth.

And it is just this sense of sin, and of being judged, that imprisons people and deprives them of hope—for who can reach perfection? And I see that you've angered me, and this was no doubt your intent, so—why?

It is just that sense of sin and of external judgment, yes. And it is impossible to be perfect in that sense, yes. And this brings us to our point. What is impossible for man is possible for God—or, in this particular example, what is impossible for our ego-self that identifies with all manner of competing and often antagonistic values, all continually a-shift with shifting time, is not impossible for the overall self that sees straight and clear and identifies not with the passing moment but with the unit as it exists beyond the reach of time.

We are sorry if that statement is not immediately clear. To some it will be, therefore we stated it. To others it will become clear upon contemplation and experience and reflection upon experience.

[In transcribing this, I realize that it is necessary to point out that the guys upstairs are equating neither themselves nor our higher selves with God, but they have often said that people often experience the higher self or the larger being and jump to the conclusion that they are in contact with the creator. In a sense it is true, but in a sense it is misleading.]

So—to circle back—self-criticism is not necessary or even appropriate *to the degree that one weighs one's life from the point of view* of the higher self, the larger being, the soul-seen-from-beyond-time-space. But only from there, and to that extent. To the extent that one identifies with the current moment's consciousness—what we are calling the ego—one cannot help criticizing and reacting to criticism. Is a very painful situation, but one that can be transcended.

It isn't transcended by the adoption of some abstractions such as "all is one," or "life is suffering" or even "God is love." It is transcended in the only way a thing *can* be transcended: by being experienced, then accepted, then loved (or, shall we say, experienced as part of one's essence) and then understood. Once understood, the charge is gone. But it cannot be understood only mentally, but through experience, transmuted by acceptance.

Thus as we have said more than once, judgment, condemnation, isolates and makes rigid. It condemns the judge in the same action by which it condemns what is judged. We say again, *don't judge, lest you be judged.* That *doesn't* mean, "if you judge somebody, we'll judge you in turn." What it does mean should now be evident.

Now, "don't judge" is usually taken to mean "don't judge (i.e. condemn) *others*." It doesn't, or does only peripherally, because you will find that as you cease to judge your own components of your person-group, your inclination to judge others—let's say, even, your *need* to judge others—drops off accordingly, and you are free.

Returning to Papa—?

We never left the subject. His life—as anybody's life, but his is well documented—shows you his inner fears, his self-doubts, his despised and rejected and besieged parts, by the evidence of his conscious ego's reaction against them. Hemingway was a man of genius and force who shaped his life to an ideal, and paid the price. (Paid it willingly and would have paid it willingly even if he had known ahead of time, but paid it.) Ideals conflict, like any other possible trait. An ideal of excellence conflicts with an ideal of acceptance, for instance. You can't expect tolerance from one who is living an ideal of perfection—and you can't expect ease or comfort, either. To find Hemingway's self's definition of the life, look to his made-up quotation in *Winner Take Nothing*.

[Courtesy of the Internet search facility, I find this, which is only a partial quote but should serve: "Unlike all other forms of lute or combat the conditions are that the winner shall take nothing; neither his ease, nor his pleasure, nor any notions of glory; nor, if he wins far enough, shall there be any reward within himself."]

Enough for today, I think. My thanks as ever.

And ours in return, to you and to all who do the work on themselves, for it is good work toward a good end.

≈ 12 ≈

Sensory Evidence

Friday, September 17, 2010

I got from the Hemingway Collection in the Kennedy Library photocopies of some pages from Ernest's sub-hunting log, and his report of one possible sighting, and other notes in his handwriting. Well, might as well stop talk-

*ing to myself. Ernest, now that I have this material, what direction should
I go with it?*

You have different things there, but the main use to you is to show
that we were serious about sub-hunting. It wasn't just make-believe and it
certainly wasn't doing as we wished when and where we wished.

But I already believed that.

Sensory evidence is always worth something to persuade other layers
of yourself that may otherwise be holding back. Besides, you have now
taken a first step, and the French say it's only the first step that counts.

I won't ask—first step to what? Time will tell.

Time will tell and your inclination and capability and actual deci-
sion will determine.

So what should we be talking about today?

There isn't any "should" about it. But we might talk about the sub-
chasing material. Read the *Submarine Manual* that ONI put out during
the war. You aren't memorizing it, but read it. You will get something out
of it, but hard to describe what or how. After you read it, we can talk.
You've already read my typed account of our seeing the Spanish ship and
the sub, and I remain firmly convinced that we gave them something of
value, there, that they never used. The handwritten notes are more for
you to read in a daydream state to get a sense of me. There is one nugget of information in the material starting Finca Vigia San Francisco de
Paulo Cuba. So read it over. And then the logbook pages are mostly to
let you look over my shoulder and see the changes over time. You don't
have any history-changing information there; that isn't the purpose of
the exercise. But it can change *you*, or start to. And of course there's no
use *telling* you what life will *show* you.

*All right. I'm still getting that this period in your life is important some-
how in a way not yet realized.*

Keep your eye on one thing. You are looking for the corrective to the Myth. To that purpose, everything you find that shows you me as opposed to the Myth of me, or your own ideas of me, serves the purpose.

And how does your material tie in with all the other material I've been getting? Or—does it?

The only way for you to see the outline of the thing is to outline it. Get a clearer sense of what has been given to you, and you will see; it will be clear, of its own nature, and what remains will be your own decisions. In other words, you will have a lot of choices, but not an infinite number. Among the possible choices will be some that appeal to you more than others. A few strategic decisions on your part will lead to more detail, and ultimately to tactical decisions and you will be done.

Just like that.

Just like that, the way *Men at War* was just like that, or any major exercise in compiling and choosing. I didn't say it would be easy, and you may not even do it. Who's going to force you? But *if* you're going to do it, that's the way. You have to start from an overview.

~13~

A Man Among Men

Friday, September 24, 2010

Last Friday I was talking to you, Ernest, and you said I should look through the Submarine Manual ONI put out during the war. I've done that.

And you just got a sense you hadn't had before, didn't you.

Yes I did. It's sort of comparing two unknowns, because I didn't experience either, but I suddenly realized, you in your 40s, during the war, must have been much like my father during the war, and I'm going to call dad in too, being that you've met a couple of years ago with me as the common ground.

[FD Sr.] Starting to get the hang of it?

Every year, I see how much I owe you, dad, and I see that among our family it was as if we were a person-group—we did hold the ring together, but maybe not that well or by all that much. We certainly were disparate elements.

[EH] All right, you're going to have to make clear to people what's happening. That means, spelling it out as we go.

Yes. Just as I'd had a sense of the young Hemingway by remembering my cousin Charlie, so this time I got a sense of Hemingway in the Q-boat era by sort of imagining my father with his friends. Dad in his 20s working in the shipyard, a man among men, sharing their lives and their amusements, their prejudices and loyalties, in a way I've never been able to do because I was never one of the boys in that way. But it gave me a sudden vivid sense of Ernest during the war in the Caribbean, a member of the team even if the driving force, gambling, drinking, competing innocuously—hard to spell out what it is that I just got.

[FD Sr.] And then you jumped from the life I led that was more like Hemingway's to the life we shared, or didn't share, because you and I were so different that we couldn't really see each other usually except through a haze of irritation.

And judgment. Yes. You had so many excellences that weren't obvious because all I could see were the things that weren't there that I needed—the understanding of who and what I was, for one thing. And of course there I was, covering up to beat the band.

[EH] The point for the moment is that between you and your father, you understand aspects of me that people sometimes miss. I wasn't either/or, I was both. Or maybe both/neither.

Perhaps you should spell that out, rather than me doing it.

By 1941 I was famous and rich; I had succeeded at my craft and I had accomplished what I wanted to accomplish in terms of bringing American literature back to a true course. It hadn't played out yet, but it was in the works. People were writing truer, and their very imitation of my style meant that even when they didn't know what I was doing—even when they wouldn't have agreed with what I was doing—they were continuing to undermine that over-refined, ornate deadened prose I'd set out to overthrow. (Not that I'd known that's what I was doing on any conscious level. We always focus on smaller things than that; it is the end result of many years of work on smaller things that accomplishes the bigger ones.)

I was living a rich life, and if I hadn't been a craftsman dedicated to his work, I could have become nothing but a wastrel, a parasite, one of the empty bored rich. But I *was* a craftsman, and that kept me focused.

The war came. No shock to me, of course. Hadn't I've been predicting it? Didn't predict Pearl Harbor, though! Never dreamed the incompetents in Washington would lose us our fleet before the war started for us.

But to stay on the subject—

First I edited *Men at War*, and that was a huge, massive job, unappreciated. I'd spent a couple of arduous months in the Pacific with Marty in 1941, and that had gotten me peripherally involved with the government, and the military in particular. Then, when *Men at War* was finished, there was The Crook Factory as a project, and then the Q-boat idea.

You've read now that it was a part of a vast effort by the government to overcome an urgent need that came about because of the government's stupidity and lack of foresight, as usual. Sinking U-boats in the North Atlantic and not considering that maybe we'd wind up at war with them! And not asking, if we *were* at war, what would subs do to us! But anyway, we were needed and we were glad to participate. It was my idea to carry it a little farther, and be ready to attack a sub if we got the chance. They went along, it not costing them anything in particular to do so, being that it was a few civilians and one Navy man risking their lives if it came to that. (Yes, [Don] Saxon was a Marine, but so what?)

The point of this is, there I was for all those months, dead serious but having our fun as we went along. I was one of the boys—they were all my friends—but I was the captain, and it was an easy fit for all of us. So, we drank and we played cards and we finished and we practiced and we lived together for a long, long time on a very small boat, and the relationship between me and them *as men* was much like the one you saw with your father and his friends in his fifties. I mean, it gives you an insight.

And, like you, dad had an extra dimension.

Yes. It wasn't so much that I was a *writer* as that I was a *reader*, or rather that I lived so much in my mind as well as so much in my body. I was their equal in what we could do as men, but I was also a resident of another world they didn't know. This sounds a bit highfalutin and I don't mean it to. It is simply that I spanned a broader span.

Yes, and I got the sense of it when I remembered dad, the reader among his friends.

[FD Sr.] If you could have let me teach you the things I knew, you wouldn't have lived so much in your mind alone, and maybe I could have followed you in your world, too. But then, if you hadn't lived a one-sided life, you wouldn't be what you are now.

Oh, I see it, all right. Life uses all our problems and even our failures, doesn't it?

[EH] It's mostly a matter of intuitive sympathy. We find our way toward each other—or away from each other, for that matter—by an automatic set of reactions that are continuously testing the acid/alkaline balance, or the salty/fresh balance, or the hot/cold—whatever analogy you like. And who do you suppose does the weighing and comparing?

I know that one too. The guys upstairs—our own particular upstairs component, I mean—move us this way and that, helping us stumble into this or that influence, giving us opportunities to decide how we're going to react. Do we need to say any more about your Q-boat time, Ernest?

You got what I wanted you to get. It was my last time as a man among men. Europe was different, and then after the war I was never the same. Concussions aren't good for you. Neither is prolonged strain physical and spiritual, for of course it is hard to be among fighting men who are going to die around you day by day. And it was hard being there more or less under false pretenses. What did I care about *Colliers*? I was researching my next book. And yet even as I researched, I saw, or felt, that it wasn't going to be the same.

Care to say more?

You already know what I'm going to say. If you read *Across the River and Into the Trees* you'll see my profound weariness and distaste for the whole business. It was necessary, because losing a war is worse than winning it, but there wasn't anything glamorous or shining about it. I wasn't 19 anymore. I loved the men and we all hated what we were doing, and we hated the fuck-ups who had made it necessary.

Anyway, in Cuba I was captain of my own little ship, responsible for our operations, and we did what we were required to do, and more. In Europe the only thing I did that was worth doing [helping our troops find the least costly way to take Paris], I had to lie about and deny, and anyway it only lasted a month or so. The rest was observing. I was always a good observer, but after a while you got sick of it.

And after the war there was no equivalent to the Q-boat experience.

That's right—and nobody has ever realized it! They think of me as a writer, and they look at the war as a desert or as research, and they forget the man who had that dimension that they—the writers—don't necessarily have. And if you hadn't had your father as a model, you wouldn't have known it even second-hand, because your life too was one-sided.

Well, we'll put out the word and see if it gives anybody a better sense of you. Ernest, dad, I love you both.

And we are living in you, you know, as you are living in us.

I hadn't thought of it that way. That's true for everybody isn't it?

That's a big question. Ask your guys on another day, but you do remember your catechism about the communion of saints.

Only vaguely. I can look it up, I guess. Okay, till next time.

≈14≈

Hemingway's Wavelength

So what do we talk about?

[TGU] Consider Hemingway's life in light of what we said yesterday about the internal rather than the external life being the center of things. Since we don't want this series of conversations to fade off into the mist, we ground it in a famous man's life, that you may see the principles in application.

If you will look in Hemingway's life not as a succession of externals to be itemized and examined and weighed and measured but as an inner expression and choosing among qualities, it will appear very differently—as will any life, of course. Same life, same circumstances. It is not the data that change, but the mind of the observer! You could do the same for your parents, or your children, or your closest friends or lovers or anyone you felt intensely about. Look at them not as walking biographies—and certainly not as extensions of yourselves—but as working expressions of combinations of qualities, working out internal compromises and alternations and squabblings and alliances, etc.

That's very interesting. Sort of a subtle change in perspective, but a real change.

That's the motto of the firm: subtle changes but real ones. Too drastic a change is hard to get integrated with the rest of your life. Too little change, or rather too trivial a change, may not be observable in its effects, though it will have them. But an important subtle change offers great new insights.

There's no great advantage in our commenting on Hemingway's inner life. You have him to do that, and in fact he has been doing it right along. But, *notice* it. Look at what he has been saying from a different perspective, and see if he hasn't been saying something different than you have been hearing.

I have noticed that often it is difficult to get people to hear what I actually say, if they are strongly expecting me to say something else. The other day, I had someone entirely reverse what I had said, thinking all the while that she was merely rephrasing, rather than reversing, my thought. And there was no easy non-contentious-sounding way to correct her misunderstanding. It happens probably more often than we realize.

Try it from this end!

Made me laugh, that time. All right, I see your problem. I feel your pain, in fact. But is there more we need to address concerning Ernest? I get the background sense that there is.

I think it is mostly that as you establish your interconnection with somebody, you get the key to their life, and that gives you a key to *your* life, because after all, you tuned in on them. If you and they weren't on the same wavelength *at least somewhere*, you couldn't.

And that "at least somewhere" is why you and the other guys had to establish a concept of us as being of many frequencies, many different people within us.

Yes, and that picture-painting is far from done. There are different *kinds* of intelligences, different *layers* of awareness, different *forms* of interaction, and they are all to be spelled out, but probably not until you express the intermediate stage of understanding you have come to.

To quote Rita Warren, "To understand A you first have to understand B, but to understand B you first have to understand A."

Precisely. It's a continuing process of understanding things more deeply by recurrently going back to what you thought you knew and seeing it with new eyes.

Now, since you hold frequencies A, D, and S, and another person holds C, H, and S, the two of you, communicating on that S common frequency, each has access to A, C, D, and H as well. So you, who have no natural access to C or H, find your range increased by your contact along the S frequency.

To put it less abstractly, if you and Henry Thoreau share a deep aspiration for self-transformation, as you do, a longing to be more and better then you experience yourselves, *Henry* can also experience (and not
exactly at second hand) your sexual experience, or your incessant reading
of different kinds of books (mystery novels, for instance) than he ever
read, or your Catholic-in-20th-century-America thread. You see? These
are just off-the-cuff examples. He never read war literature, never heard
of Appomattox, let alone San Juan Hill or Verdun or D-Day. But these
mean something to you, and so—because you and he share an interconnection in that line—they in *attitude*, or maybe I should say in *key*,
mean something to him. It isn't the external event or influence on you so
much as you having been affected by it. Similarly, he was deeply versed in
religious—mystical—English poets of the 1600s and 1700s. They don't
mean anything to you, but what *he* is, because he also had that thread
nourished, does mean something to you.

*I sort of see. This is a little more complicated than I thought it was going
to be when we set out.*

Well, you should be used to that.

I am. Shall we go on, or are we a place convenient for stopping?

Perhaps it is worthwhile to hammer on one point, once again. Your
TGU concept has made it possible for you to receive a maximum of content with a minimum of Story. You never meet save intuitively or via a
persona—Yeats's mask—and even intuitively you might be said to be talking persona-to-persona. In the absence of having to define in advance who
you're talking to, you have a lot more space to receive rather than con-
strict your reception to what you think is possible, what you think is likely.
(This—may we say—afflicts much channeling. It is why the language is
sometimes a parody of another time's rhythms. It is a mostly or entirely
unconscious attempt to fit the communication into a preconception.)

*Okay, point taken. Time to wrap up, I think. My thanks as always for
this enriching continuing conversation.*

You're welcome—and perhaps sometime we can discuss how your endless reading of biographies and history—and of fiction no less—has facilitated this work.

Well, you know where to find me.
That's more than you do sometimes! Farewell.

≈ 15 ≈

The Garden of Eden

Friday, October 15, 2010

Papa, let's talk about [his posthumously published novel] The Garden of Eden. *Was that your happy ending, or hadn't you decided?*

It is as I wrote it. I couldn't leave him unable to recover. Perhaps artistically I should have—I hesitated over it—but I couldn't do it. On the other hand I hadn't let go of it. I never got to finish it fully; it had to be abandoned as my life had to be abandoned.

It is satisfying, this way, in a way it couldn't have been if he had wound up having his new love but having lost what he had written—which might mean having lost the ability to write into the future. The fact that his recapturing it added detail, and that he had a surer knowing of his father then he had had on writing it initially, showed that he had not been truly permanently damaged by the body-blow.

That's right.

You had Fitzgerald in mind, didn't you.

Among other people. Zelda wanted to put him out of business as a man and as a writer, and she tried her best—and she was crazy as a loon after a while, though not in the way David's wife Catherine was.

It seems to me that you were very carefully giving David a background very different from yours—his father a white hunter, David an air-war veteran—in an attempt to distance yourself, so that perhaps people wouldn't assume that all that sexual experimentation was your own experience.

Besides, it *wasn't* only me.

No; I hear the word "only." We don't have to talk about it unless you would prefer to.

No, you zeroed in on the heart of the book in one respect—the writer living the life he was writing, and his immediate circumstances being by contrast sloppy and surreal.

Oh yes. I think your description is the finest description of living in Focus 27 and C1 simultaneously that I've ever seen. It deserves wider circulation.

David's girl could appreciate the result—could sincerely love the writing—but neither she nor anybody could accompany him into that territory, as you, and all writers, know.

A writer's lovers must live married to a sailor, seeing him only when he is in port between voyages, even if that is every day.

And if he is voyaging every day, a part of him will be away even when he is not. It is the price you pay, living with a writer.

Is there any reason for people to know of your own sexual experimentation? I got hints of something going on with Mary over some time—I forget where— but it is your own business unless you have a reason for talking about it.

There would be things to say, but no real purpose would be served. Let it lie, or lay, there.

Okay. There is some of that novel that I can't intuit anyway, it being written pretty elliptically.

Necessary in the times I wrote it.

I understand. By the time it was published, though, in 1986, it could've been pretty explicit and still get published.

At 87, I'd have been a lot less interested!

∽16∽

Roger and Thomas

On finishing Islands in the Stream this morning sometime, I had a thought of another theme to pursue about the reality versus the myth of Hemingway. Like a fool I didn't write it down except on the Akashic record. Papa Hemingway, what was it? Or, rather than putting words into your mouth (no, wait, what else am I doing?)—Well, go ahead.

By reading [as a short story in the *Finca Vigia* edition of his collected short stories] the chapters where Roger and Helena (Audrey) travel from Miami to New Orleans on their way west after leaving Thomas Hudson, and then returning to *Islands* to read the second and third parts, set six or seven years later, you drew a connection that I couldn't find a way to draw if Roger [hadn't] stayed in the book, but couldn't find a way to integrate if he did. The *Islands* that was published wasn't finished because I couldn't work out the problem involved. Putting it out as it did worked well enough, but left out the troublesome element that I was working on.

Roger says he has to go fight fascism at some point, but has competing responsibilities and has a right to enjoy himself as he goes along.

It is that balance that is at the core of it. In the 1930s Thomas Hudson had achieved a precarious balance of responsibility to his work and to his status as a father, on the one hand, and took his pleasure as he went along, on the other. He read, he drank, he fished—he was a physical and intellectual man in a physical and mental world. He tried to stay in harmony with himself. The outside world he let be, or ignored, or tried to stay unmired from. So, the fight on the dock that Roger got into. Roger's life in general.

It seemed to me that Roger and Thomas Hudson are different aspects of you, not so much different ways of looking at you as different ways of your experiencing yourself. Making Roger both a writer and a failed painter was a good idea that might have gone farther.

You see the problems I couldn't figure out how to fix. It blurred the focus.

Sure. Like, what was the relationship between Roger and one of Tom's wives. It seems clear that he was living with Andrew's and David's mother for a while—clear from the chapters not used—but not clear from within the book as published.

You could list the elements if it makes it clearer to you.

Roger is both writer and painter. He is politically aware, and prescient as to the absolute danger that fascism represents. You as shown in your letter in Esquire, for one example.

Yes. Thomas doesn't try to do both; he settles for appreciating writing while practicing his painting as an art, measuring his effectiveness by the popularity of his sales, but not needing to tailor anything to affect the sales.

You as writer going your own way with Scribner's support and outlets such as Esquire available to you.

And eventually TV and movies, yes, without my changing to meet what they want—and without my having to watch what they produced.

Later in the book, you as weary but doing your duty. No sense of Roger's attitude at all.

Well, you could say that Thomas Hudson's attitude was about what Roger's came to be by then. For all you know, Roger may have been killed in Spain. It killed enough idealists, even cynical ones. But by 1943, who could be idealistic about our side who knew the score? It was still an absolute given that fascism had to be destroyed if possible. But the corrupt French and the corrupt British and the corrupt American political establishments had managed things so well by repeated betrayals of each other and of themselves that you'd have had to be a total idiot not to see—

I know where you're going, but I lost the thread.

The West's governments—including Franklin Roosevelt's, don't kid yourself otherwise—represented the rich. That's all they ever represent except very occasionally in an emergency. The rich—especially the established rich—regarded it as their right, and sometimes as the obligation, to govern.

So World War II amounted to having to help the reluctant rich put down the fascists and Nazis they had tried so hard to appease for fear of the Communists, internally as well as in Russia. How hard was it to see that any victory dependent on the rich was going to leave the rich in charge? And yet that was better than letting the Nazis win. And the joker in the deck, the thing that complicated everybody's calculations, was Russia. In the heat of the battle in Spain, when nobody else was doing anything for the Spanish Republic—was strangling it, in fact, in the dark—Russia was there. At that time, criticizing Russia or Russian politics or Russian crimes was the same as treason to the Republican cause. But as soon as you were away from the war—especially once it was clear that the war was lost, and partly because of the NKVD and everything that went with it—then there was time for a balanced reappraisal, and you could see that after the Nazis were beaten we'd be faced with a bigger problem. And where was the shining moral example between the world's governments of the rich and the Soviet government of the secret police?

So, no, Thomas Hudson wasn't engaged in the war with his heart, only with his head. Maybe he was Roger with a few more years of illusions knocked out of his head by observation and experience.

≈17≈

"What was I supposed to do?"

You really did make your separate peace after World War I, didn't you?

Too simple. Put it this way, after a war that has cost you something, you have to ask yourself what you bought. I had gotten that wonderful sense of comradeship in the months between July 1918 and the end of the year, even if I didn't *quite* deserve it, and had to hide it from the others as best I could. My industrial accident had lifted me out of the anonymous ranks because I was the *first*, you know? Who remembered the *second* American to be wounded on the Italian front, or the 2000th?

But it was fragile.

Yes, Reynolds brought that out in The Young Hemingway, which I didn't understand for a while. You were in danger of sinking back into a life too small for you, unless you could invent yourself a new role that would give you a way out.

And I was lucky—that's what it looked like at the time, I not suspecting stage management because I didn't have the concepts you do—to get that job nurse-maiding the boy in Canada. That led to everything else, eventually.

But when I had gotten myself married, which solved my emotional problem and then solved my immediate financial problem too, and when I had gotten myself to Paris in an official capacity for the Toronto paper, which gave me standing among the newsman who could see what was really going on, I could see how little peace we were going to have in my lifetime from the peace that ended the war.

Now, there I was at—pick a date, say 25—there I was with all my life ahead of me, and no glimpse of peace ahead *In Our Time.* What was I supposed to do? Do you remember Roger telling Helena how impossible it was to go up against the stacked deck that was Florida politics in the 1920s? Should I have spent my life in politics? Or in advocacy journalism?

Emerson's "pretended siege of Babylon."

Exactly. I had my life, I lived it.

Everyone says you left Hadley much better off than you had found her, because—I take it—you showed her how to live rather than just exist.

We were very good for each other, and to each other, and maybe another smarter version of me stayed married to her and maybe that path didn't turn out to be without bumps either.

So in the 1920s, if not before, you could see that the war to end war wasn't going to.

It never was that except in Wilson's mind and in America's heart. Now, I don't mean to disparage that—ideas have consequences. But if it had been possible to tell the people the economic facts that had caused the war and were shaping the war and were going to dictate what could or couldn't be accomplished by victory, we wouldn't have had that terrible sense of betrayal and futility that came with a few years of headlines and consequences.

Newsman, you know, are cynical, and I was a newsman among them. We knew the score, or thought we did. For one thing we knew the difference between what we could learn and what we could get printed. That alone is a terrific education. You find out what people don't want you to say, and you can figure out why, easily enough. Of course not all your calculations are going to be correct, but you'll be miles ahead of the people who don't have the inside dope.

To sum this up, if I ever in my life thought of war as anything more than a sometimes unavoidable but always sordid and wasteful charade, it wasn't after I got out of the hospital in 1918. Oh, I still had use for the reflected glory, and I was as proud as anybody else of being on the winning side—assuming we could be considered to be the winning side, but anyway we weren't among the obvious losers—but four months of close association with and observation of real veterans was enough to dilute any remaining posturing that kid still had. And it didn't take long after that to see that however useful the war had been to me, it had bitched the world, well and completely, and there was no going back.

And then came the fascists.

An annoyance, at first. A joke politics, as Italy had been a joke front. But then Hitler copied it, and nothing the Germans do is ever going to be a joke. It may be heaven or it may be hell, but it isn't going to be a joke. And everybody could see it and nobody would look at it.

Because of Russia.

Because of Russia as a perceived threat to the rich, yes, but because of exhaustion, too. Winston Churchill lost his post when he tried to get involved for the Greeks against the Turks. He was calculating correctly in terms of The Great Game, maybe, but he was out of step with his times. The West was *tired*.

And besides, that was reminiscent of Gallipoli. [World War I military operation that turned into a disaster for England and was blamed mostly on Churchill, and cost him his position as first Lord of the Admiralty.]

That too, so nobody trusted him to look at things calmly and impartially. But mostly, people were tired. And that was an opportunity to Germans knew how to use.

My handwriting is deteriorating badly. Got to go. Thanks for the chat.

Any time. I'll be here.

Keep your cell phone on.

I will when you will.

VI

January—December 2011

In the Keys • Fatherhood • Biography • Hemingway's Range • Ideals and
Shortcuts • The Value of Time • Isolation and Connection • Hemingway's
Iceberg Method • An Industrial Accident • Alone • Fukushima and War
• The Sun Rises, Too • Revolutionary Politics • Land, Sea, and Air • The
Purpose • Hemingway's Catholicism • Fears • Viewpoints • Time and
Dimensions • Mind to Mind

In the Keys

Friday, January 7, 2011

[A friend and I took a vacation to the Florida Keys, and on our first
full day there went to Key West to see Hemingway's house. The next day,
I hauled out my journal to rehash the visit.]

You connected with the space, didn't you?

*I did sort of, in a slipshod way as usual. I mean, we took the tour through
the house, we saw the study, I glanced at the swimming pool, I felt for the
right books to buy in the gift shop, and that was about it.*

No it wasn't. Think.

Already, I get it. Slow down, you mean. And that is what has been wrong these past couple of months, isn't it? Too revved to communicate here in this way.

There is an art to anything. You can't go fly fishing by rules that work for—

I dried up on the analogy. I don't know fishing.

No, you don't—and you're forgetting that you're supposed to be letting stuff *come through*, not *providing* it.

I am indeed. Boy am I rusty. Okay, let's try recalibrating. [Pause]

We got our tickets and went to the living room. The guide came in and started his spiel. In the living room I noticed the photo of Gregorio Fuentes. I noticed the size of the room, the height of the ceiling, the light and air of the room. And I remember realizing that Hemingway had actually lived there, that he had been there.

We crossed to the room at the front of the house on the opposite side of the central hallway, the dining room, which was dominated by photos on the walls. The Hemingway wives, etc. Started to notice the disrespectful undertone in the guide's "funny" comments. Then the kitchen, then upstairs to the master bedroom. My memories aren't very specific. Wasn't I paying attention, or was I paying attention in a different way, to different things?

When you try to absorb the atmosphere of something, you are blanking your mind of specific associations and thoughts—in fact, thought interferes with the process. The memories are there, of course—they are there for everything in your life—but they are not memories of *words* or *thoughts* (which you were not recording or registering) but of connection. If the thing was recorded in one mode, how could it be played back in another? If you *think*, you remember *thought*. If you *feel*, you remember *feelings*. If both, both.

Let's skip to your study, then.

You were at first disappointed that you could go only a couple of feet into it before you were stopped by the metal barrier. But this had its advantages. No one else was in there too. The room was empty of people.

It was a composition of scene. *And people's energy did not disrupt the built-up energy* that the reconstructed scene creates.

I don't quite understand that. If you had left the room and it was as you had left it, I could imagine that your presence had left an imprint. Not so easy to imagine that, given that you left before 1940, and it was only reconstructed as a model of your writing life decades later, after Pauline's tenure and the new owner, etc. But this is assumption on my part, and I begin to see it.

Yes, you're getting it. My imprint on that room does not depend upon the visual cues left around or deliberately placed, any more than a ghost's appearance depends on a photograph of him remaining on a wall. We leave our energy on our surroundings as we live, or, to put it another way, we *merge* our energies with the world, continually. It is one more way in which people are not as separate from the world as they think they are.

Now, you can see the assistance that visual cues provide. Auditory cues, too, would help if there were any. Recorded voices or sounds help to produce that composition of place. But neither visual or auditory nor any other kind of cue—smells, for instance—are *necessary*; it's just that they can be *helpful*.

I well remember walking through London by the Nelson column, actively trying to allow David [a past life] to re-experience London. We walked down to the river embankment—I suppose "we" is about the best way to say it—and I looked at one monument that said, merely, "July 1, 1916," and I—he?—was filled with this ghastly flood of grief, indignation, etc. when I didn't even know what battle it referred to, or why the monument should have needed nothing beyond the date itself.

As I said in *A Farewell to Arms*. After a point, after enough suffering, words like "glory" and "sacrifice" can't mean what they are used to mean, and only dates and other concrete specific markers retain meaning—and that partly because they have meaning only to those who know *why* they have meaning, where words like "valor" don't mean anything specific to they *sound as though* they do, and people think they feel or understand something when in fact it is merely abstraction. David didn't respond to the conventionally worded tributes, did he? For one thing your own overlay of thought and reading—secondhand memory, call it—got in the way. But mainly, he wouldn't be in the mood to hear patriotic speeches, and *was* in the mood to connect who he was then and now with who you were at the moment.

Now, when you went through the house, in feeling for my presence you were not listening to stories about dead people, you were doing something entirely different. You were there, in that moment, willing to connect with me in that moment. That couldn't be a sensory experience; I am not there anymore. But it *can* be a non-sensory experience, because I am a part of the place not in any metaphorical sense but as a real living (though not living in 3-D) person. All the visual cues are designed for people trying to imagine what it was like, and they do assist in the process. But imagining can be either (or both) of two processes.

You can imagine as a sort of what-if exercise, in which you assume that the people who lived there are dead, and so it is only a sort of petrified memory that helps you to fantasize a story. Or you can imagine as an extension of your senses, in which you assume that the dead remain there non-physically (but not *only* there, of course, not tethered there, so to speak), available for you to interact with non-physically. In that case, imagination is not storytelling, or fantasizing. You did not wander around thinking that you were hearing me talk to you, or were even talking to me then. You went around in an open and receptive state, open to the interesting physical cues like photos on the rooms themselves, but open as well to whatever might come in between the lines.

≈2≈

Fatherhood

Wednesday, February 2, 2011

So, Papa, let's talk about the aspect of your life that was fatherhood. I am enjoying [eldest son] Jack's book Misadventures of a Fly Fisherman: My Life With and Without Papa. He seems such a good and cheerful man. Between you and his mother and Paul Mowrer, he seems to have gotten what he needed. And I read [books about Hemingway's youngest son Gregory, by Gregory's wife Valerie and son John]. It seems like he didn't get what he needed, but I don't know that it was anybody's fault particularly. Your views on them, and on [middle son] Pat?

You know first hand the competing demands on your time between career and family. Now, in one way I was freer than most, because I never had a nine-to-five job in my life, and once I married Hadley and we started to live in France, I could work on my own career instead of devoting energy to other people's business—my employers', in other words. But the other side of that is that my career was increasingly my sole responsibility, and quite a responsibility that was! If I was going to succeed, it would be on the back of my own work, my own decisions, my own strategy—and that is all very high-stress over time, something people don't always factor in when they see my letters to Max or my explosions in various directions. None of that makes it easier to concentrate on family.

Then there was the factor of women. Everybody has noticed that I always had to have a woman in my life—and that means all sorts of crosscurrents. I'm not talking about how ex-wives got along or didn't, I mean the emotional toll they took and the emotional nurturance they provided. Women take a lot of attention, not because they are greedy for it—some are, some aren't—but because when they are in your mind, they are front and center.

And speaking of that, don't forget my tremendous power of concentration. I could hone in on whatever I was doing and do *that*, and nothing else existed while I was doing it. You have some of that. I suppose all writers do. I had it in an extreme degree. But this means that if you weren't in my focus at the moment, you might as well not exist. Nobody senses this more than kids. They're usually pretty philosophical about it, in the way kids accept whatever life dishes out to them, but the more sensitive ones need more attention sometimes than they get, and some of them need it from one specific person—Papa, or Mama—and if they don't get it, they can't get an acceptable substitute.

And while we're listing things, we can't forget selfishness. I was the center of my world—who isn't?—and for long periods I didn't really think of the kids if they weren't around. So much easier to have Gigi taking care of by a paid employee than to do it ourselves, since Pauline had her own selfishness. That particular failure of imagination hurts, because it *had* consequences, and didn't have to be that way.

It is clear that life with Papa was vivid and memorable, though.

I could teach them things as much by how I lived as by what I instructed them in. Jack, say. Mr. Bumby [Ernest and Hadley's early nickname for their child] was born to be a fisherman, apparently. I didn't steer him to it, and other things like hunting that he had equal exposure to did not go to his core like fishing did, from his earliest days. But I could teach him, by example, to *enjoy* what he was doing, and to make his own fun by planning it. He picked that up, all right.

I guess what I was concentrating on is that when the boys were with you, they were very much with you—or I suppose I mean, you were very much with them, and they knew it.

Children tend to think they should be the center of their parents' world, and in a way they are and in a way they aren't, and as you grow up you get used to it.

Sibling rivalry, I suppose, could be looked at as each child wanting to be the center of the world for the parents. It isn't just a matter of attention. I hadn't thought of that in just that way.

But it doesn't happen, and can't happen, and wouldn't be healthy if it did happen. The mother who can't let go is as bad for the child as the father who has no interest. Nor will those children have children in their turn who will be the center of *their* world. *A* center, maybe. *The* center, no.

Except maybe.

Except maybe, agreed. I didn't see it even in Sara Murphy, say, who was a good mother whose experiences with her children were tragic. Even she had other interests, and had to have, and should have. It's only natural. It is only that infantile I'm-the-center-of-everybody's-world attitude that expects anyone to have no interests but them.

Speaking of that—

Oh, I know. Don't think I don't, and didn't. Is *your* life under *your* conscious control?

I'm not meaning it as a criticism.

But you weren't sure I'd noticed? Don't worry, I always had plenty of people volunteering to tell me how self-centered and thoughtless of others I was.

Well, since we're on these waters, let's touch on the subject. Many people have said you got increasingly arrogant and caught up in your own myth as years went by. In fact, I noticed a careful line in Jack's book, speaking of early 1942:

"Before I left in early January to return to Chicago, much of the glamour of the Finca had gone. Somehow, without consciously knowing why, I was becoming aware of the ever-more strained relationships and the occasional gruffness Papa was wont to vent on anyone in the line of fire. On the other hand, he was never unkind to me, except for his natural roughness which I was sometimes oversensitive to." [Pages 101-2]

Jack loved you, was fond of you at the time and retrospectively and was not so much critical as sometimes coolly observant. I found that telling testimony, in context, as I might not have from someone with an ax to grind.

It became more difficult all the time, once I left Key West, to be a man among men. You can't treat unequal things equally and come up with a proportionate result, you know that. The longer things went on, the more I was the most famous, the most resourceful, the most accomplished man in my circle. That's why I valued Wolfie, say, or Paxtchi. They had their own center and weren't dependent on me. And it's why I got increasingly suspicious. Sometimes it seemed that everybody around me was along for the ride, and sometimes it was pretty nearly true. And, come to think of it, it's probably why I drove my older friends away: They knew a different version of me, and they and their unadjusted attitude no longer fit.

And you couldn't break out of the closing circle.

Even now it's hard to see how I could have.

You'd have had to have been surrounded by your equals, or rather by people who were each superb in something. And there was your competitiveness.

I know, I know. But it never let me alone. And maybe without it I would never have accomplished anything.

But we are looking at the down side.

What were my choices, realistically? If I'd lived in New York so that I could be among the equals, what kind of physical life could I have had? And which of them was my equal anyway? And if I stayed in Cuba, increasingly I was on my own turf and people came to me—wanted or not wanted—and so I lived in a sort of very public isolation. Should I have gone to the West Coast and lived among the [film] Industry types? I can't see that that would have helped matters. I like fishermen and bullfighters and people who could *do* things, but even though I could fish, I wasn't a fisherman for a living, and I certainly wasn't a *torero*! So any friendship was still going to be with Papa as the celebrity and the head of the table.

I am put in mind of Einstein telling somebody that as an old man he lived happily in the solitude that is so painful in youth.

If you're going to make sense of my life from within, you're going to have to remember that other strands don't cease to exist merely because you are examining any one particular strand.

Yes. It's a complicated puzzle you were.

You can tease it out. It's just a matter of time and careful attention and an instinctive sympathy.

≈ 3 ≈

Biography

Thursday, February 3, 2011

All right. Papa, I finished your son Jack's book, and I did get a couple of valuable clues from his book, not least a confirmation of my feeling that

*Hotchner was not just a hanger-on but a real friend, and that Mary was—
well, you tell me.*

There isn't any point in setting out to prove a thesis when you come
to write up somebody's life, but people *will* do it, and it's very misleading to themselves and to whatever readers believe them. Maybe the only
way to learn about somebody you didn't know is to read a lot of different
points of view, and make allowances, the way you are doing. But what if
nine out of ten of your sources are reciting the party line, and the tenth
is the one with the truth?

If you have the same basic story through enough points of view, you
will form your own point of view. The longer you can hesitate to do it,
the more sophisticated your portrait is likely to be. After a while you
become so firmly rooted in the general environment of it that every new
fact takes its place to confirm or contradict or add a shade of color to
the picture you have been constructing. So you read Mary's book and
some things didn't ring true, and other things seem clearly to be writing
around something she wants to be silent about, and some things seem
to be firmly rooted and some seem likely to be true from her point of
view but not necessarily from others. And maybe you read Hotchner
first, and so you wonder if you were wrong about your weighing of his
account. And now you read Mr. Bumby's, and it confirms your uneasi-
ness about some things about Mary, and your confidence in Hotch, and
reminds you that perhaps you are being too hard on Marty, or seeing her
only from one limited point of view. Now, if that becomes the last book
you read, the temptation will be to assume that you have what you need.
After all, you've read Baker, you've read Reynolds, Myers, Mary, Marty,
you've read Hotchner and Jack and Gigi's son John—you know.

And nobody can read all the important books on anybody's life, if
they keep coming out! And if any given book, good or bad, may have
just one nugget, but a real nugget, obviously there's no hope of putting
together a complete picture that way.

Beyond that, in anybody's life there are going to be aspects that you
just can't relate to, so can't really understand. It's one of the things that
makes you different from him, or her. In your case, hunting and fishing. They just aren't part of your makeup, apparently. Or, if they are,
they've never had a chance to emerge—which is pretty much the same
thing. Or riding horses. You know, a host of physical things. If you are to

understand me, you are going to have to *imagine* somehow the effect on a life of such a different makeup.

You can imagine, perhaps, how little a scholar in the library is able to do that, or even to understand the need for it.

Oh, I don't know. When I was studying history, I remember reading somewhere that a prime requisite for any historian was the ability to imagine a world different from ours—before mechanization and urbanization, for instance. How different is that from remembering that people are different and spend their time in different ways, and have different mixes of sensory input?

Maybe more different and more difficult than you are allowing for. If you are studying the 1700s and you know what you are doing, you don't expect trains, let alone cars, and so you adjust your picture of how big the world was, and how much slower. But if you don't think about people being *really* different, and you read about somebody's words or actions, you may easily misread what you think you learned.

I've lost my grasp on whatever point we were pursuing.

You are sort of wanting to get me to talk about Mary and other such complications. But maybe that isn't the best thing to do. One more source of gossip, and what good does it do anybody? Would you want anybody prying into your life? Would you want them trying to reconstruct what you must have thought, must have felt, must have wanted or needed or love or hated? You know it can't be done, not really.

I see where you're going. Let's talk about the limits and scope of biography.

Let's talk about sources, while we're at it.

Okay, let's.

If the scholars would remember their limitations, they would do a better job. If you will realize and remember yours, which are somewhat different, you will too. It is only when people exceed the limit of their knowledge and expertise that they run into trouble.

For instance. A Carlos Baker digs and digs for the facts, and he amasses quite a lot of them, and puts them into a sort of order that gives other scholars a starting point. He works first-hand with some people who knew the person Baker is writing about. He gets their impressions. He knows the books, the articles, the letters, the points of view accessible to him. He *digs*, in other words, and to that extent, well and good. But is he a novelist? Is he a fisherman or hunter or drinker or pugilist? Did he grow up where and when I did? Does he know my temperament from inside? Was he there, as the old comedian used to ask? ["Vas you *dere*, Charlie?"]

Nobody can reassemble anybody from the outside. Every thing you don't understand, or don't know, is going to distort the picture. So is everybody's first-hand account from another point of view that may be deliberately or unconsciously slanted to put me in a bad light. So is the lack of proportion in realizing that the incidents are less than the tip of the iceberg that will forever be underwater.

And it isn't really any better when a person goes to write his own biography of himself. In a way you wind up writing an outside view of what you saw from inside, *because you can only write about what you know happened* (or what you think happened, anyway) and can't write about what you did while unconscious of it, or what you did that had effects you didn't realize, etc. Try doing that and you're putting together an apology, a statement for the defense, and you're doing it from an outside perspective, responding to what people said about it, because *you* weren't there!

You're talking about state-specific memory.

I'd have never called it that, but I am. Spell it out a little.

One of my friends—Bruce Moen, I think—once pointed out that different memories are associated with different states of mind, and were not necessarily available in other states. I would tend to associate it with what the guys say about different strands taking turns running the show. Let's say one part of us functions while drunk or drinking and another functions under some deep emotion, and another when we are being coolly analytical. What we say and feel and mean when we are deeply in love may not be available or even able to be remembered when we are in a state of towering rage, say, or are obsessed with financial worries or whatever.

Yes, and this is only common sense, after all. Everybody knows this. But scholars may tend to forget it unless they are acute psychologists as well, *because they always come to their work in the same state of mind!* They're always in scholar mode. How can they connect to other parts of me?

Well, I'm not sure that's true, Papa. I don't see why a scholar might not daydream about you and your life and times even when he isn't at his desk. And you have people like Terry Mort, who pretty clearly understand that side of you.

Then let me say it a little more carefully.

To write a true biography you would need to be able to do impossible things, such as

> *See and feel and think and react as the subject would have done.*
>
> *Contain within yourself all the subject's background, including people, places, books he'd read, things he'd done, the news of the day (day by day), the daydreams he had, the talents and aversions and every aspect of his personality.*
>
> *Know everything that had ever happened to him and some that happened only around him, and from multiple points of view.*
>
> *Know every strand that operated within him, and in what proportion and in what circumstances, including the tremendous amount he didn't realize himself.*
>
> *Know at least something of why he came into life (or, you might say, what the potential of that particular mixture of elements was) and see how one thing could express only at the expense of others, and hence what tensions this set up.*

I could go on, but you can see, it's an impossible task. You'd have to transcribe the Akashic record—and for what? Who could listen, let alone record? It would take a lifetime to absorb, as it took a lifetime to live—and at the end of it, you'd *still* be on the outside looking in.

Everything you say makes sense, but still there is a need for biography.

Of course. But my point is that it is important that the biographer remember that he—or she—can't really do what he or she is trying to do. They can present *a point of view* of the subject, and it can be more sophisticated or less, more profound and sympathetic and discerning or less, depending on the biographer, but they aren't going to catch the bird himself, only the shadows he cast. As long as they remember that, what they do may be of great value.

≈4≈

Hemingway's Range

Friday, February 4, 2011

Well, Papa, if you're interested in talking some more, let's talk more about your life.

Let's talk about my range.

Fine, let's do so. As you will know, sharing my mind, I have thought about it quite a bit.

If people realized that I knew classical music, opera for instance, and haunted art galleries and read all levels of current and classic literature, if they knew that the cultured end of our heritage was not closed to me, they would be able to put prize fighting and safaris and deep-sea fishing and *corridas* and other more physical pursuits into more their proper context in my life. Then add unrelenting devoted work writing, which is enough full-time career for anyone, and add strenuous friendships, romances, antagonisms, and family connections, and add the everyday occupations such as news and correspondence and gossip and drinking with friends, and add daydreaming and remembering—certainly necessary to any storyteller!—and you have a better-rounded picture of the life I led. And even that, of course, necessarily omits the time I spent thinking and brooding, time not less part of my life just because it may have left no record.

You see? There was tremendous breadth of interest, of accomplishment, there. I didn't exactly stretch myself thin—but I did keep stretching. That list doesn't even mention business letters, and negotiations, and schemes of one sort and another, all the way from schemes to have fun and add intensity, like our syndicate on Bataclan II, to things that truly were important, like using *Pilar* to fight Nazis, or setting up The Crime Shop.

And what of the poetry I wrote? Okay, it was lousy poetry, but it expressed a part of me that wanted expressing. You can't expect to be a genius at poetry as well as prose, but like the saying you like, "a thing worth doing is worth doing badly." Better if you can learn to do it well, but if you can't, you can still do it, if it is important to you somehow.

Supposing I had become a painter, or a sculptor? Maybe I'd have become good at one of them, but there are only so many hours in the day. The point is, I extended that far.

Yes you did, and it's no wonder you aren't really very well understood, but are more or less caricatured. People see one aspect of you, or two, and in all good faith they think that that is (or they are) the only important thing or things to concentrate on, and the rest of your life more or less an irrelevance.

Consider someone writing your life and see how many strands would have to be considered to truly understand you. And maybe most of the strands are invisible. This goes for everybody.

So—since we are talking of you because you are famous and accessible through your writing—what is the point for people to come away with?

What good is a writer who has talent but does not take pains to tell the truth? I'm not talking about facts, now, I mean truth. To sell a false image of life because The *Saturday Evening Post* is willing to pay for that and not for something true is to lie for pay. Worse—much worse—is to sell your talent an inch at a time, because whoring destroys your ability to say anything real—and it *should*.

I was a tremendous storyteller in my personal life, as you already know, and it is strictly Biographer Beware when it comes to concluding that what I said happened must have really happened. But in my stories and novels I told truth! The facts were made up, the characters were made up, or modeled on real people, or were scrambled from various models— but the description of the world was true, or as true as I could see it.

This is the one central fact about my work: I wasn't a journalist, I was a storyteller, but the picture I drew of the world was a true one, as best I could manage it with my power and intent.

Well, I see clearly, and I know that many critics and biographers must see, that your one area of life where you never compromised was in your art. You didn't take shortcuts and you didn't tailor your message to make a sale.

⁓5⁓

Ideals and Shortcuts

Now—speaking of range, let's get into trickier ground. Extend what you just said about writing to the rest of my life. Can you say the same? That I never compromised or took shortcuts or tailored my message?

Well expand upon it. I don't think many people would be able to agree. I don't know if I could, yet—but I'm open to argument.

"Never is a long time," you always say, and it would only take one example to invalidate an absolute statement. But broadly speaking, I would say that "I" didn't compromise or take shortcuts or tailor my message to my audience in order to gain something from them. But then we are playing the same old song, which "I" are we talking about?

It seems clear to me that you lost control of yourself and did things that you were ashamed of, or were unable to admit to yourself that you had done. But should we include such moments as compromises or shortcuts or pandering? Personally, I don't think so unless they were conscious choices.

Your audience is going to think we are splitting hairs, here, but it is an important distinction. On the one hand, intent; on the other, execution.

I agree, and I was sort of there already although I hadn't ever put it that clearly. Your conscious intent was to live with integrity and honor, and you stuck to it despite lapses caused by alcohol or paranoia or robots surfacing.

And in that, I am as much a model of the world as in anything else.

Yes, clearly. One final connection to the question of range, before we wind up for the morning?

The ideals you have provide the horizons of your life. The wider your horizons, the richer a life you can have.

You'd better spell that out a little, if you don't mind.

You could look at ideals as your ambitions for life. If your ideal is a sound mind in a sound body, an intellect continually nourished, a body continually educated and exercised, you're going to have a more fulfilling life—*to the extent that you try to live your ideal*—than if you're content to just get by.

You know how competitive I was. It hasn't struck you that I was in competition with myself, even in a way with God. If you want to get into the habit of settling for second best, the habit widens into other areas of your life. And if you get into the habit of always wanting and needing to be number one, your result improves.

If my ideal had been to be the best-selling author in America, or the one who commanded the highest magazine prices, or the one that all the ladies knew and read, or the one who was on the vanguard of social change (whatever that meant), it would have been an ideal much more easily attained, maybe, but it would have warped my life. Instead, it was to write true and hold my good opinion of myself by continually earning it. That wasn't a day-to-day accomplishment, necessarily, but it *was* the ideal, the pole star.

It served you well. And perhaps it can still serve us well as a reminder. You were the prime example of a man whose values were shaped before World War I, met the disconnect between those values and the new reality that followed, and lived them into the new era. We need the example.

≈6≈

The Value of Time

I get the impression, Papa, that you knew very well the value of time, and you used your time.

Suppose you had come within an ace of being killed before you were 19 years old. Do you suppose it might put you in mind of irreplaceability?

Well, but I remember that sudden impression of you as a young reporter in Kansas City, just like my cousin Bub, all nerve endings and adrenaline and irrepressible enthusiasm. That was before the war, and the shell.

True enough. But I didn't want to get cheated. That's what the shell did.

Okay. It kept that impatience alive.

Not impatience, exactly. That sounds more like I couldn't wait to get somewhere I wasn't. Just sucking the juice out of life as I went along. That's what I was doing.

Not a bad way to live.

Nope.

≈7≈

Isolation and Connection

Don't let yourself slide into the idea that you, or I, or anybody, is singular in the way people think of it. In other words, don't be a Sunday Christian about it, living your mental life one way usually and another way only in a certain context. If you're going to understand a thing it has to really sink in within you, and if it does that, it is going to change the way you see everything, without your being able to help it, or wanting to help it.

Just remember that the Hemingway you are talking to is not the isolated mind who lived his life on earth moment by moment. Just as I don't have the same limitations of viewpoint produced by temperament and living moment to moment (that is, reacting in isolation rather than reacting to the lifetime as a whole), so it is not the Hemingway who lived in isolation from other viewpoints.

> *Separation in time, separation in space.*

Yes. It's a condition of life on earth, and it has its uses or it wouldn't be a condition, but by its very nature it produces limitations that don't apply once we are no longer in the body. So—you see a Hemingway who is not the Hemingway that was, or I should put it, not the Hemingway that he and others experienced. But what may not have occurred to you and to your friends is that I am not experiencing the DeMarco that is in isolation—the DeMarco you and they know and experience—but another version of you, put it that way, the version that is not limited by time and space. Thus our connection.

> *I think you mean to say that Hemingway 1899-1961 and DeMarco 1946-20whatever do not touch, and that I have been thinking that DeMarco-46 was touching the spirit of Hemingway-99, but it may be more accurate to say that the larger being of which DeMarco-46 is a part is communicating with the larger being of which Hemingway-99 is a part, and the two time-bound parts are having a sort of virtual conversation.*

You might look at it this way. When you are engaging in Intuitive Linked Communication, as your guys rightly call it, DeMarco-46 is communicating with *his* larger being, who communicates with others and seamlessly passes the contact through, itself usually remaining invisible or at most to-be-inferred. Your larger being may contact Hemingway-99 through Hemingway's larger being. How else can it be done? If mind is non-physical, and it is, your link to others can only be non-physical in nature, however it may seem to be bound by the laws of physical life. Hence, instant hatreds and instant attractions.

Remain aware of when things in your life work out smoothly and when they don't, and see if you can deduce or rather *feel* a difference within yourself that corresponds to and precedes each type of smooth or rough patch. This is *not* to say that anyone's life could or should be lived without rough patches, and it is not to say that if you hit a rough patch it's your (or anybody's) "fault"—but look. You know the saying, when your luck is running good, push it. There's a reason for that saying. When you hit a smooth patch, don't go to sleep; take advantage of smooth water and either paddle like hell or rest and look around and enjoy it or drop a line into the water or whatever you want to do—*but be aware of it* while it's there, and remember that there's no guarantee that smooth water is going to last forever, or *should* last forever.

As I'm writing that, a part of my mind is thinking of your life's end, and how people are tempted to read all sorts of inevitable tendencies into it. It may be it was just taking the rough with the smooth.

That's part of the secret of the good life—you take the rough with the smooth and you don't think life owes you a ride that's all smooth. And it's better if you realize that you wouldn't necessarily like it, or profit from it, if it *were* all smooth, any more than you'd do better if every day was Tuesday, or every month was March.

≈8≈

Hemingway's Iceberg Method

Tuesday, February 8, 2011

Well, the fruit stand is open. Papa?

Continue with the exercise.

And that is?

To see your life to this point and see what it has led you to, so that you can begin to express what you have never felt able to express. For, this lack of ability to understand your life (partly because you can't express what you know, which would make you more able to understand more) is a very common problem. As people see somebody working it out in public, they will get their own ideas on how to do their own sums.

Is this a particularly appropriate time for the exercise?

Can't you feel it?

I do, actually. The vacation in Florida, which already seems a good while ago, marked a sort of intermission, a time away from normal, and was dominated by thoughts of moving, and by a strange sickness that wasn't asthma, and a sort of gathering of forces, maybe.

That last statement. It doesn't really *say* anything. Say it, or give up hope of understanding what you mean and what you're only half perceiving.

I begin to see what you are doing. You are showing me how you worked and why you did what you did.

But do the work.

All right. Gathering of forces. What did I mean? I had a sense that both Charles and I were preparing somehow for a new phase in our lives. There was a sense of anticipation of change, and a readiness for change, in fact an impatience with a continuation of the old.

How? How did you feel that?

It's beyond any "how." I just felt it.

If you're going to communicate, you're going to have to hand the reader something definite. The by-product will be that you will hand it to yourself, at a deeper level of understanding than you have ever known. How did the sense of anticipation of change manifest?

I don't know, really.

Remember specifics.

I would sit on the deck looking out at the water. I had books about Hemingway. I had just been to Key West (the first full day in the Keys). I had this journal, and I see that we had some substantial conversations. It looks like my time went to reading, talking to you, planning to move, and talking with Charles. And being sick, and a little sightseeing, not much.

How did the sense of anticipation manifest itself?

I don't know!

Yes, you do. Or, you will, when you do the work.

I am put in mind of sitting in the chair on the deck. That's what keeps coming up, sitting on the chair there. It wasn't when I was reading, or even writing, but when I was just sitting.

You're getting there. Pursue the thread. *This* is the work I did in silence that never showed. *This* is the iceberg beneath water.

But in regard to different subject matter.

Do you think so? Different externals, yes. But a man's internal experience of life can be experienced with superficial understanding or can be deeply understood, and mine was as deep an understanding as I could achieve. Yours to now has not been.

I can see that. Partly it was not knowing how.

Or that is your cover story. Just be willing to see. What happened when you were just sitting?

Things were going through my mind, probably, but I don't remember what.

So remember the water and the island and the sky at night or in early morning or in midday or evening. It all changed continually.

Yes, of course it did, and particularly after I got sick, it wasn't always entirely comfortable, but usually more comfortable than being inside. I don't see how to get to whatever you're trying to get me to, here.

You tell others about state-specific memories. Doesn't it apply to you?

Oh sure, it isn't an intellectual thing at all, it's a matter of getting back to the emotion that will connect up to the memory of where I was when I felt that emotion.

Isn't that what I said when I advised people to remember what specific detail had caused an emotion in them? The water jumping off a tightened fishing line, for instance?

I didn't understand it that way. In fact I didn't understand it at all. I could see that it was giving you something, but I couldn't see what.

So now that you know, apply it. Do you remember what you were looking at?

I remember the wading birds. Charles thought they were always waiting for dinner. I figured much of their day involved other things that birds might understand but we don't. But for all I know they do think about food all day long. My eyes aren't very good for distance anymore—I often saw only a blur where Charles would see birds—but I'd see the ones close—

You know, thinking about it, that inability to see detail or even clear outline was on my mind that trip. I've come to accept it but it was getting in my way. I could see color changes, but even color is off when you can't see in focus.

So your life was out of focus?

You could put it that way. So—how out of focus? In what way? Telling, I guess, that I can always read, with or without glasses, even if I can't read road signs or see birds or trees or anything else clearly. Yes, in fact, my life was feeling somewhat out of focus. I'd just finished The Cosmic Internet book, so I should have been feeling pretty good about that, and in fact I did. But I was feeling impatient about the time I waste. I was feeling, obscurely, that I was on the verge of stagnating. Can't say why I was feeling that.

Oh? Can't you?

Can't if I don't know why.

State-specific memory. You don't remember the individual thoughts, you get back into the emotional place where you connected to those thoughts. Watching the blurred but pleasant scenery, enjoying the day or night. Waking up, that time, to the intense star shine that you'd never experienced before. Why were you feeling you were stagnating?

For some reason the idea of living in town was growing on me, and had been for a little while. Somehow it seemed that the townhouse I was thinking of at the time (which didn't materialize) was going to encourage and force me to consolidate, to concentrate. I would center more on myself and less on my surroundings—which is ridiculous, as I center on myself continually, practically to a pathological degree.

Follow, don't judge. Judgment automatically cuts off access; it is not a mode of perception.

There was this feeling that I wanted to concentrate on expressing what I know, and somehow to continue to live on the New Land as I had for more than a dozen years would not aid but hinder that process. I had a strong sense of "more lives to lead," like Henry leaving Walden. It was time to put some things into the past so as to see them more clearly.

Oh?

Yeah, I heard that. To see more clearly. But I think I'm pretty much done for the moment.

Maybe you learned a skill here, though.

Maybe I did. We'll see. Thank you, Papa, I do appreciate it.

≈9≈

An Industrial Accident

Wednesday, March 9, 2011

Papa, using this cane yesterday and this morning [having injured an ankle in a trivial accident], I was thinking about you. It was romantic, that limping around—but it wasn't only romantic.

No, it wasn't only romantic. It was a damn nuisance, as well. And it was a loss that was bearable because it had meaning as an honorable war wound. Only with the coming of time did I start to feel it as an industrial accident, and then saw the other woundeds as equally the result of industrial accidents, regardless of their valor—an important point people often miss. And from there it became possible to see the entire war not as a crusade of right versus wrong—which is how it had been sold to us, how we had sold it to ourselves—but as one colossal industrial accident that had maimed us for no particular reason.

If you understand how I came to see it that way, you'll understand better my attitude toward the second world war. I went into that one without illusions. The men at war were a fascinating phenomenon, and the war had to be won, but as evil as the Nazis were, they were only evil in a different way from the people running England and France, not to mention Russia and the little dictatorships all over Europe. The little countries weren't so much to blame, but their sufferings were as much the result of geography and history as of anybody's evil intent. You might say that the invasion of Belgium both times, and Holland and Denmark and all the second time, were another form of industrial accident.

That's a lot of insight to get from your wounding.

From my wounding, but also from some reporting for the [Toronto] Star after my wounding. The Turkish war showed me World War I in miniature and in retrospect. It is all there in Farewell to Arms and The Sun Also Rises, but you have to be able to see that my perceptions were neither simpleminded nor trendy nor the party line. And God knows, I wasn't advocating that anybody live like Brett or Mike or even Jake. I was just describing the emotional aftermath of one giant industrial accident. With time it became clear that this accident was still in progress. As you've seen and see and are going to continue to see. It's hard to get too excited about Progress and the Rights Of Man and the Victory of this or that principle, when you see that it is mostly illusion on some people's part and deception on other people's part and what you would call general unconsciousness on everybody's part living through it. It's just that I was wounded so quickly that I had just what I had wanted when I shipped out! I was a hero, or as much of a hero as you can be when you are wounded out of the blue—or out of the black, to be more accurate—with no combat involved. And isn't that how nearly all the boys and men were injured and killed, after all? If you are torn apart—a little bit or extensively or entirely—by high explosive thrown at you from a distance, by somebody you never saw, who knew or cared nothing about you except maybe as an abstract representation of "the enemy"—the valor involved is entirely different from a cavalry charge, say, or a sword fight or even a duel of rifles at point-blank range. They saw it—the soldiers saw it, whether the officers did or not—in the Civil War, 50 years earlier. Getting blown to bits by artillery fire while you hide from it in trenches was exactly what was happening in France and Italy in 1918. It was a world of difference from warfare as it existed in 1861, let alone in the Napoleonic era, say.

And when you were wounded you were a little embarrassed that you hadn't been doing anything heroic.

Exactly. The experience didn't match what we had been fed about it—mostly lies, of course, as usual in war—so at first I assumed there was something wrong with *me*. So, I dressed up the story to make it bearable, so I wouldn't feel like a pretender.

You had to pretend to avoid feeling like a pretender.

Yeah, crazy, isn't it? But I didn't see it that clearly then, and maybe you weren't so clear yourself when you were 19.

You don't have to tell me! But, continue.

The real soldiers, the ones who had gotten wounded after long service, saw through me at once when I paraded through all decorated. They knew, you see. I was still seeing through civilian eyes, and the eyes of a kid who had just arrived, like a new recruit in 1864 would have been among men who had been wounded at Gettysburg and were still recuperating, or who had just been wounded at Forts Hell and Damnation. *They knew*, and I didn't, even though my industrial accident had given me a spurious membership in the club. It was okay for me to use the clubs facilities, but I was an honorary member, and they knew it and made it plain.

Now, it's funny how life works. I was an innocent, though I didn't quite realize it because I was such a fast learner. My few months as a reporter in Kansas City had given me enough of a peek into the lives of the men who kept things going, like police and firemen, and the lives of people who had had their own industrial accidents (though I didn't think of them that way yet) that I thought I had become hard boiled. I *felt* toughened and knowledgeable. And of course I was so green, so much living in image and illusion, and everyone around me knew it, but I didn't know it. So—I pretended my way through a succession of roles, altering the part as I went, learning from observation how the real heroes acted, figuring out how they felt, and mimicking them when safely not in their presence. This whole sequence was invaluable when I came to become a writer, for what is a writer of fiction if not somebody who gets inside somebody else's skin and describes how the world looks from there?

And the result was that even when I was back home, or in Chicago, and I was still playing the role, I was feeling my way to a reevaluation of what I had expected to feel and what I really had felt; what I thought was the way things are, and what I had really found them to be. I pretended, or posed, maybe we should say, and it gave me cover, and with time I learned what had happened to me, and then I could start to express it.

I get that as others wrote their experiences, you learned from that too.

Well, sure. You think writers can always write and never read? I know you don't, that was rhetorical. Reading other people's stuff is a prime window on their world, and some things are going to be obvious, and some you'll reject and some are going to surprise you and lead you to think about things differently.

It's only been an hour, Papa, but I'm pretty tired. More another time, I hope.

It's up to you as always—*we* aren't going anywhere!

Enjoy your fishing.

You enjoy yours, too.

≈ 10 ≈

Alone

Wednesday, April 13, 2011

So, Papa, talk to me about loneliness. For I got a clear sense, last night, of how lonely you got, and how often.

Loneliness is a writer's life, after all. Or, let's say aloneness. You're living in a world you're bringing into existence, and you can only do it by sitting with it for hours at a time, day by day in a long disciplined effort. Right there, that guarantees that some of your life is going to be lived very much alone. Writing isn't the same as script conferences for Hollywood.

But you're referring to a loneliness that didn't have to do with writing, so much as with living in the world, being very much a part of it and yet being apart from it, at the same time. Isn't that everybody's experience of life? I observed and I described, and I imagined and guessed, and I tried to make things happen. It isn't like I was passive. I shaped my life as I went along, and it was my realization toward the end that I no longer had the strength and clarity and endurance that would have been needed to *keep on* shaping my life that told me that my road was coming to an end. This, as much as any physical or mental difficulties. Or maybe we should say the realizations stemmed from them, or perhaps caused them.

But even when I was in my prime, sure I was lonely. That was the hell of it in my relations with women, you know. I couldn't live without them; something inside me got so lonely without them—but I couldn't live with them either, not for long. There was something between them and me that kept getting in the way.

A sort of competitiveness?

Well, maybe. I wouldn't have called it that. Perhaps it was. Certainly there was a sense of jockeying for position all the time, working to be sure I didn't get dominated the way my father had been. But that wasn't exactly competition. Competition is two people doing the same thing and seeing who does it better. That was *very* deeply ingrained in me. But what do you call it when you have two people who are two different *kinds* of people—because one is a man and the other is a woman? In your time, you pretend there isn't any difference, so there isn't any problem, but it isn't true and everybody knows it. Your time has gotten all tangled up thinking that equality means identical twins.

There is something different between men and women and it isn't just sex organs. It's fundamental, and if your time doesn't want to see it, well, it'll just keep going farther and farther off the beam. There is something absolutely fundamental about the difference—and this even though, beyond male or female, we all have in common that we are human, and that we comprise strands that themselves expressed as male or female.

May I rephrase?

Feel free. You bought the pen and the pad.

I hear you saying that the strands that comprise our person-group of which the conscious self is the ringmaster are, themselves, past expressions of male or female identities, and that therefore nobody is all one thing, but there is nonetheless a difference. Each of the strands—insofar as it was a past life—was a mixture of male and female, as we all are and have to be, and the balance is different in each person because everyone is composed of different combinations of strands.

That's beyond what I actually said, but I agree with it, and it is what I would have meant if I had thought in those terms. You can see that human sexuality expresses in a long bell-curve line—not a concept that I remember ever hearing, but a useful one—from asexual on one end to pansexual on the other, with every possible variation included—by definition. Homosexuals and bisexuals and transsexuals are as "normal"— that is, as normally occurring—as heterosexuals, and heterosexuals themselves come in many flavors.

I knew all that from observation. What I approved of or disapproved of had to do with social behavior more than private sexual behavior, and my attacks on homosexual assumptions of superiority had as much to do with social hypocrisy and rottenness as it did with what they did in private, which I didn't care about.

But you can see how hard it is to stay on the subject without veering off. We're talking about the fact that there is a difference between men and women that goes beyond the physical. That difference *is real*, and everybody senses it, and each sex makes jokes and complaints about the other because of it. Men and women can't be friends except by stepping around it, or dealing with it, or even by rejoicing in the difference, as the French say. But that difference is *there*, it is *inmate*, and society's organization and taboos and license can't remove it.

You may think I've gotten off the subject of loneliness. I haven't. If you're lonely without women but are not really comfortable with them because of that core of difference that is so obvious to you, you're going to be in a position where you have to live *as if* things were in a way that they aren't. And that is going to set up tensions. Even if you're deeply in love, you don't spend all your time in bed, and you don't spend all your time thinking each other's wonderful. Sometimes you're just doing the same thing together and you're doing it differently. Fishing, say, or trophy hunting, or even reporting.

If it's a comparable activity and muscles or endurance don't enter into it—in other words if the physical differences between men and women don't enter into it, or if they balance off like strength versus endurance— you're still going to see a difference in the way men and women go about it, and if you have a woman who has a lot of man in her, people will say she goes about things like a man. I don't mean she'll necessarily be mannish, but she'll be masculine in some essential. Beryl Markham, for instance, or Marty. And of course the same for men, the other way around.

I'm saying, there are *male* expressions and *female* expressions, and everybody knows it, and they aren't *created by* society but expressed how-ever each society finds it convenient to express them—and this is true even though any individual man or woman expresses a different combi-nation of male and female traits. There isn't anything startling about this way of putting it, in the real world. It is only in the world of theory and of sexual politics that it may seem strange or new. It isn't anything every-body doesn't know anyway.

So if I was living with Marty, say, and she was so much into compe-tition and judgment, that was an uncomfortable thing and yet it was a familiar thing. The familiar part of it was sort of comforting; it was like being with one of the boys, only with sex. But when it wore off—when the comfort of the familiar feel wore off, I mean—it grated. You know the saw about a bore being someone who deprives you of solitude with-out providing you with company. That's what it was like, and at the clos-est quarters there are. But if I was with somebody like Mary, who still had that area of familiarity but in a different mix, other things still got in the way, and we fought for position regardless.

You had to be sure you wouldn't be dominated. But—loneliness?

If women couldn't hold it off, and friends and structured play-time, and reading, and creation, and drinking and other sensual pleasures—what could? It seems to me anybody is going to be lonely if he's awake enough, alive enough.

Don't you suppose your loneliness is connected to your connection to the church?

Sure—though I didn't know that I did [know it] then. But, sure. When you can feel that something is missing, isn't it natural to go looking for it? And if you've sensed a connection that is the opposite of loneliness and so you know it's there, isn't it just common sense not to join in with the crowd saying it doesn't exist? Brett says God never worked, for her, and Jake says God works for quite a lot of people, himself included. But just because there's this broad trail claiming to be the way to get back to that connection you felt, doesn't mean it does you any good. It might, it might not. And the rules don't have anything to do with it unless the rules are the way to make the connection. So, Jake goes to church and tries to pray and doesn't really accomplish anything in the way of connection; he has winds up thinking and free-associating. He knows what he wants and what he needs, but he doesn't know how to get it.

Were you lonely like Jake?

Yes, and for the same reason, come to think of it. He didn't live in the same world the people around him did, although it looks like it to them, so you could say he never had company. Or, you could say a certain part of him never had company.

You [unlike Jake] could look for it in relations with women.

Yes, and did. And it's true that dealing with the other sex brings out part of you that maybe you never see otherwise. But women aren't a cure-all, nobody is or could be. You've got to deal with your loneliness on its own terms.

What does that mean?

Loneliness is a part of life like hunger or thirst or anything else. If you were to try to live your life never being hungry or thirsty, how practical would be? How fulfilled would you be? Nero Wolfe is an interesting creation, but would you want to be Nero Wolfe? Hungers are good for the body—they add interest to your life.

Well that's a thought I've never had.

Anything carried too far is—well, it's carried too far. But everything in life has a place.

≈11≈

Fukushima and War

Thursday, April 14, 2011

[While I was engaged in a routine household chore (which occupied my surface mind) I got this from Papa, nearly in direct, specific words rather than my usual knowing-which-translates-into-words: "If you want to understand my attitude toward war, just combine your admiration for the men who are doing their heroic best at Fukushima, and your sympathy and pity for them and their families, with your anger and disgust at the decisions that made this all possible, and the people (and their motives) who made the decisions. Nothing is different."]

≈12≈

The Sun Rises, Too

Monday, May 2, 2011

So, Papa, the thought that came to me a few minutes ago—did you inspire it, or if not where did it come from? The thought is, you named the book "The Sun Also Rises"—and I don't know that I ever really absorbed the implications of the title.

Thank you. It certainly has taken long enough for that to penetrate. I would have thought it so obvious as to need no comment, but 90 years on—or nearly enough—apparently it still isn't obvious to people.

I feel like you want me to say "none of the critics ever noticed," and it makes me nervous lest Hemingway scholars might be able to say, "not only did they notice, but the real Hemingway knew they noticed."

Well, it's understandable, but I don't see what you can do about it. If you're going to go exploring, you're going to have to take some risks. I don't remember *anybody ever, anywhere*, seeing the title in its proper light. They all saw Gertrude's comments, and somehow they read right by the quotation beneath hers, reading it as "vanity of vanities" rather than as, "this too shall pass away."

It also rises, meaning the war was the end of something but something else was going to take its place?

You can't confine symbols to one meaning, you should know that. It also contrasted Spain's continuity with France's *dis*-continuity, and with the West in general. Nobody would have to tell the Spanish that the sun also rises; it's only the degenerate sophisticates who get stuck in a moment as though the world was created that morning and would go on in that condition forever.

So you were painting a moment. Shooting a photograph.

All my work was photographs.

Whose idea was it, then, this morning? Mine? Mine by way of you? Or what?

You don't have the right definitions to talk about it. Ask your guys, some time. They do good theory.

All right. Tell me, is there any reason I couldn't do the book on you and the myth? Starting now, I mean?

You'd need to give some thought to the predominant emotion, or feeling, you want to convey. Get that firmly in mind and the rest is exposition.

And I need to do that.

It's the only way it will be yours and not borrowed.

≈13≈

Revolutionary Politics

[Reading Norberto Fuentes' *Hemingway in Cuba*, not well organized or thought out but a valuable point of view.]

Papa, how does it strike you?

It provides good leverage to turn your attention and your insight in ways I probably couldn't do directly. And this is worth a line or two of explanation.

Sometimes you may get an impulse—buy this book! Read that weblog! Re-read this or that! Generally you're pretty good about following such impulses. Think of such suggestions as pointers. Here, if you will look over here you will learn a fact or hear a point of view or see an unsuspected connection or—mostly—make an unsuspected connection because your two connected bits are common to your mind but not necessarily anybody else's. It would be much more difficult to put these extended thoughts into your head. So—leverage. You know more now about my life in Cuba. I can tell you more subtle, more complicated things that otherwise I couldn't.

I understand. My reading the information has rearranged the neurons, so to speak, and so I have a prepared field for new information that has to take that newly acquired information for granted.

Yes. The more you know, the more you can be told. My politics, for instance. Do you think Mary was burning personal correspondence only so it wouldn't be published because I didn't want it published? No. A lot of it was dangerous.

Dangerous to her? To your reputation?

To many people I had worked with who were not all protected by death or distance.

You're talking revolutionary politics.

Twenty years of it. And some of it, published in Cold War times, would have been very damaging, though if it were to come to light now it would reflect to my credit. We couldn't very well hope to stash it secretly away for fifty years until the time should be right.

I'm getting the same nuances as when we discussed the Cuban and the infantry scouting episodes of the war.

I was by profession a writer. You don't see me doing anything amateur in regards to my profession. Even things like doing my own negotiating that may look amateur, I had my reasons for. You understand what I am saying? I was a professional, in discipline, in knowledge, in the business aspects of it, in weighing the markets, in considering what I was doing against what others have done or were doing. How many things can you be professional at? You can try to bring a professional's attitude, but can't hope to have a specialized knowledge that only a professional learns over a lifetime. I wasn't quite a professional fisherman, certainly not a professional hunter. Fishing and shooting are not the same thing as having all the background knowledge and skills of professionals. I was a good boxer, too; that doesn't mean I could have gone into the ring as a professional.

All that is background to say this: At revolutions, I was an amateur and couldn't become a professional. Do you see Castro writing classic novels, or playing orchestral level violin, or—oh, anything? To become a revolutionary is like becoming a soldier. You could be a volunteer, and that's one thing. To be a professional is another.

So, politics. The same subject, you see. I knew a lot of background, I knew a lot of people, I could see a lot of what was wrong and knew some of why it was wrong. I knew many of the players, good and bad. I knew some of the hidden springs. Still, I was an amateur, subject to an amateur's misjudgments.

If I hear you right, you are saying Mary burned a lot of evidence of misjudgments that could have gotten you into a lot of trouble, post-facto.

Well, let's be careful, here. You are going to have to bring your discernment to another level now, because what you're getting is now a mixture of my input, your reading, your thinking, other peoples second- and third-hand reports, and it makes it on the one hand richer and on the other hand more susceptible to distortion. What you've learned about Hemingway has given you a great store of referents. But maybe it risks hardening the picture so it is harder for me to provide the unexpected.

I can see the problem. But seeing it isn't the same as overcoming it. I'll try.

If I was drawn to the left in the 1930s, it was in reaction to what I could see happening. Not merely in terms of fascism but of Wall Street. You yourself have seen how I was lured into conspiring against those bastards—that's what it amounts to—for a while, before I moved back to a more neutral or let's say a less naïve position. You're always in danger of forgetting—as Norberto Fuentes forgets, or doesn't mention—that at the same time we were faced with Hitler, there was Stalin with his show trials killing off the old Bolsheviks, clamping down the entire country under the great terror, shooting some of his best generals like Tukhachevsky.

Now, Churchill and Roosevelt weren't troubled about dealing with Stalin in the war years. They did it out of calculation. They needed those Russian soldiers! And if Roosevelt projected New Deal over Soviet agriculture, that made it easier to swallow, but he sure needed those soldiers, and to the very end he and Churchill were worried that Russia would sign a separate peace again, though they needn't have worried. It's one thing to go to Brest-Litovsk because your soldiers wouldn't fight any more. It would have been a second thing to do it when you were carrying the field.

But—to stick to it—my own politics was revolutionary but cautious. I had a lot to lose, including a position from which I could and did contribute assistance. And, I knew how difficult and uncertain any struggle must be. Not much advantage in being defeated and removed early when you might have been preserved and used to great effect later on.

Notice a couple of things. My sympathies were never on the side of reaction. From *In Our Time* on, my books and stories always said, we've lost the past—for good or evil or both—and it isn't going to be re-created. I was interested in Communism, I was interested in Mussolini as a phenomenon at first, until I saw through them. And I was continuously interested in any force of nature or force of personality or social force that looked as though it might crack the crust of hardened convention and let life come through. But which wars to play to win, and which to hope for as a long shot and which to shake your head at and wait for another day?

You know how it is. You wait your whole life for things to get better while you see them always getting worse.

It would take a real optimist to think that World War II was a happy ending to anything.

And so, during those years of waiting?

You just read that I had to get out of Cuba in a hurry in the 1940s. That blew over, and only the fact that I was publicly named by the government of the Dominican Republic is the reason it was remembered—and even so, how much is it remembered? Not much. If you hadn't been able to get a hold of Fuentes's book, how much would you know about it? And that was the merest toehold.

Papa, I'm hearing a recurrent theme, here. You as a man were involved in things that aren't necessarily on the record—just like U-boat hunting and getting information as to the safe approaches to Paris—and reflect a more serious side to you than is generally recognized. Did you knowingly contribute to the Hemingway myth because it was good cover?

People don't do things for just one reason usually. But if you have a place owned by a celebrity and he holds parties all the time, it's easy for people to meet there while holding drinks. Let's say that.

So Batista's police weren't so far wrong.

Hell no they weren't wrong, and the nice thing is, they knew they weren't wrong, but they couldn't do anything much about it, because I was too famous. It would have hurt them. That's why they killed my dog, as much as anything. They could get away with that much. I don't say they planned that, it's just that they were frustrated and they were going to go on being frustrated, and they knew it.

∼14∼

Land, Sea, and Air

Friday, June 22, 2011

Papa, why did you conceive of the land, sea, air book? The scope was way too big to be accomplished. As you recognize, you didn't have time enough to learn air warfare let alone air realities in the first place. But was Across The River the land book, and Islands part of the sea book?

You're confusing yourself a bit. Yes, *Across the River* was my land war book, and maybe I could have done better to leave out the love story—though I don't see how I could have, and to have [protagonist Richard] Cantwell fall in a less impossible love wouldn't have fit in either. But the indirect description of the aftereffects of battle and warfare was as well done as I could. If it was a bridge too far for my critics, I can't help that. In time the book will rise or sink, and it won't have much to do with the judgment of the critics of 1950.

Islands in the Stream is a different case. I intended to begin in the prewar years, describe the transition into war, and show the war at sea, unknown as it was. The chapters I couldn't figure out how to include—Roger going west while watching the war in Spain—would have been part of that transition. But I couldn't figure out, finally, what to do. I could've sent Roger off to fight in Spain and maybe get killed, but, what was there to say that I haven't already said? And how could I split the focus between Thomas Hudson and Roger?

There were minor discrepancies in your account of Havana in the "Cuba" section. The boy and the kitten, for one thing. He was set too young for the first Christmas of the war.

I was still adjusting everything. That could have been fixed in a few words.

Oh, I know. But it shows me it was still a work in progress.

Ideally here's how it would have gone. A prewar section, culminating in Thomas Hudson losing the boys. A transition from peace to war section, probably putting Roger at the center of it but coming back to Tom. A section on the onset of the war, maybe Roger mostly but not entirely. The war as it went on—Cuba, then the chase. I thought about putting in a chapter introducing the men and the venture, to go before "Cuba" and explain it better, but hadn't decided.

Somehow it seemed too much death, to kill Roger in Spain and then Tom in Cuban waters. There was plenty of death all around in the war, but it would have been adding up too much: Roger, the three boys, Thomas.

I should've had a section, too, on Tom hearing about young Tom's death—and to do that, I would've had to have the air section that I couldn't write without faking, or I would've had to set it up in some way that didn't repeat the peacetime section, and didn't repeat his reaction to the death of the first two boys. Couldn't come up with a formula, and put it off too long.

How about a word for those who assume that if you weren't publishing you weren't writing, and if you weren't writing you wasting your life?

How you answer that depends on how you read where the question is coming from. If they're sincerely interested, you just say that a writer has to live in order to write, and some things can't be put off beyond a certain point. Our [1954] African safari, for instance. Yes it ended badly but it had been good until then, and every year that went by would have been one more reason why I wasn't likely to ever get back to Africa. So even though the crashes cost me my health and my youth (what was left of it) and thus probably some good writing that I'd no longer be able to do, how could I know ahead of time that was going to happen?

And, you know, writing is one thing; publishing is another. If you don't need the money and you don't need to protect your career, publishing is more trouble than it's worth sometimes. I thought I'd have another 10 or 15 years of productive time, and I could put the manuscripts in the bank. There wasn't any hurry about it.

Did I owe it to anybody to keep on publishing? If Charlie was gone and Max was gone and I had all the money I needed and I'd made my reputation by 30 years' worth of work—why should I *have to* write anything, for anybody? Some critics seem to think an author owes them something new every so often. It doesn't occur to them, an author's work is a gift, and it's up to him whether he wants to do the work to present it or not.

≈15≈

The Purpose

Sunday, July 10, 2011

A little bit discouraged, Papa. I have just about roughed-in the first draft, and I am wondering if I am not on the wrong track. What I'm putting out isn't all that new, most of it. Remind me, what's in it for the reader.

Just because everything you're saying could be found here or there, or could be inferred by reading between the lines of enough books, doesn't mean it's going to be available to anybody else. Not, necessarily, to scholars, even. You have the irreplaceable thing you were told about when you were very young—a viewpoint. That viewpoint can't be duplicated anywhere, by any means. It is the same as your description of minds in *The Cosmic Internet*—any mind is irreplaceable and can't be duplicated exactly. The thing is, is that mind *different* enough, is what it knows special enough? Yours is. You know me from the inside, you've had quite a bit of experience from the outside—reading books about me, I mean—and your other experiences give you a unique view of what is going on. Plus—who else could bring Carl to the subject?

You're going to have to let go of the idea about something the scholars take seriously. *That's the wrong set of scholars!* Not Hemingway scholars, but scholars investigating transpersonal communication. *There's* your audience. You aren't going to convince the Hemingway scholars because you and they will talk right past each other. Your evidence—my point of view, our conversations—is just no evidence at all to them. They could agree with everything; it would still not be evidence, just opinion.

But your conversations *are* evidence of something else. They show how conversations may occur and become habitual and provide increased access to knowledge and to understanding. They ground a subject that too often flies off into the air. And the point of view you begin from is in itself a reorientation. Historians and amateur students of history do not tend to be the same people who explore nonphysical realities, as you well know. So, exploring from that viewpoint in itself is it a departure; in itself. Can you see that this in itself would prevent Hemingway scholars from taking this book seriously *in their own terms*? And Jung scholars, too, of course.

I can now that you mention it, yes.

Well? That being so, doesn't that refocus your intent on showing what is or isn't possible?

What isn't possible is a little clearer to me than what is possible.

Settle in. Think in images. What image arises when you think of this project?

Me sitting here writing, early in the morning, day after day, and quite happily.

Convey that.

And yet, a straight transcript of our conversations wouldn't work.

Too much life in between; too much explanation needed of what you'd been reading, how it had affected you, what other conversations you've been having. So what can you do about it?

Well, I thought I was doing it!

Go back to images.

The image that is right in front of me is all my loose-leaf binders and all my journals.

Why do you suppose you chose that image?

There's a sort of continuity there—a lot of years of work.

Could you publish them as they are? Of course not, nor would you want to. They are your *source material*, not your finished product. So are our conversations—yours, mine, Carl's, Abraham Lincoln's.

The various famous men—mostly men—are all queued up for a different book on society, I have assumed.

They could be. But first the fact and the value of the communication has to be established, and that is the purpose of *this* book.

It is?

It is. Look at it. Your career has its own logic, although it hasn't been obvious to you. *Muddy Tracks* is your initial exploration. It's the one that gives newcomers entrée. *Sphere and Hologram* carries it forward—here's what you can get moving forward. *Chasing Smallwood* starts the next phase, that of direct communication *about life* as it is lived. *Cosmic Internet* sets out a theoretical structure *for* it, *using* it. And *Hemingway* shows you moving out a little farther, addressing a subject well enough known to draw attention and to serve as a check on your statements. After all, if you produced a book like that channeled biography of George Washington that had all its "facts" wrong, it would be ridiculous and would be seen as ridiculous. When you come up with something that holds water and occasionally startles by bringing new clarity to a subject that seemed well understood, you help bring the two sides of the veil slightly closer. And that is the primary purpose, remember, not any correction of the Hemingway Myth, however desirable that would be.

≈16≈
Hemingway's Catholicism

Sunday, September 25, 2011

So, playing Free Cell while waiting for the coffee to brew, I thought, Papa's Catholicism is an angle that hasn't been explored properly, probably because it isn't properly academic to explore it seriously. Papa?

"This is Ernest Hemingway." The voice keeps coming back to you as a sort of anchor. Why do you suppose?

Well, is a recording of your voice. It has whatever it is we read into voices—or maybe read out of voices, I don't know.

It is a touch stone. Books are others. Now, you are reading *Hemingway's Boat* and finding it unsatisfactory. Why, do you suppose?

Much of it seems like twice-told tales, yet I know that isn't fair. Just the chapter on Arnold Samuelson alone would be an original contribution. Could it be that my concern with fishing and boating is so much less—oh, I see where you're leading me.

Yes. Your center of gravity is what we might call the centering effect of the Catholic religion, the thing I found, and you understand that part of me as only a member of The Club [of ex-Catholics] could—and only a member who was not embittered by his experience.

Some center on boats, some on hunting or fishing, many on the writing of books, some on the reading of books, some on politics, some on the personal interactions that make someone else's life so colorful or untidy or reprehensible. Some center on aesthetics, some on careerism, some on the connection between my life and the life of my society, some on my influence on writing or on popular culture. Who has ever focused on Hemingway's religion? *Your* Hemingway is unique. Everyone's is, to the degree that they concentrate their attention.

Yes, I unpack that to mean—we each resonate to different strands, and different combinations of strands, and so what we can perceive is different. It explains why so many people psychoanalyze you so assuredly and come to similar but different conclusions.

To stick with you—the insight is this. I was not a Catholic in doctrine—"a very dumb Catholic" I said. I was a Catholic in the sense of being emotionally connected to the great body of churchgoers, but that doesn't quite say it.

You felt yourself part of the mystical communion of believers, except it isn't really belief either, any more than it was ritual.

Keep going. We're feeling our way to it.

*It's connected—
your fear of death*

your lure toward death

your superstitious nature

your intense aliveness

somehow, your need to hunt and kill, although I can't quite see how it's connected

your connection to the other side as a writer

your near-death experience, your OBE

your sense of hollowness in yourself, your society

your instinctive respect for the peasant soundness

your rejection of the rich even as you lived among them

It's all in there, but it isn't clear.

It is a reaching out for wholeness, for communion.

You wanted to be a saint, and your overwhelming, suffocating sense of guilt and unworthiness had you in a continual state of tension, fighting it all the way. I think one key is in Islands in the Stream where Thomas Hudson says to his first wife, do you have to rub it in that I made a mistake and then a worse mistake? In other words Pauline, first, and then, even worse, Martha.

That's true as far as it goes, but it doesn't touch my guilt for my father's suicide, or for the war between my parents, or for my children's failures and problems and my part in them.

In other words, you had to help the sun come up every day.

Someone who could emotionally identify with my rages and my most boorish, bullying behavior and could explain what they felt like from the inside could perform a service.

Who better than you yourself?

Well, that's what we're doing.

≈17≈

Fears

[Reading a lot of books about Hemingway! Skimming some. Papa really did become prisoner of paranoia as time went on. I see I have to be more careful of sources if I wish to bring my material to a new level. This book, *Fame Became of Him: Hemingway as Public Writer*, by John Raeburn (1981: Indiana University Press Bloomington), is very insightful. It hadn't occurred to me that of course his *Esquire* articles made people see him as glamorous at least as much as any book he published.

Nine roles set out in *Death in the Afternoon*, Raeburn says: sportsman, manly man, exposer of sham, arbiter of taste, world traveler, *bon vivant*, insider, stoic and battle-scarred veteran, and heroic artist.] (Page 44)

Listed that way, Papa, I can see that you painted yourself into a corner, for there is little room to blend in scholar, reader, thinker, religious mystic, social critic, open-hearted sympathizer with the sufferings of others, open-handed dispenser of lavish but quiet assistance, would-be family man, puzzled lover and husband, or admiring/resentful observer of the lives of scholars, critics, and other possessors of expertise to which you could not pretend. That's a long list, and it seemed as though you contributed to it. In any case, it does come clear to me—as hasn't been clear till now—how you enmeshed yourself in your myth and therefore cut yourself off from at least any public acknowledgment of how much more complicated you were.

Take only religious feeling and religious guilt, to say nothing of the all-pervading sense of sin that all but crippled your ability to let yourself accept responsibility when your self-described responsibility was more than you could bear. I don't think most people believe your Catholicism was more than tactical. Esquire articles did not present you going to confession, or receiving communion, or expressing a sense of being one among many or of being one in relation to God. How could they? What do you think? How far off the mark is this?

The other thing that could be alluded to but not dramatized is the hours of work, for those hours are impossible to describe and are too far removed from people's ordinary experience for them to relate to.

I could take a stab at describing it; you already have, in that piece that came to me that day.

Yes, but it requires as background and understanding of the mental world that people didn't have. So, it looks like thinking and rearranging commas.

Should mention, too, your true humility, your shyness, your gentleness, all of which surprised people (Marjorie Rawlings, for instance) because so out of your public persona.

Papa, I can see that my work is being sabotaged by my own self-doubt. (Is it really Hemingway online? Will anybody believe it? If they do, will they care? If they would, can I put the material into an enjoyable, accessible format? Etc.)

How would you expect to avoid such doubts? That's part of the territory. You know the writer's three fears.

I do. "I have nothing to say, I can't say it, nobody would care anyway."

Well, if you know they are common fears, why give it to them when they visit you? Or dwell within you, if that's the case?

It takes a monumental self-confidence, it seems to me, to be so sure that what you're doing is worthwhile and can be done.

Yes, or courage to do it *without* being sure.

All right. Sort of like me working on the novel, not really knowing how I'm going to do it, not having any surer footing—at all—in what I am doing now.

So? That's part of the admission ticket.

$\approx 18 \approx$

Viewpoints

Frederick Henry is not a hero, just an ordinary man. If anything, less than an ordinary man, living disconnected from everybody as he did. I never realized that—my habit of throwing myself wholeheartedly into allegiance with the narrator of the story blinded me to that. Obvious once pointed out. Really, the Italian army deserted *him*. He didn't desert it. It was leave by running or leave by being shot. Out of his hands either way—and was he then to return and say, it was all a misunderstanding? There was no way back; it was out of his hands. He had had no choice in being arrested, and had no choice in proceeding out of the country as best he could, only he went to find Catherine, for she was now his country. "Morire non e basta." [To die is not enough, the war slogan said.] "What else do they want?" somebody asks angrily. No sacrifice is ever enough, is it? And they're sick of it.

Papa?

You are reading multiple perspectives on someone's life, and seeing that they are viewpoints, and therefore not to be despised. What are the characters in the novel or short story, but viewpoints? What are human lives, but viewpoints?

There is more to some of the scholarship than I had thought. Initially I had some impatience. But they're just essays; just editorials. As such, worth considering.

It's only when they represent a viewpoint that is not real that they are toxic, but even they are instructive sometimes. For instance, if a perspective is Marxist or feminist or the latest (or non-latest) literary fad, the person holding the viewpoint may be less than the abstraction. How valuable is that? But maybe the person gets free of the straitjacket and in that case they find something to say.

Looking at my viewpoint as just another viewpoint.

It takes the pressure off. You don't have to be infallible, just articulate. And if your experience of talking with Hemingway is critical to your story, who can quarrel with it? They may invalidate it, or refuse to deal with it, but they certainly cannot refute it. How do you refute experience?

I feel like such a babe in the woods, though.

Nothing wrong with knowing it.

[I should say explicitly that I have not read all the criticism of Hemingway, and no one could. In fact I am quite ignorant of it, of literary theory, and know only what I know, which is my reading of the work, my thoughts on it, the biographies I have read, and, primarily, the dialogues with Papa—whatever they are in fact.]

≈ 19 ≈

Time and Dimensions

Papa, the fourth and fifth dimensions [that he said he tried to achieve in his writing]: Time, and then Beyond Time?

Close enough. Or you might say viewpoint over time, viewpoint beyond viewpoint, or overall viewpoint, or really view without the distortion of viewpoint. Now, you can see that to write in such a way as to hint at (for you cannot actually do it) going beyond viewpoint is very difficult, and requires not only skill and luck in the writer but, let's say, skill and attention in the reader. Luck, too, perhaps, for the reader has to be in the right mental space to be able to comprehend it.

That's what I was trying for in *Across the River*. I told the story seemingly from inside Colonel Cantwell's head, but not precisely. Within his mind—the nonphysical mechanism we all live in, as you recognize—he moves across elements of his past, both what he has experienced and what he has experienced second hand through reading or other instruction or from appreciating, as in a picture. I believe I achieved that fourth dimension, and it was disappointing to have it not recognized—because of Renata, of course.

Now here is something nobody sees. I achieved the fifth dimension with Santiago, who lay dreaming of the lions at the end. My achieving it was not at the end, though, but throughout, because in careful recounting of his moment by moment actions, and his moment by moment thought or memory, and his moment by moment emotion, I was so close to the moving present that we get *beyond time* to the timeless. Where else do you think that strange aura around the story comes from? It is *not* told from Santiago's viewpoint, or from Manolin's. It may be said to be narrated by God, or the guys upstairs, or the part of Santiago that lives outside time and space. It is our life described neither from within it nor from without it.

Yes, there is the story itself—the old man striving, and winning, and losing, and remaining himself. There is the effect on the boy. But beyond all that is the strange penumbra that people feel but don't quite understand, and this is because the story's atmosphere talks to us of things beyond the story.

I could not have produced the story to order. And it came as a gift, and I passed on the gift. Those who think it's simple or simpleminded are only one eyed; they cannot sense the presence of that extra dimension.

It is a curious paradox, isn't it? To get beyond time, one way is to sit on the very edge of the moving line. There are other ways—Tolstoy did it on a mammoth scale—but this was mine.

≈ 20 ≈

Mind to Mind

Tuesday, December 13, 2011

Papa?

The effect on me of peripheral involvement in revolutionary politics was that on any rich man whose sympathies were for the poor rather than the rich—but whose eyes were open from experience. I wrote about political violence from my earliest years. It was the defining element in my years in the way religious-political violence had been at the time of the great religious wars. My anti-fascism never wavered from the first time I saw Mussolini and knew him for what he was. But it was devilishly hard to be on the side of the poor and not let yourself be used by first Stalin and then Stalin's successors. I could generalize that to say: It is always impossible to get involved with revolutions and keep your hands clean. But sometimes sitting by and doing nothing isn't so clean either. Also, sometimes you get used without your knowledge. Sometimes your name gets used. Sometimes you do a thing thinking things are one way when they are really otherwise.

This matter of conveying information mind to mind isn't as straightforward as you sometimes like to think it. Suppose I know something from you, and someone else asks me to convey it. (And suppose it isn't something you would object to my conveying, for the one person's wishes have something to do with it too, even if they never know about it on a conscious level.) If I convey the sense of your mind *perfectly* from my end, does that mean they necessarily receive it perfectly? Just as my thoughts get clothed in your grammar, they get changed or retranslated by what we could call the atmosphere of your mind—the context new information fits into.

For instance, revolutionary politics. Surely you can see that the more you know about such things, the more you can convey. If you know a little, you may get [only] the broadest of generalities. If you have more, you may get more. If you know a lot, you may be able to receive nuances that would be totally invisible otherwise. How much different is this than anything else in your mental life? There's good reason for it.

If you were a trance medium, you could be used to receive very specific messages that could be far removed from your own knowledge, and the messages could be transmitted without distortion or omission or unintended addition. But the more your personality is involved, the more you get involved with very specific advantages and limitations. The advantage is that your surface mind, or your surface mind and certain deeper but still consciously-formed levels of your individual mind, helps shape and texture the incoming information. You and it become intertwined on an emotional level, not merely a mental level. If you know enough, this means you gain a second perspective (and potentially others if you wish) on a firmly rooted set of facts. In other words it becomes a part of your normal functioning mind. It is not walled off needing to be integrated from the small end of the telescope. Something *felt* as it is being brought through is yours in a way that something *understood* never can be. *Only* understood, you understand.

I do.

The disadvantage, of course, is that subjectivity always blurs out lines. You get tempted to think, "that isn't reasonable, that isn't a safe conclusion, probably that's just me putting that in, I don't think that can be right." At an extreme, you wind up with people starting with a genuine gift but ending up faking. So—disregarding privacy rights, which do exist—if I hear someone saying something and I try to convey it to you, we have to go through your mind with all its established patterns. They're going to color the materials just as they color the language I express in, and the way you write, and the specific words you use.

Yes I understand this, at least abstractly. It explains why you couldn't communicate with me in Spanish or French or Italian.

And it explains why I can't easily give you facts you don't consciously know but can give you perceptions, feelings, reactions, or suggestions on what you do know.

So I guess I am not going to get much about revolutionary politics.

You know what you need to know. I was more or less on the sidelines, but with special connections, specific sympathies, unusual opportunities. When I was sufficiently tempted, I'd put a toe in the water, but I was very much aware of how much I had to lose and how little my sacrificing myself would do for anybody. I got a couple of good scares, of course never being certain. Transcribing this, you suddenly understand that I had this background tension in my life for *years*—half the time I was in Cuba, not even counting the war years—and you see that colored my emotional life.

I do. It must have been a terrific strain, and I can see that it would come out in temper among other things.

It isn't that it was often front and center. Mostly it was a background presence. But it remained there, and yes it was a continuing strain, background noise that never went away, like my headache when I was in England.

Thank you, Papa.

If I am Papa, right?

Smiling. Right.

Index by Hemingway Chronology

(1899-1918) Before the War

(1918) Italy

(1919-1921) Recuperation and Marriage

(1922-1923) Paris (I)

(1924-1929) Paris (II), Publication, Pauline

Fitzgerald III • Fitzgerald And His Talent III • Reflections on Fitzgerald IV • Being in Training V • Consequences V • Outlandish Stories V

(1929-1939) Key West Years

Hemingway's Catholicism VI • Hunting, Fishing and Our Primitive selves II • Harry Morgan and Paul Potts I • The Edge I • Harry Morgan, Values and Rules II • The Code II • How to Work and What to Work For II • Understanding Your World II • Learning II • Life and Interpretation II • Men and Women II • Hemingway and Jung on Sex II • A Path Less Skewed II • Hemingway's Reaction to Jung II • The Image Machine II • Hemingway's Sons IV • Fatherhood VI • Pain IV • Person-groups V

(1936-1941) The Spanish Civil War and Martha

For Whom the Bell Tolls I • Spain and the Modern World I • The 20th Century and God II • Spain and Modernization II • Choices III

(1942-1943) War in Cuba

Unfinished Business I • Opening Pathways I • The Hemingway Patrols I • Q-boat II • Sensory Evidence V • A Man Among Men V

(1944-1945) War in Europe

A Shipboard Romance II • Fukushima and War VI • War without Illusion II • Part of the Army II

(1946-1960) Years in Cuba with Mary

Land, Sea and Air VI • The Old Man and the Sea I • Beisbol and Santiago I • World War II in Europe II • Recuperation II • Land, Sea, and Air II • Roger and Thomas V • Postwar Isolation II • The Old Man and the Sea, and Perkins II • Paranoia II • Spiritual Causes of Mental Disorder II • Units and Rage III • Psychological Models III • The Individual as a Society III • Disturbing Evidence III • The Invisible Aspect of Writing III • Different Exiles III • Individuals as Communities

(1961) "The Family Exit"

(1961-) Posthumous Life

Appendix: Meeting Hemingway

I think you get a better idea of how much Hemingway did by seeing his work merely listed by publication date, rather than broken up into categories like novels, short-story collections, non-fiction, etc. Note that *Men at War* is an anthology that he edited, with an introduction that deserves more attention than it has received. And, of course, more than fifty years after Papa killed himself, the Hemingway machine continues to grind away, producing books from previously published material ("Hemingway on ___") and continues to find a marketplace.

(1923) *Three Stories and Ten Poems*
(1925) *In Our Time*
(1926) *The Torrents of Spring; The Sun Also Rises*
(1927) *Men Without Women*
(1929) *A Farewell to Arms*
(1932) *Death in the Afternoon*
(1933) *Winner Take Nothing*
(1935) *Green Hills of Africa*
(1937) *To Have and Have Not*
(1938) *The Fifth Column and the First Forty-Nine Stories*
(1940) *For Whom the Bell Tolls*
(1942) *Men at War: The Best War Stories of All Time*
(1950) *Across the River and Into the Trees*
(1952) *The Old Man and the Sea*
(1961) *The Snows of Kilimanjaro and Other Stories*
(1964) *A Moveable Feast*
(1969) *The Fifth Column and Four Stories of the Spanish Civil War*
(1970) *Islands in the Stream*
(1972) *The Nick Adams Stories*
(1985) *The Dangerous Summer*

(1986) *The Garden of Eden*
(1987) *The Complete Short Stories of Ernest Hemingway*
(1999) *True at First Light*
(2005) *Under Kilimanjaro*

What Others Have Written About Him

Odd to make his acquaintance first-hand, then read about him afterwards, but that's how it happened. An interesting process, to read the same man's life as seen through so many filters, receiving so many external views after, or in some cases before, hearing how a given situation looked from inside. Of course, objectivity is as unattainable in biography as in the rest of life. Those who write about another's life thereby provide portraits of themselves, perhaps without realizing it, for what they see is only what they *can* see, and how they *can* see it. Yet each one's filters help us construct a more complicated, nuanced picture.

Here are some of the books I have read and profited from. I omit the usual apparatus of scholarship, a detailed bibliography, as being unnecessary in this day of search engines.

Full Biographies

Carlos Baker	*Hemingway: A Life Story*
Peter Griffin	(2 volumes)
Kenneth S. Lynn	*Hemingway*
James R. Mellow	*Hemingway: A Life Without Consequences*
Jeffrey Meyers	*Hemingway: A Biography*
Michael Reynolds	*Hemingway* (5 volumes)
Peter Griffin	(2 volumes)
Kenneth S. Lynn	*Hemingway*
James R. Mellow	*Hemingway: A Life Without Consequences*
Jeffrey Meyers	*Hemingway: A Biography*
Michael Reynolds	*Hemingway* (5 volumes)

Baker's biography came first and remains an excellent source, and I learned things from Lynn, Mellow and Meyers, but I'd give first place to Michael Reynolds. Griffin's books I came to only after this book was substantially finished, but they were as good as Reynolds.

Other Books I Found Particularly Interesting

Matthew Bruccoli, ed.	*Hemingway and the Mechanism of Fame*
Morley Callaghan	*That Summer in Paris*
Gioia Diliberto	*Paris without End*
Norberto Fuentes	*Hemingway in Cuba*
Martha Gellhorn	*Travels with Myself and Another*
Jack Hemingway	*Misadventures of a Fly Fisherman*
John Hemingway	*Strange Tribe*
Leicester Hemingway	*My Brother, Ernest Hemingway*
Mary Welsh Hemingway	*How it Was*
Valerie Hemingway	*Running with the Bulls*
Paul Hendrickson	*Hemingway's Boat*
A.E. Hotchner	*Papa Hemingway*
Bernice Kert	*The Hemingway Women*
Stephen Koch	*The Breaking Point*
Leonard J. Leff	*Hemingway and his Conspirators*
James McLendon	*Papa: Hemingway in Key West*
Peter Moreira	*Hemingway on the China Front*
Terry Mort	*The Hemingway Patrols*
James Nagel, ed.	*Ernest Hemingway: The Oak Park Legacy*
Mark P. Ott	*A Sea of Change*
James Plath & Frank Simons	*Remembering Ernest Hemingway*
Michael Reynolds	*Hemingway's First War*
Arnold Samuelson	*With Hemingway*
Henry S. Villard & James Nagel	*Hemingway in Love and War*
Alex Vernon	*Hemingway's Second War*
Rene and Raul Villarreal	*Hemingway's Cuban Son*

Books put together from things he wrote, collections of his letters, and volumes of literary criticism, are found easily enough via libraries and search engines. An excellent resource not to be overlooked is The Hemingway Society: http://www.hemingwaysociety.org/.

About the Author

FRANK DEMARCO was co-founder (in 1989) of Hampton Roads Publishing Company, Inc. and was Chief Editor there for 16 years. Besides *Afterlife Conversations with Hemingway*, he is the author of two novels and four previous books of non-fiction.

Fiction

Messenger: A Sequel to Lost Horizon (1994) carries James Hilton's classic 1932 tale of Shangri-la into the 1960s and 1970s. How do you weigh the outer world against the inner world? What would be important to you if you could live forever?

Babe in the Woods (2008) describes two dozen people at a week-long residential course designed to bring them to states of higher consciousness. Sometimes when you go exploring, you get more than you bargain for.

Non-fiction

Muddy Tracks (2001) is an account of various psychic explorations and experiences. If one person can do it, presumably others can do it, so what does that mean to the world around us?

Chasing Smallwood (2009) starts out as conversations with a past-life individual about 19th-century America and progresses to a discussion of the huge task ahead of us in our time.

The Sphere and the Hologram (2009) consists of transcripts of 22 altered-state conversations with "The Guys Upstairs," centering on our possibilities, problems and opportunities.

The Cosmic Internet (2011) widens the exploration of themes from the previous three books, as the Guys Upstairs provide a new model of consciousness and life on both sides of the veil.

In addition, three books of poetry, *The Marsh*, *Death and Resurrection*, and *An Unsuspected Life*, are available as downloads free from Hologram Books, *www.hologrambooks.com*.

Related Titles

If you enjoyed *Afterlife Conversations with Hemingway*, you may also enjoy other Rainbow Ridge titles. Read more about them at *www.rainbowridgebooks.com*

The Cosmic Internet: Explanations from the Other Side by Frank DeMarco

Conversations with Jesus: An Intimate Journey by Alexis Eldridge

Dialogue with the Devil: Enlightenment for the Unwilling by Yves Patak

The Divine Mother Speaks: The Healing of the Human Heart
by Rashmi Khilnani

Difficult People: A Gateway to Enlightenment by Lisette Larkins

When Do I See God: Finding the Path to Heaven by Jeff Ianniello

Dance of the Electric Hummingbird by Patricia Walker

Coming Full Circle: Ancient Teachings for a Modern World
by Lynn Andrews

Thank Your Wicked Parents by Richard Bach

The Buddha Speaks: To the Buddha Nature Within by Rashmi Khilnani

*Consciousness: Bridging the Gap Between Conventional Science
and the New Super Science of Quantum Mechanics* by Eva Herr

Jesusgate: A History of Concealment Unraveled by Ernie Bringas

Messiah's Handbook: Reminders for the Advanced Soul by Richard Bach

Blue Sky, White Clouds by Eliezer Sobel

Rainbow Ridge Books publishes spiritual and metaphysical titles, and is distributed by Square One Publishers in Garden City Park, New York.

To contact authors and editors, peruse our titles, and see submission guidelines, please visit our website at *www.rainbowridgebooks.com*.

For orders and catalogs, please call toll-free: (877) 900-BOOK.